SUNDRY EXTRAS

England *v* Australia

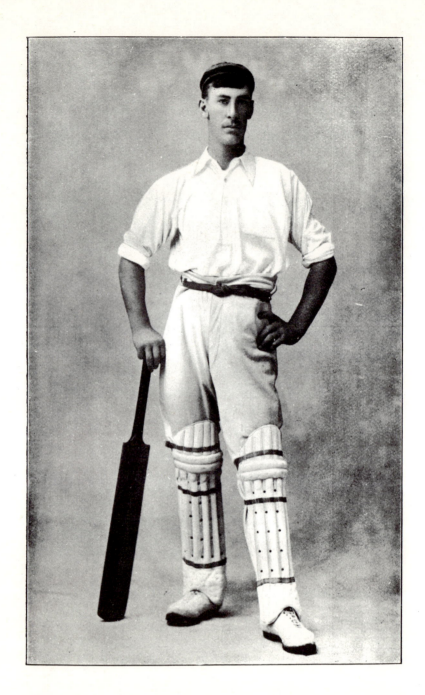

Albert Trott (Victoria) played three Tests in Australia in 1895. His batting average of 102.50 is better than Bradman's and the highest for either England or Australia. He also took nine wickets at an average of 21.33.

SUNDRY EXTRAS

England *v* Australia

PETER MAHONY

THE HAMBLEDON

PRESS

Published by The Hambledon Press
35 Gloucester Avenue, London NW1 7AX

ISBN 0 907628 48 6

British Library Cataloguing in Publication Data

Mahony, Peter
    Sundry Extras: England v. Australia
    1. Cricket players – England – Biography
    2. Cricket players – Australia – Biography
    3. Test matches (Cricket)
    I. Title
    796.35'865   GV915.A1

© Peter Mahony 1984

Printed and Bound in Great Britain by
Robert Hartnoll Ltd., Bodmin, Cornwall

CONTENTS

LIST OF ILLUSTRATIONS

PREFACE

Cricket has always fascinated me. From an early age I was absorbed by the deeds of great cricketers, especially English and Australian ones. In the 1930s there was a marked difference in importance, interest and intensity between Ashes matches and Tests against other countries. For me that difference still holds good, despite the post-war advance of the West Indies first to parity with, then to superiority over both England and Australia.

At the time of the Centenary Test I decided to mark the occasion by producing a definitive book on England versus Australia, to be more an appraisal of the players than an account of matches and rubbers. The original scheme was grandiose, envisaging a trilogy: the first volume on the great names of cricket, the second on the nearly greats (such as Charlie Barnett, Frank Iredale, L.O.B. Fleetwood-Smith and Ken Farnes), the third encompassing all other players who had contested the Ashes. Like most grandiose schemes it had soon to be scaled down to manageable proportions. When I discovered that nearly two-thirds of all the players fell into the third category, I realised that I had an opportunity to look at the series from an unusual angle and to recount the achievements of a large number of forgotten, and in many cases underrated, cricketers. While very little new can be written about Don and Jack if their surnames happen to be Bradman and Hobbs, a good deal more is possible if they are Kenyon and Iverson. Consequently I moderated my transports and gave full attention to these Sundry Extras.

The task required strictly defined limitations. Only cricketers who have played for England against Australia and for Australia against England were to be included, and only their performances in these Tests were to be taken into account. Only players who took part in less than ten matches have been examined, with a few exceptions being made for men who played more games but never established their place in the side.

In modern times the narrow focus on England and Australia has inevitably led to some distortion, in that it excludes from consideration players' records against other cricketing countries. My only defence to this, other than a belief in the unique glory of the England versus

Australia series, is that to do otherwise would have made this book twice as long, and would have tended to make it a miscellaneous catalogue rather than a considered record.

I have allowed myself one deviation from the main plan. In order to set the series in its proper perspective, I have begun the book with an account of the first series in 1877, and a consideration of the twenty two players who started it all. Of the twenty two, seventeen fall clearly into the category of Sundry Extras (eighteen if Billy Midwinter is included, who played 12 Tests in all, but less than 10 for either England or Australia). This book embraces all Tests between England and Australia up to the end of the 1982-3 season.

I have greatly benefited from the work of other cricket writers. I should particularly like to acknowledge my debt to *England v Australia* by Ralph Barker and Irving Rosenwater; *A History of Cricket* (2 vols.) by H.S. Altham and E.W. Swanton; *With Bat and Ball* by George Giffen; *The Croucher* by Gerald Brodribb; and, above all, *Wisden's Cricketers Almanac*. The Cricket Society's excellent library has been a rich source of material.

I should like to thank my wife Dorothy for typing and proof-reading the bulk of the manuscript, ably assisted by my son, Patrick, and my daughter, Eileen; Peter Hill for his indispensable work on the statistical tables; Kay Saunders for her sustained application to the detail of production; and Martin Sheppard for sifting my parentheses. I can only hope that readers will obtain as much enjoyment from the book as I have had in writing it.

PETER MAHONY

May 1984

One crowded hour of glorious life
is worth an age without a name.

(Thomas Mordaunt)

To
Dorothy

INTRODUCTION

Just over 100 years ago in Melbourne, Australia, the first international cricket contest was staged. Since then there have been 250 repeat performances, involving a cast of perhaps not quite thousands, but certainly several hundreds. 626 cricketers have so far taken part in these England versus Australia Test Matches. 342 have represented England, 283 Australia, and one man, William Midwinter, contrived to play for both countries — though not at the same time of course.

Among the 342 English several 'Immigrants', apart from Mr. Midwinter, have been included. 'Gubby' Allen came from Australia; 'Ranji', 'Duleep' and the Nawab of Pataudi (Senior) from the Indian sub-continent, (which could also technically lay claim to Colin Cowdrey); Trinidad provided 'Plum' Warner; and more recently, Basil D'Oliveira, Tony Greig, Phil Edmonds and Alan Lamb arrived from Southern Africa. Derek Pringle and Norman Cowans, born in Kenya and Jamaica respectively, made their debuts in the most recent series. In addition, there have been 5 canny Scots: Douglas Jardine (none cannier!), Gregor MacGregor, Ian Peebles, Mike Denness and the MacKinnon of MacKinnon; a Welsh quartet: Cyril Walters, Alan Watkins, Gilbert Parkhouse and I.J. Jones; and a trio of Irishmen: Sir T.C. O'Brien, L. Hone and Charlie McGahey. Indeed, the net may be said to have spread even further, embracing a 'Peruvian' (Freddie Brown, born in Lima), and a 'Maltese' (Wally Hammond, born in Malta), as well as an Absolom, a Schultz and a Subba Row (born in Croydon). Quite an international flavour.

A curious feature of this 'Immigrants' list is the disproportionate number of captains amongst them — Allen, Jardine, Warner, Walters, Denness and Tony Greig — and we could add Brown, Cowdrey and Hammond for good measure. (The Nawab captained India later on, as well.) Perhaps it all serves to underline the English penchant for self effacement.

The Australians have relied very much more on the home-grown product. (Of course it could be claimed that they are all immigrants, but one can hardly start a book like this on such a contentious note.) Ignoring the numerous 'Wild Irish' contingent — the O'Reillys, O'Neills,

Horans, Burkes etc.) and the smaller Scots group (Bannermans, McDonalds, McLeods), there has been a thin sprinkling of 'foreigners' in the Australian ranks, mostly of European origin. Hans Ebeling and Dr. Otto Nothling are clear examples; not to mention Coulthard and Hartkopf and Jim De Courcy; and what about Harry Moses? Len Pascoe, born in Yugoslavia, completes quite a cosmopolitan lot for such a comparatively small population.

Many of the earlier Australian Test players were indeed emigrants from the Old Country, but the only traceable Commonwealth immigrants are Clarence Victor Grimmett, who arrived from New Zealand in 1918, and Keppler Wessels, from South Africa, who is their current opening bat. Therefore the Australians can claim less 'foreign' influence than the English, but they are by no means immune. The variety of names in the roll-call of the six hundred-odd Anglo-Australian players is an eloquent testimony to cricket's capacity for transcending national boundaries.

The 343 Englishmen have been drawn from all of the first class counties. Yorkshire leads the way — naturally — with 44 representatives, closely followed by Middlesex with 42, Lancashire with 40, and Surrey with 38. Kent (31) and Nottinghamshire (24), the remaining two of the Big Six have also been well favoured and the remaining counties have had their share. Glamorgan, with only 3 representatives, is bottom of the list, apart from L. Hone of Ireland, the sole non-county representative.

The Australians, with only six states to draw from, have relied most heavily on Victoria. After all, it all began in Melbourne, didn't it? 105 Victorians and 97 from New South Wales have constituted the bulk of their teams. South Australia (39) comes next, then Queensland (23) and Western Australia (18). Tasmania, recently accorded state status, already had two representatives — K. Burn and C.J. Eady — before 1900. (The ubiquitous Mr. Midwinter played for Victoria and Gloucestershire and is therefore included twice.)

The pattern of selection revealed by an analysis of the appearances of these 626 players is indeed intriguing. 124 men (just under 20%) played in only one Test Match each. Another 78 managed one extra appearance before incurring the selectors' disfavour, so that just under one third of all the protagonists have been cast as extras; mere walkers-on. 60 more played in just 3 Tests and another 34 got as far as four; the minor supporting roles. A few of these aspired to greater things, but the Fates — and the selectors — combined to disappoint them.

The remaining players, 330 of them, have had the privilege of acting out the main drama of this continuing saga. 132 were picked between 5 and 9 times — for parts, at least, of two rubbers — and these constitute the major supporting players, some of them very effective. 115 more were selected for from 10 to 19 Tests, leading players whose influence on the Tests has been considerable; leaving a final group of 83 who have played in 20 or more matches — the Super Stars.

This book is concerned with the performances in England-Australia Tests of the largely unsung heroes who played in less than ten matches. They all contributed in varying degrees to the drama of the Greatest Show on Earth, the struggle for the Ashes. They all deserve commendation (again in varying degrees) for the pleasure, thrills and anguish which they have helped to give the lovers of the game during five generations of Test Match cricket. But, first of all, let us give some attention to those who started it all.

The Lillywhite Boys: (Back row) H. Jupp, T. Emmett, R. Humphrey, A. Hill, T. Armitage, G. Ulyett. (Middle row) E. Pooley, J. Southerton, James Lillywhite (capt.), A. Shaw, A. Greenwood. (Front row) H.R.J. Charlwood, J. Selby.

2

THE LILLYWHITE BOYS

In 1876 James Lillywhite of Sussex, professional cricketer, organised the fourth cricketing tour of Australia. In partnership with Alfred Shaw of Nottinghamshire, the famous length bowler, Lillywhite undertook to finance the tour – no doubt expecting to net a good profit from the venture. They recruited ten other professionals and set sail for Australia in the autumn of 1876.

The personnel of Lillywhite's team constituted an interesting collection. The hard core of the side consisted of five Yorkshiremen: George Ulyett, Tom Emmett, Allan Hill, Andrew Greenwood and one T. Armitage. Lillywhite and Shaw each brought a county colleague: H. Charlwood of Sussex and J. Selby of Notts. respectively. The party was completed by Harry Jupp, James Southerton and Ted Pooley of Surrey. Though a competent bunch, they could not really pretend to be representative of England's best cricketing talent. The bowling was fairly strong, but the batting was at best mediocre. Four of them, Lillywhite, Southerton, Jupp and Greenwood, had visited Australia 3 years earlier with W.G. however, so the side was not short of touring experience.

There had been three previous tours of the Antipodes. In 1861-62 H.H. Stephenson captained a side sponsored by Spiers and Pond, the caterers; then in 1863-4 George Parr of Notts. led a powerful team which returned unbeaten; and in 1873-74 W.G. Grace took his 'honeymoon' side. Parr's and Grace's tours had been at the invitation of the Melbourne C.C., but the Lillywhite Boys went at their own risk. The three previous sides had played all their games against odds and Lillywhite's side expected to do the same. Towards the end of their tour, however, developments occurred which almost by accident established the future pattern of Anglo-Australian cricket. The tour's itinerary included a visit to New Zealand which was to take place from January to March 1877. Just prior to embarking for New Zealand, the Englishmen had much the better of a draw with eleven of New South Wales. This was the first occasion when England and Australia met on equal terms and it whetted the Australians' appetites. While the Lillywhite Boys were struggling around New Zealand, Sydney and Melbourne agreed to co-operate in choosing an Australian XI to play the English when they returned to Australia in March 1877. The twelve English professionals certainly had no idea that they were setting a precedent which has now lasted more than a hundred years. Their main reason for agreeing to play the fixture was, no doubt, financial. A large attendance could be expected at Melbourne and they probably anticipated no great difficulty in disposing of the Australian challenge.

If Julius Caesar (of Parr's team) had been touring with Lillywhite, he would indubitably have pointed out the folly of arranging to begin such a match on the Ides of March. However a working knowledge of Shakespeare was possibly somewhat lacking among the 1877 men. Anyway the game was scheduled to occupy the four days — 15th-19th March 1877 — immediately after the Englishmen's disembarkation.

The crossing from New Zealand to Melbourne was extremely rough. Half of Lillywhite's army took the field suffering from *mal-de-mer*, and to add to their troubles, Pooley, their only keeper, was languishing in a Christchurch gaol. An inveterate gambler, Pooley had offered to back himself to nominate correctly the individual scores of the Christchurch Twenty-Two opposed to the tourists. A local gambler offered 20 to 1 in shillings against the possibility; which meant that Pooley would have to pay a shilling for every wrong forecast, but collect a pound for every right one. The Surrey keeper promptly predicted that each batsman would score a duck. Local Twenty-Twos invariably included a number of batting rabbits and, sure enough, nine of the Christchurch men failed to score. Pooley thus stood to collect nine pounds less thirteen shillings, a tidy sum in those days. Claiming that it was a trick, the local gambler welshed on the bet, fisticuffs ensued, and the protagonists were gaoled, pending a trial.

Pooley was later acquitted and the Christchurch people collected £50 for him and presented him with a watch; so eventually he did very well out of the seedy business. Unfortunately, by that time his colleagues had been beaten in the First Test. With their forces reduced to the bare minimum required, almost inevitably Lillywhite lost the toss.

The Englishmen tottered into the field at 1 o'clock and fielded until close of play, by which time Charles Bannerman, of New South Wales, had scored the first ever Test century. On the following day Bannerman continued to 165, before becoming the first Test casualty of fast, short-pitched bowling. A ball from Ulyett split Bannerman's finger and he retired hurt, having made nearly three quarters of the Australian total off his own bat.

Lillywhite's men never caught up. A solid fifty by Jupp could not prevent Midwinter capturing 5 wickets for the colonials. Australia led by 49 and, though Shaw and Ulyett skittled them for 104 in their second knock, they emerged as comfortable winners. England's final effort foundered against some fine fast bowling by the left-handed Kendall, who took 7 for 55 in 33 unchanged overs. First blood to the Australians.

A return match was arranged for a fortnight later. An unchanged England — Pooley was still in New Zealand — fitter and acclimatised, gained a sweet revenge by the margin of 4 wickets. Honours were even and the pattern for the future was established. Despite their comeback in the Second Test, the Lillywhite Boys were probably the weakest English team ever to visit Australia. Seven of the side never represented England again, while Ulyett was the only member to become a regular Test player. Alfred Shaw was a class slow bowler, but Lillywhite and Southerton, the round arm bowlers, were over the hill . Most of the rest were just not of Test standard. They were fortunate to return home with honours even.

James Lillywhite was a left hand medium pace bowler of some skill, but by 1877 he was approaching the veteran stage. Between 1862 and 1881 he captured over 1,000 wickets for Sussex. His prowess at representative level was, however, suspect. He appears to have been a shrewd captain; the general opinion being that he was tactically superior to Dave Gregory, his Australian counterpart. Probably the side's tactics were jointly decided — the whole tour seems to have depended largely on a happy-go-lucky spirit of mucking in . Lillywhite's test record of 1 win, 1 loss, places him as a captain, on a percentage basis, above A.C. MacLaren, Walter Hammond, Peter May and a number of others. He failed to use his own bowling sufficiently in the first match — possibly he was one of the sufferers from sea-sickness — but in the 'revenge' game he captured 6 wickets.

Alfred Shaw, Lillywhite's co-organiser, had a more distinguished Test career. Everything points to him as being the real brains of this side. During his career he contributed a number of practical ideas for the betterment of the game; he was the first to suggest that creases should be whitewashed. His prowess as a bowler was unquestioned. Known as the 'Emperor of Bowlers', he was the apostle of length.

Sundry Extras

Slow-medium right handed, he wheeled up 25,700 overs in his career at a cost of less than one run per over. Two thirds of these overs — mostly 4 ball affairs — were maidens and he captured more than 2,000 wickets. To achieve such figures he must have known a thing or two about field placing as well as bowling. To his nagging length Shaw added flight and clever changes of pace, while his off-break was sufficient to beat the bat. Shaw managed, in conjunction with Lillywhite and Arthur Shrewsbury, four further tours of Australia in the eighties. He was captain in 1881-2 and again in 1884-5 (though not in Tests). In 1886-7 he was joint captain with Shrewsbury, again not playing in the Tests; while in 1887-8 he acted mainly as manager. His experiences on this last tour, which clashed with another tour led by Lord Hawke, led him to advocate that the M.C.C. should sponsor future tours, a suggestion almost twenty years ahead of its time. In the first of all Test matches, Shaw collected eight wickets (his 6 further Tests only brought him four more) including 5 for 38 in the Australians' second knock; the first Englishman to bowl unchanged through a Test innings. His phenomenal accuracy produced 50 maidens in 89.3 overs which cost him only 89 runs. Indications are though that Shaw, like so many English slow bowlers, lacked sufficient bite in his bowling to reap a rich harvest of Test wickets in Australia.

George ('Happy Jack') Ulyett was the side's star performer. England's first genuine all-rounder played another 21 Tests after this original tour and was a regular choice, at home and abroad, throughout the eighties. A hard hitting bat, fastish bowler and a fearless fielder, he sired a line which has passed down through Jessop, Tate, W.J. Edrich, Dexter and Greig to Ian Botham. In this first series Ulyett averaged 30 with the bat and 17 with the ball — impressive figures. He was a comparative batting failure in the first game (the New Zealand trip may well have taken its toll even of his renowned strength) but he came to the fore in the second with two fifties. His bowling in the second innings of the first match accounted for Bannerman, Horan, Midwinter and E. Gregory, and one of his lifters had caused Bannerman's retirement in the first innings. He continued to give England yeoman service for the next decade.

Tom Emmett, Yorkshire's famous fast bowler, only distinguished himself as a batsman with 48 in the match. He played in 5 more Tests, all in Australia, but, except for the 1879 'Lord Harris' Test when he took 7 for 68, his left-hand bowling was found wanting at international level. A disastrous tour in 1881-2 which brought him only 2 wickets in

4 matches at 90 apiece, ended his Test career. The only other player in the side to play in subsequent Tests was John Selby the Notts. batsman. He top scored in the second innings of this first game and kept wicket in place of the absent Pooley. He also played well in the first game of the 1881-2 tour. However, like Emmett, he could never command a place at home.

None of the other players ever appeared in Test Matches again. Jupp contributed England's first half century in the first innings of the first game, but achieved nothing else. Charlwood, a fairly sound county bat, scored only 63 runs all told. Southerton, at 49 years of age a real veteran, bowled his round armers tidily in both games, taking seven wickets, but was a negligible bat. Armitage's only contributions were to drop Bannerman before he had reached double figures in the 1st innings of the first game and then to indulge in an abysmal spell of lob bowling. He tried to bombard the bails with a series of high-tossed deliveries and merely succeeded in giving Bannerman 10 runs in his first over. He then resorted to grubbers (more often labelled 'shooters') but failed to make any impression — other than an hilarious one. Greenwood and Hill, Yorkshire's other representatives, fared better. The former's 49 and 22 in the second game were major factors in the win, while Hill batted well in both tests. Hill's fast bowling provided him with the first of all Test wickets when he bowled Nat Thompson, and later it established England's ascendancy in the 1st innings of the return match. He was probably superior to both Emmett and Ulyett as a pace bowler and was unlucky not to play in subsequent Tests. A severe shoulder injury in 1884 ended his career. The remaining tourist, Ted Pooley, never played in a Test match and his absence from the first game was probably the single most decisive factor in England's defeat.

These then were the English pioneers. Their defeat encouraged the Australians to try their luck in touring England. The Australians were successful in their 1878 venture, thrashing the M.C.C. at Lord's and establishing the precedent for regular trials of strength with the full England XI. The Lillywhite Boys probably accomplished more for the rapid development of Anglo-Australian cricket by losing the first Test match than would have been the case if they had won. An English victory might well have retarded regular international encounters by a decade. So, even in defeat, the Lillywhite Boys served cricket well.

The Australian Team of 1878. (Back row) Spofforth, Conway, Allen. (Middle row) Bailey, Horan, Garrett, Gregory (capt.), A. Bannerman, Boyle. (Front row) C. Bannerman, Murdoch, Blackham.

3

THE AUSTRALIAN PIONEERS

The colonials opposed to the Lillywhite Boys proved far more formidable than the tourists had anticipated. They won the first clash because they possessed a superb batsman in Bannerman, a fine bowler in Kendall and a top class stumper, John McCarthy Blackham. These three were sufficiently superior to their counterparts among the tourists to make the vital difference, for Bannerman played the first great Test innings — still one of the most dominating knocks ever played — Blackham kept wicket brilliantly, and Kendall, in England's second innings, turned in a top-class bowling performance.

New South Wales and Victoria were almost equally represented in the Australian side. The former contingent comprised Dave Gregory, the captain, his elder brother, Ned, Nat Thompson, Garrett and Bannerman; while, apart from Blackham and Kendall, Victoria supplied Horan, B.B. Cooper, Hodges and Midwinter. In the second game Spofforth, and Murdoch, of N S.W. and one T.J. Kelly (Victoria) replaced Ned Gregory, Horan and Cooper. (One shudders to think what might have happened to the sea-sick Englishmen if Spofforth had played in the First Test.)

Like the tourists, the home side contained a number of semi-passengers. David Gregory, although winning 2 of the 3 Tests which he captained, achieved little until the second innings of the second game when he top-scored with 43. He captained the 1878 team which toured England but led the colonials only once more in a Test Match before fading out of the game. His brother E.J. recorded the first duck in Test cricket and never played for Australia again. Neither did Cooper of Victoria, whose contributions were a paltry 15 and 3. Thompson and Hodges lasted only one match longer, as did Kelly and, very surprisingly, Kendall. Thompson, the first Test Match victim, batted well as an opener in the second game, and Hodges captured 6 wickets for 84 in the two matches, but neither of them seemed to have the required class. Hodges, a left-hand medium pacer, owed his place to the withdrawal of the redoubtable Spofforth from the original side and he only played 4 first class games all told. Kelly, Cooper's replacement, scored 19 and 35 in the return game and was picked two seasons later against Lord Harris's side. He dropped from the Test arena with a batting average of 21; not bad going for that low scoring era.

Kendall's disappearance from the Test Match scene after this first rubber seems inexplicable at this distance of time. A fine left-handed fast bowler and a fore-runner of Alan Davidson, he followed his 8 wickets in the first game with 6 more in the second; a better return than the much-vaunted Spofforth. He was a member of the side selected to tour England in 1878, but he only played in the preliminary matches in Australia and New Zealand and never made the trip. Perhaps his tendency to put on flesh rapidly was the reason for his exclusion. 14 Test wickets at 15 apiece surely merited further recognition.

William Midwinter, the Bendigo Infant, has a number of claims to fame. A hefty six-footer, he was a good medium-pace bowler with a high delivery and he captured 5 for 78 in England's first innings at Melbourne; the first achievement of '5 in an innings' in Test Matches. top-scored with 31 in Australia's first innings of the return game. A good all-rounder, he returned to England with Lillywhite's side and played for his native county, Gloucestershire, in the 1877 season. He was selected to join D.W. Gregory's 1878 tourists and played 5 matches for them before W.G. Grace insisted that he should honour his Gloucestershire commitments. Midwinter took no further part in Test Matches for 4 years, and is on record as having regretted his defection from the 1878 team. When he reappeared, he was representing England! He played in all 4 Tests for Shaw's 1881-2 side, scoring only 95 runs and taking 10 wickets at 27 each. One season later, Midwinter changed his allegiance again. He represented Australia in the extra match against Ivo Bligh's side which had regained the Ashes. His feat of bowling throughout the first morning into a gale-force wind earned him much commendation and he had the best analysis of all the Australian bowlers in this game. This performance earned him a place in the 1884 touring side and he played in all 3 Tests, top-scoring at Old Trafford, but achieving little else of note. Two years later, Midwinter played in both Tests against Arthur Shrewsbury's tourists, but he was over the hill by then and his performances were poor. His 12 Tests brought him 269 runs for an average of 13, and 24 wickets at 25 apiece, workmanlike, unsensational figures. He was on the winning side, both Australian, in only 2 games of his 12 Tests. Perhaps he never really belonged to either team. His sad end only four years later was caused by a series of family tragedies which left him alone in the world.

Tom Garrett of New South Wales was only 18 when he played in the inaugural Test. No one younger has yet appeared in these games. Garrett played in a further 18 Test Matches during the next decade but with only moderate success. A lively medium pacer, he attacked the off-side, keeping a good length and worrying batsmen with his pace off the pitch. He toured England in 1882 and 1886, capturing over 100 wickets each time, but his returns in Test Matches were negligible. His best rubber came in 1881-2 when he accounted for 18 wickets at 20 runs each in 3 Tests and topped the Australian averages, above Palmer, Boyle and Spofforth. As a batsman Garrett's usual place was number 9, but he did bat higher on occasion. He was instrumental in winning the Second Test of 1881-2 at Sydney, when a sensibly compiled 31 not out carried Australia home by 5 wickets. Later, in 1885 — the Third Test at Sydney — Garrett batted at number 10 and scored his only Test 50. In a last wicket partnership of 80 with E. Evans, Garrett made 51 not out and retrieved a first innings collapse. Ultimately Australia won by a mere 6 runs. Garrett's 339 Test runs and 36 wickets in 19 games are poor figures for a man chosen so often. He was on the losing side in 10 of these matches so his value as a talisman must also be doubted. Australian selections in those early days were often dictated by expediency and Garrett, a popular player, may have been luckier than his playing prowess merited simply because he was not troublesome like some of his more talented contemporaries. Perhaps, too, his selectors were constantly hoping for his early promise to be fulfilled.

Another Thomas — Horan of Victoria — also appeared very frequently during the first decade of Tests. He was rated in his prime as Victoria's best batsman, but his Test average, in 27 innings, is less than 20. He scored 12 and 20 in the opening Test and then was dropped to make way for Murdoch. In 1881-2 Horan compiled his solitary Test century in a drawn game at Melbourne. His only other innings of note was a 63, again at Melbourne, in 1885, in his first match as captain of Australia. Horan became captain by default, since Murdoch, skipper in the first game of this rubber, was involved with a number of other players in a dispute with the Melbourne Club over the distribution of gate money. Horan led a patchwork side which was soundly trounced by Shrewbury's professionals. In the last Test of this series (at Melbourne once more) Horan again led the side, won the toss, batted first on a wet wicket, and was beaten by an innings and 98 runs. Thus his two ventures in captaincy ended in crushing defeat, though the inter-state dissensions did leave him with a weak team on both occasions.

Curiously Horan blossomed forth as a quick bowler in the third match in this series, taking 6 for 40 in the first innings at Sydney. He exploited a spot caused by Spofforth's follow through and paved the way for the 'Demon' to bowl Australia to victory by 6 runs. (This was the same match in which Garrett scored his only Test 50.) Horan toured England in 1878 – when he struggled to average 10 with the bat – and again in 1882, when he completed his 1,000 runs and finished third in the averages behind Murdoch and Massie. Like Garrett, he played in the 'Ashes' match without distinction. It would seem that, again like Garrett, Horan was favoured by the selectors, particularly Melbourne's, to a greater extent than his play deserved. Nevertheless, he was on the victorious side in 9 of his 15 games.

The remaining pioneer Australians all have definite claims to greatness. Spofforth, Murdoch and Blackham played Tests regularly over a lengthy period. Their achievements have been fully discussed in other books than this. Oddly Spofforth refused to play in the First Test because Blackham was preferred to Murdoch as wicket-keeper and Spofforth did not rate the Victorian as capable of doing as good a job as Murdoch. All of them played in the return match with Blackham doing the stumping. He acquitted himself rather better than the N.S.W. pair who did not live up to their reputations. Nevertheless, these three were to make lasting contributions to Australia's advance to Test parity with the full might of England in the Old Country .

The man who played the most important part in the first Test only played twice more for Australia. Charles Bannerman toured England in 1878, when there were no Test matches played, and headed the batting averages, compiling over 1,200 runs in all matches in a low-scoring season. In the solitary Test against Lord Harris's side the following winter, he scored 15 and 15 not out. 'Illness' – Charlie was apparently over-fond of the cup that cheers – then removed him from the first class game, but his Test average of 59.75 from six innings places him fourth in Australia's all-time batting list. Only Albert Trott, with a freak average of 102.50, Don Bradman and Sid Barnes have outscored him. There is no doubt that Bannerman, with his ability to score heavily by keeping his strokes on the ground was the first of Australia's great batsmen. He was on the winning side in 2 of his 3 Tests and did more than any of his contemporaries to establish the Australians' claim to cricket equality with England. His historic debut innings justified Australian confidence, whetted the English appetite for revenge, and made the necessary dramatic impact to stimulate public interest in the continuing series of England versus Australia.

4

LUCKLESS LIONS

The biggest thrill for any cricketer must come when he is asked to play for the first time in an England *v.* Australia Test. And his biggest disappointment must be not being invited to do it again. 71 Englishmen and 53 Australians have undergone this once in a lifetime experience. For seven of them — Paul Allott, David Bairstow, Paul Downton, Paul Parker and Bill Athey of England; Dirk Welham and Carl Rackemann of Australia — their England-Australia involvement only began in recent series; but for the remaining 117 opportunity knocked but once.

Most of this 117 failed to make any impact on the game in which they played, so they were probably not surprised to be dropped from the side for the next match. Some, however, acquitted themselves well and had every right to feel scurvily treated by the selectors' fickleness. (There are, of course, legions of good players who were never selected at all for Test Matches, but due consideration of their claims would certainly fill a separate book. Here we must concern ourselves with those who did play.)

Dealing with the Englishmen first, there are a number of cricketers of doubtful quality who made up the number in early touring sides. Lord Harris's 'Gentlemen of England', beaten by 10 wickets at Melbourne in 1879, contained six men — A.J. Webbe, Vernon Royle, the Mackinnon of Mackinnon, L. Hone, the Irish stumper, S.S. Schultz and C.A. Absolom — who never played another Test. Spofforth's bowling was much too good for the majority of them; Royle and Mackinnon were the first two victims of the first Test hat trick, and only Schultz had any pretensions as a bowler. However Charles Absolom, an audacious hard-hitting batsman, sporting a W.G. type beard, hammered 52 out of England's paltry 113 in the first innings; so he, at least, had claims to further recognition.

Two other early tourists were G.F. Vernon of Middlesex and W. Newham of Sussex. Vernon played — batting at number 11 — in the First Test of Ivo Bligh's tour. He scored 11 not out and 3. Newham, six years later, was one of the combined team picked from the two English sides which toured Australia in the same season. His first innings of 9 had him relegated to number nine for the second knock where he scored 17. Another amateur, L.H. Gay of Somerset, was given the stumping spot in the First Test of Stoddart's 1894-5 tour at Sydney. Gay was England's soccer goalkeeper, but he was much less deft as a wicket-keeper. He dropped several catches, depressing the team in general and Tom Richardson, the unfortunate bowler, in particular. Australia made 586 and though Gay contributed 33 to England's fighting recovery, he was replaced by Philipson of Middlesex for the rest of the Tests.

Probably none of these Gentlemen would have been called on by England if all the leading cricketers had been able to tour in these early years. None of them had a hope of playing at home, for the Graces, Jacksons, Steels, etc − as well as the full range of professionals − were available and were much better players. Probably they were lucky to have been able to afford to tour and gain selection in somewhat sub-standard sides. But I still think Absolom was hard done by.

Back home in England, another sprinkling of amateurs was selected for single Tests. W.G's brothers E.M. and G.F. played at the Oval in 1880 − the first Test in England − and both carved a niche in Test history. E.M. assisted W.G. in an opening stand of 91, scoring 36 himself, but he made 0 in the second innings. As he was already 39 it is probably not surprising that he was passed over for further Tests. No doubt he complained about it bitterly to the Champion, but had to put up with it. Fred Grace, on the other hand, was a good prospect for future Tests. In this game he recorded the first pair in Test Matches − but he held that much described catch off a skier from the mighty Bonnor, who was on his third run when the ball was pouched. No Fred would have been forgiven his pair and selected for future Tests on the strength of that catch alone. Two weeks later he was dead of pneumonia. Poor Fred and, who knows, poor England.

Frank Penn of Kent played in that same Test alongside the Graces. He scored 23 in his first knock, and top-scored with 27 not out in the undignified second innings when England lost five wickets in scoring the 57 required for victory. Penn had toured with Lord Harris' Gentlemen but had not made the Test side in Australia. He later suffered from a heart disorder, so perhaps his omission was due to ill-health. His form at the Oval in 1880 surely justified some further games.

Stanley Christopherson of Kent was given the place of the redoubtable Billy Barnes for the Lord's Test of 1884. His quick bowling (1 for 52 and 0 for 17) hardly justified the change and the selectors promptly recalled Barnes for the Oval.

John Shuter, captain of Surrey's powerful side in the late eighties, was called on as a replacement for T.C. O'Brien of Middlesex for the Oval Test of 1888. (O'Brien had played at Lord's which seems to imply that selectors were choosing horses for courses or at worst pandering to local interest.) No less than 5 Surrey players appeared in this Test. Granted, Abel, Walter Read and Lohmann were automatic choices anywhere at this period, but Shuter's selection and that of Harry Wood the stumper were challengeable. England won by an innings, but Shuter's 28 and Wood's 8 (plus 1 catch, 1 stumping and 1 bye) could not be said to have made a major contribution to the victory. They were both omitted from the final Test at Old Trafford.

In 1890 at the Oval England was sadly depleted by county calls and injuries. J. Cranston, a left hand bat from Gloucestershire and 'Nutty' Martin, a left hand bowler from Kent, were two of the stop-gap replacements. Cranston did not set the world on fire, scoring 16 and 15, but Martin, replacing the injured Briggs, turned in a performance which is an English record to this day. He captured 6 wickets in each innings for 50 and 52 respectively, and his match figures of 12 for 102 constitute the best bowling debut by an Englishman. 'Nutty' hit the stumps 8 times, outshining the great George Lohmann, and was the chief architect of England's 2 wicket victory. Even when the competition of Briggs and Peel is considered, Martin should have merited further recognition. This one performance has placed 'Nutty' at the top of the all time English bowling averages.

In 1896 the irascible Captain E.G. Wynyard of Hampshire was in the side for the final Test at the Oval. He probably got the batting place vacated by an unfit Andrew Stoddart. Anyhow Wynyard did little with it, scoring 10 and 3.

Another stop-gap was a certain R. Wood of Lancashire who turned out in the Second Test of Shaw and Shrewsbury's 1886-7 tour. Wood got his place because Billy Barnes had injured a hand. (Legend has it that Barnes took a swing at Percy McDonnell, Australia's skipper, missed, and hit a wall.) Wood's chance came and went with but 6 runs to show, batting number 10. Wood, curiously enough, was not a member of the original touring side; being resident in Melbourne he was pressed into service, and signalised the honour by demolishing his own wicket in the second innings.

Walter Mead of Essex played at Lord's in 1899. How he came to be preferred to J.T. Hearne on his own midden is a mystery. It is said in cricketing circles that to do well at Lord's is twice as valuable to a player's future prospects as a similar performance elsewhere. The converse is equally likely to be the case. Mead bowled 53 overs to take one for 91 and Australia won by 10 wickets. Mead was never called on again despite a lengthy and successful county career.

By the turn of the century it had become firmly established that England required its best players to combat the Australians at home and abroad. The M.C.C. took over the responsibility for touring sides in 1903 and the number of birds of passage in the Test sides was radically reduced. Nevertheless, several found their way into the pre World War I home teams, usually with good reasons for their selection, but occasionally with disastrous results.

The first of these was the ill-starred Fred Tate. In 1902, England's 'best ever team', to quote Sir Neville Cardus, had managed by injudicious changes of personnel to go one down with two to play against Joe Darling's second Australians. (It is highly debatable that this side was England's best. For a start they were led by that mixed blessing Archie MacLaren. I also suspect that the fielding was not as skilled — nor as well managed by captain and bowlers — as it should have been. My money would be on Chapman's 1928-9 side, Hutton's 1954-5 team and Brearley's 1978-9 bunch, to give them a pasting.) It was into this delicately poised situation that the 35 year old Tate was thrust, summoned by the lordly MacLaren at the last minute to replace Schofield Haigh whose release had been refused by Yorkshire. One might have expected MacLaren to nurse his protege in his first Test. But that wasn't MacLaren's policy He sent Tate to field deep, though fully aware that the Sussex man's experience was solely in the slips. Tate dropped a vital catch, was hardly needed as a bowler despite the wet conditions, and then had to go in last when England required just 8 runs to win. Tate made 4, then he was bowled. England lost by 3 runs and poor Fred was never allowed to forget it. Tate's 2 for 7 in 5 overs in Australia's second innings was forgotten however, and he withdrew into county cricket to hide his diminished head. But what was MacLaren doing, one might ask, to play a 35 year old bowler, suspect in the field and a poor bat, when George Hirst was in the squad for the Test? Tate might have made an England bowler, but this traumatic start ensured that he would never again have the opportunity.

In 1905 David Denton of Yorkshire played his only Test. He made 0 and 12 in the third game at Leeds, so he was hardly a success as a substitute batsman for MacLaren. In the same match, A.R. Warren of

Derbyshire was brought in as a fastish bowler in place of Arnold of Worcestershire. Warren captured 5 for 57 in the first innings, giving England a lead of 106, but Australia salvaged a draw. He was promptly dropped to make way for Walter Brearley at Old Trafford. Brearley did even better there than Warren at Leeds, so perhaps the change was justified. But why did the selectors recall Arnold at Old Trafford? Surely Warren deserved a further chance in tandem with Brearley?

After this relatively settled spell, MacLaren got in on the act again in 1909. What power he wielded at Lord's to be granted the captaincy once again is difficult, at this distance of time, to assess. As in 1902, the selection system if it can be called a system was bizarre. 25 players were used, of whom eleven — a whole side — made just one appearance. Four of these played their only Test against Australia. G. Thompson, Northamptonshire's sturdy all-rounder, scored 6 and bowled four overs for 19 runs at Edgbaston in the First Test. England won, thanks to Hirst and Blythe, but Thompson was discarded without having been really tried. He was entitled to feel aggrieved, as indeed was the next debutant, J.H. King of Leicestershire. Aged 38, this left handed bat had probably long given up hopes of Test status. However his experience helped him to a top score of 60 in England's first innings at Lord's, and though he failed second time round so did several more notable personages. He achieved further distinction by opening the bowling in Australia's first innings, but his slow left-arm trundling was heavily punished. England lost this time, by 9 wickets, and King went to the scrap heap.

For the next two games England relied on more experienced players, but in the final match at the Oval two more tyros were called up. England, one down, needed a win to square the series — so they left out Blythe, the series' best bowler, and brought in D.W. Carr of Kent, 'a 37 year old googly merchant, inclined to stoutness'. They also played Ernie Hayes of Surrey in place of J.T. Tyldesley. (Local interests again.) Hayes made 4 and 9, but Carr opened the bowling, and captured 3 early wickets. Then Victor Trumper, Bardsley and Macartney got at him, and Maclaren, of course, over-bowled him so that his final figures were five for 146 in 34 overs. His match haul, after 35 more overs was seven for 282. Carr had his money's worth. He bowled half as many overs again as the great Barnes and conceded over 40% of Australia's runs. MacLaren was a very suspect handler of new recruits. The last one-timer of the Golden Age was S.P. Kinneir of Warwickshire. On Plum Warner's second tour of 1911-12, the 40 year old Kinneir had the privilege of opening the innings with J.B. Hobbs in the First Test. He acquitted himself well with scores of 22 and 30, but his poor fielding told against him and Wilfrid Rhodes was promoted to partner Hobbs in the next Test. The rest is history — and poor Kinneir never got back.

The advent of Warwick Armstrong's Australians after World War I spread panic in the English ranks. No less than 34 players were tried in the course of two rubbers, without success. In Australia in 1920-21, Dolphin, the Yorkshire keeper, replaced Strudwick for one Test, scoring 1 and 0, allowing 6 byes (in 600 runs) and making one catch. Another Tyke, E.R. Wilson, played in the final game at Sydney, scoring 5 and 5, taking 3 for 36 and antagonising the Australian crowd by writing some forthright comments in the newspapers. His non-selection for further Tests was probably as much due to diplomatic considerations as to doubts about his form.

The most advanced case of selectorial madness came in 1921. 30 players were picked (with a pin?) to represent England against Gregory and McDonald; they still managed to leave out the best player of fast bowling in the country, George Gunn. 10 unfortunates were required to provide instant success — which, not surprisingly, was not forthcoming — and were then discarded as rapidly as they had been summoned. The ten were Percy Holmes (Yorkshire), Nigel Haig and Jack Durston (Middlesex), Charlie Parker and Dipper (Gloucestershire), A.J. Evans and Walter Hardinge (Kent), T. Richmond (Notts.), Andy Ducat (Surrey) and Charles Hallows (Lancashire). All of them, except Durston and Hallows were aged thirty plus. Holmes made 30 and 8 at Trent Bridge, Durston captured five for 136 at Lord's, Dipper — a steady opening bat but a clumsy field — scored 11 and 40 in the same game; Charlie Parker's left arm spin bagged 2 for 32 at Old Trafford in 28 overs; but the rest did very little. Evans and Ducat failed dismally as batsmen; Hardinge was not much better; Richmond's and Haig's bowling was expensive; while poor Hallows had his solitary innings curtailed by rain at Old Trafford. England's depressing run of defeats was extended to 8 straight Tests and the selectors must shoulder the lion's share of the blame. The unfortunate captains, Douglas and Tennyson, were never given a chance to weld a team. Holmes was held to have 'flinched' from the fast bowling and a selector is said to have vowed that he would never be picked again. He wasn't.

Never again did such profligate selection take place. In 1926,

George Macaulay (Yorkshire) was chosen at Leeds as an opening bowler and took 1 for 123. He then top-scored in England's first innings with 76 excellent runs. Reasonably the selectors decided that bowling was what they needed and looked elsewhere. Still a Test batting average of 76 was something for Macaulay to treasure. Maurice Nichols, the Essex all-rounder, played at Old Trafford in 1930. He opened the bowling with Maurice Tate, captured 2 for 33 and scored 7 not out in a game restricted to one innings apiece by the weather. In view of his county record and performances in other representative games, Maurice merited a second chance. He didn't get it. Neither did Tom Goddard, Gloucester's off spinner, who played in the same game and captured 2 for 49. Goddard, a better bowler than most, should have been used again. The success of googly bowlers, Grimmett and O'Reilly, probably influenced selectorial thinking at this period and Goddard was passed over in favour of a succession of expensive leg-spinners: Mitchell, Peebles and Robins spring to mind. Goddard was probably born 20 years too soon. He was still among England's top half dozen bowlers after World War II, when he was well past 40 years of age.

Walter Keeton, Nottinghamshire's opening bat, made one appearance in 1934. Keeton was never quite in the top flight of batsmen, but he was given his chance at Leeds as a replacement for the injured Herbert Sutcliffe. He scored 25 and 12. Naturally Sutcliffe, now recovered, was restored for the final Test.

Experiments occurred again in 1938. Reg Sinfield, another Gloucestershire spinner, took 2 for 123 at Trent Bridge; and Arthur Wellard, the Somerset hitter and pace bowler, took 3 for 126 at Lords and outscored Denis Compton, of all people, in a second innings stand of 74; what does one have to do to retain a Test place? Fred Price, the Middlesex stumper, took the place of the injured Leslie Ames at Leeds, scoring 6 and 0, allowing 6 byes out of 349 and taking 2 catches. This obviously was not good enough for the selectors, for they called on 39 year old Arthur Wood (Yorkshire) to do the keeping at the Oval. Wood rose nobly to the occasion. He scored 53 out of 106 added with Joe Hardstaff for the seventh wicket, rescuing England from the parlous state of 770 for 6. Wood also made 3 catches and conceded 5 byes out of 324. The advent of World War II effectually ended the Test careers of these four, who were all approaching the veteran stage when they made their debuts.

The post war Tests produced a spate of one time losers. Laurie Fishlock of Surrey took the place of the incapacitated Wally Hammond in the Fifth Test at Melbourne in 1947. It was asking too much of a 40 year old to cope with Lindwall, Miller & Co. He made 14 and 0. The first match at Brisbane had found Paul Gibb, then of Yorkshire, later of Essex, behind the stumps. 5 byes in a total of 645 and one catch, plus 13 and 11 with the bat was a nondescript return, and Godfrey Evans was waiting in the wings. Gibb, who had been a very promising player in 1938 and 1939, lost his place, and Evans remained a fixture for the next decade.

In 1948 Bradman's side emulated the triumphal progress of Armstrong's 1921 team. England's selectors repeated the clutching at straws method of their 1921 predecessors — but fortunately, not on the same Grand Guignol scale. The search for a fast bowler to counter Lindwall and Miller led to the choice of Arthur Coxon (Yorkshire) for the Lord's Test. He took 3 wickets for 172. The Fourth Test at Leed's saw Ken Cranston, the Lancashire skipper, drafted as an all rounder. He made 10 and 0 and captured 1 for 79. 36 year old George Emmett, of Gloucestershire, came in to take Len Hutton's place at Old Trafford. (Hutton was dropped because he seemed to have lost confidence.) Poor Emmett made 10 and 0, Lindwall getting him both times. Hutton was immediately reinstated. Alan Watkins, Glamorgan's first ever representative against Australia, played at the Oval. He scored 0 and 2, bowled 4 overs for 19 runs and failed to gather any of the short-leg catches which had built his reputation. Four 'new boys', all found wanting.

Lastly Eric Hollies of Warwickshire — the same age as Emmett — got into the side for the final Test. England's spin bowling at Leeds had been poor and Hollies had a golden opportunity to make a name for himself. This he did in no uncertain manner. In the best English bowling performance of the rubber, Hollies took 5 for 131, including Don Bradman, in his last Test innings, for 0. If Hollies had not been such a bad traveller, he would have continued in the 1950-51 side as a front line bowler. As it was, he made the tour but sickness ruined his form and he lost his place in the Test side. Like Coxon, Emmett and Cranston, Hollies' prime years were lost to the War. This same series of 1950-51 found Arthur McIntyre of Surrey, deputy wicket-keeper to Godfrey Evans, playing at Brisbane as a batsman. McIntyre's 1 and 7 did not rate further consideration, particularly as he was one of several batsmen blamed for throwing away their wickets in the helter-skelter of this close-run Test.

1954-55 came, and Evans' new deputy, Keith Andrew (Northants.)

stepped in at Brisbane because Evans had been injured. 11 byes, no dismissals, 6 and 5 in an innings defeat for England were no insurance at all against the inevitable return of the Kent stumper. In 1956 Alan Moss of Middlesex bowled at Trent Bridge to return figures of 4 overs, maidens, 1 run, 0 wickets. He had got his place because Tyson, Trueman and Statham were all injured. By the next Test they had all recovered and Moss didn't have a look-in. 10 years earlier or later and he would have been an automatic choice. In the same series at Leeds, Douglas Insole, the Essex captain with an unorthodox batting style, scored 5. He was replaced by David Sheppard.

1961 saw the only appearance of Les Jackson, a fine opening bowler from Derbyshire. His 4 for 83 at Leeds put him at the top of the bowling averages for the rubber, so the selectors immediately supplanted him with Jack Flavell of Worcester for the last 2 games. Jackson's county record demanded far more recognition than he ever received; a black mark against all the selectors of the fifties and early sixties. In 1964 Ken Taylor (Yorkshire) was chosen at Leeds. His fine fielding improved England's out cricket, but his scores of 9 and 15 were too disappointing to merit further selection as a batsman. Fred Rumsey, left arm paceman from Somerset, had the privilege of bowling in this same series on the lifeless pudding of a pitch produced at Old Trafford. His 2 for 99 was the best return among the England bowlers in the innings which contained Bobby Simpson's 311.

One of the saddest of stories was that of Eric Russell, the Middlesex opening bat, in the 1965-66 rubber. At Brisbane he began the game with a fractured thumb securely strapped. He then split his hand fielding, had to bat last to try and save the follow-on, made 0 not out and never again graced the Ashes scene.

Pat Pocock, Surrey's off-spinner, and Roger Prideaux (Northants.), an opening bat, played one Test each in 1968. Pocock captured 6 for 79 in the second innings of the first game at Old Trafford (6 for 156 in the match), but England's poor first innings left them with over 400 to get to win. They didn't make it. Pocock, rather unjustly, was one of the scapegoats. Prideaux was called up to replace the injured Geoff Boycott at Leeds. He made 64 of an opening partnership of 123 with John Edrich — a sterling start. Although he only made 2 in his second knock, Prideaux had shown real Test potential. He was never given the chance to exploit it. Graham Barlow of Middlesex scored 1 and 5 at Lord's in the First Test of 1977 so, despite his first-class fielding, was dropped for the rest of the rubber.

He has not been called on since. Two debuts were made in the 1980 Centenary Match at Lord's. Bill Athey of Yorkshire made no impression as a number 3 bat. His lively fielding in the covers was only small consolation for his meagre scores of 9 and 1. Consequently his future chances must be highly problematic. David Bairstow, the Yorkshire stumper, did rather better. Two catches, plus a superb stumping off Emburey, claimed 3 victims for him out of the paltry 9 dismissals which England managed in the two innings. He also conceded only 2 byes in a grand total of 574 scored by the Aussies during the game. Bairstow probably anticipated more caps, but the selectors ignored him for the 1981 and subsequent rubbers.

In that 1981 series, three young men — all named Paul — made a solitary appearance against Australia. Paul Downton, the Middlesex (ex-Kent) wicket-keeper, failed to distinguish himself in his first Test and he was supplanted by veteran stumpers, Bob Taylor and Alan Knott, for the rest of the rubber. Paul Allott, the Lancastrian pace-bowler, got his chance in the Fifth Test because of an injury to the experienced Chris Old. Paradoxically Allott scored an unbeaten, fighting fifty at Old Trafford, enabling his side to reach comparative respectability in their first innings. He then helped Willis and Botham to skittle Australia for 130, capturing 2 for 17. England were well on the way to defeat by the time this game had reached the half way stage. Allott claimed 2 more wickets in the second innings, so his final contributions to England's victory were 66 runs for once out, and 4 wickets for 88 runs in a highly encouraging debut. Somewhat short-sightedly the selectors replaced him with the veteran Mike Hendrick for the last Test. Nevertheless, even though he was omitted from Willis' 1982-3 tourists, Allott may reasonably expect more Test calls in the near future. The third Paul — Parker of Sussex was played for his batting in that last match at the Oval. He succumbed to his third ball for a duck in the first innings; and scratched his way to 13 in the second before he fell to the same combination (caught Kent, bowled Alderman) as in the first innings. Parker will need to show a return to his best form if he is again to do battle with the Aussies.

While it is possible to argue that all of these 71 Englishmen should have been given a second chance, the really unlucky ones were 'Nutty' Martin, Warren, Durston, Hollies, Jackson and Pocock — all bowlers. Charles Absolom, J.H. King and Roger Prideaux were the only recognised batsmen who succeeded, each of them scoring a half-century; as did bowlers George Macaulay and Paul Allott and stumper Arthur Wood. If most of the 71 were not hard done by, these, at least, could validly claim that fate — or the selectors — treated them unkindly.

The England Team of 1878-9: (Back row) F. Penn, A.J. Webbe, C.A. Absolom, S.S. Scultz, L. Hone. (Middle row) F.A. Mackinnon, A.N. Hornby, Lord Harris (capt.), H.C. Maul, G. Ulyett. (Front row) A.P. Lucas, V.P.F.A. Royle, T. Emmett.

5

ABANDONED AUSSIES

The Australian selectors generally speaking, have been much more reasonable in granting extended opportunities to their Test players. Nevertheless 53 Australians have leaped in and out of Test cricket in the space of one match. The first to go were Ned Gregory, maker of Test history's original duck's egg, and B.B. Cooper of the 1877 side. They were quickly followed by Frank Allan — 'the bowler of the century'. Allan toured England in 1878, but his only Test was against Lord Harris' team at Melbourne in 1879. Allan captured 4 for 80 in the two innings, but was completely outshone by Spofforth and hardly lived up to his reputation. Perhaps his flippant attitude towards the First Test, when, having been selected, he withdrew at the last minute, deserved a come uppance.

The general pattern with Australian cricket has been to produce settled sides for quite long periods and to intersperse these with short spates of experimental selection. Sometimes the experiments have been forced upon them, as for example in 1880 at the Oval. This Test was arranged almost at the last minute of their tour. Spofforth was injured and the side included three players — T. Groube, W. Moule and J. Slight, all of Victoria — making their sole appearance in a Test. Groube and Slight both scored 11 and 0, and Moule scored 6 in the first knock. But in the second innings the latter enjoyed his finest hour. Billy Murdoch, the captain, fighting a noble rearguard action in the follow on, was partnered by Moule in a last wicket stand of 88 which saved the innings defeat. Moule, who had captured 3 for 23 in England's innings — his total bag of wickets for the tour was 4 — kept his end up to the tune of 34 invaluable runs before falling to Billy Barnes. Murdoch, meanwhile, had advanced to 153 not out and England had to fight hard for the 57 runs needed for victory. Moule had deserved well of his country, but further recognition was not forthcoming.

In the Second Test of Shaw's 1881-2 tour at Sydney a certain G. Coulthard from Victoria batted number eleven for Australia. Previously he had been a central figure in the riot at Sydney in 1878 when his umpiring was considered to have favoured Lord Harris' 'Gentlemen of England' side. Graduating to an active role, Coulthard scored 6 not out and didn't bowl — Palmer and Evans being on the rampage. He wasn't required in the second innings, Australia winning by 5 wickets, and bowed out of Test cricket with a batting average of infinity. A year later Coulthard was dead of consumption, so further opportunities — as player or umpire — were denied him.

1885 witnessed one of the upheavals which seem to occur periodically between Australian Test players and the authorities of the various grounds. The 1884 side which had toured England demanded 50% of the gate money at Melbourne in January 1885. The authorities dropped the whole team and substituted a weird-looking combination containing no less than 5 players destined to make their one and only appearance for Australia. S. Morris, H. Musgrove, and W. Robertson of Victoria and R.J. Pope and A.P. Marr of New South Wales, scored 37 runs between them in the two innings. Morris the first black man to play for Australia (he was of West Indian origin) did manage 10 not out in his second knock, but their combined average of 4 was abysmal. Marr, Robertson and Morris bowled in England's large first innings of 401. Morris took 2 for 73 (Arthur Shrewsbury and Billy Barnes) in 34 overs, while the other two trundled 23 overs for 38 runs; economical but not incisive. Of these, perhaps Morris should have had another chance. Later in the same rubber F.H. Walters of Victoria scored 7 and 5 in the innings defeat at Melbourne. He also made a couple of catches without looking up to Test class. His penchant for slow scoring allowed bowlers to dominate him and it was no surprise that he toured England in 1890 with very moderate success.

The 1886 tour of England saw H.J. Scott's side beaten in all 3 matches — twice by an innings. In the last of these games John McIlwraith, who had experienced a mediocre tour with the bat, was chosen to make his sole appearance. He scored 2 and 7. Though capable of brilliant stroke play, McIlwraith's defence was suspect, particularly on English pitches. Business interests removed McIlwraith from the cricket scene after his return to Australia. The winter of the same year at Sydney found a number of regular players unavailable. This gave an opportunity to R.C. Allen and J.T. Cottam of New South Wales. Allen scored 14 and 30 — in totals of 84 and 150 — and played well enough to merit further consideration, but Cottam's efforts only came to 1 and 3. Neither of them bowled, though Allen made 2 catches and Cottam 1. Cottam never played a match for his state, so this Test provided him with his only opportunity in first class cricket, a unique experience.

Stoddart's side of 1894-5 shook the Australians by taking a 2-0 lead in the rubber. The home side again experimented, trying 21 different players in an attempt to stem the tide. Jack Reedman, the postman from South Australia, played at Sydney in the First Test, the one when Australia made 586, forcing England to follow on, yet lost by 10 runs. Reedman with 17 and 4 and 1 for 24 did not set Sydney alight. He was replaced at Melbourne by Coningham, the redoubtable Queenslander who had toured England in 1893. Coningham achieved instant fame by getting Archie MacLaren with his first ball in Test cricket, a kicker which Harry Trott pouched safely at point. Later on Coningham had Brockwell for 0 to return 2 for 17 in 11 overs, but his second innings spell cost 59 runs in 20 overs, with no further victims. Since his batting realised only 13 in two knocks and his attitude to authority was somewhat antagonistic, it is not too surprising that he gave way to Albert Trott for the remainder of the series. Coningham had toured England in 1893, but was given little opportunity to shine in Jack Blackham's cliquey side.

The Third Test at Adelaide gave all rounder Jack Harry of Victoria his chance. Harry, ambidextrous enough to bowl efficiently with either hand, was only required as a batsman. He scored 2 and 6, falling each time to Tom Richardson, and was unable to hold his place, even though Australia won by a colossal 382 runs. Harry was chosen for the 1896 tour of England, but an injured knee forced him to withdraw from the side. He then made the trip to England privately and obtained an engagement with Lord's ground staff, but success eluded him. Another lone performer of pre World War I days was J.F. Travers, of South Australia, who played in the last match against MacLaren's 1901-2 side. With Trumble and Noble capturing 15 of the wickets, Travers only bowled 8 overs for 14 runs and 1 wicket in the first innings. He didn't get a chance in the second knock.

A good performance by **J.W. McLaren** in the final Test at Sydney against Johnny Douglas's victorious side, could have established him for the Triangular Tour of England in 1912. His 1 for 70 in 24 overs and not out 'spectacles' hardly constituted the credentials of a Test player. The aftermath of the rumpus between the leading players and the Board of Control left Australia woefully short of tourists however, so it was not too surprising that McLaren — a diabetic — was chosen for the tour. His record was one of the weakest in a weak side and he never regained his Test place.

Another 1912 tourist was Edgar Mayne of Victoria. At Old

Trafford he failed to get even one innings in a rain-ruined match and was never honoured again. He fielded out to an English total of 203, the main feature of which was a fine 92 by Wilfrid Rhodes on a bad wicket. Since Mayne is reputed to have used his position on Australia's Board of Control to vote himself a trip to England, perhaps sympathy is misplaced. Mayne toured again, with Armstrong's team in 1921, but he was unable to regain his Test place; the competition was too strong. Poor Mayne — he didn't even have the opportunity to fail!

Between the wars, Australia had a regular side for most of the twenties. Apart from Dr. R.L. Park who made 0 in his only innings at Melbourne in 1920 — he was out first ball — the only one matcher of the twenties was the 35 year old A.E. Hartkopf of Victoria. Hartkopf played an excellent innings of 80 at Melbourne in the Second Test of 1925, and though he scored a duck in the second knock, it was his ineffectual leg-break bowling — the chief reason for his selection — which cost him his place.

The final break-up of Armstrong's team occurred in 1928-9 and ushered in another period of experiments, mainly on the bowling side. The first of these was Otto Nothling, of Queensland, a medium pacer who took the place of the injured Jack Gregory at Sydney in 1928. Nothling took 0 for 74 in 46 overs — economical but ineffective. His 44 (run out) in Australia's second innings helped to make England bat again but Australia lost by 8 wickets.

The Bodyline Series had four one Test performers. H S. Love kept wicket in place of Bertie Oldfield, injured by a Larwood delivery, in the Fourth Test at Brisbane. Love scored 5 and 3 and made 3 catches, but he had to give way to Oldfield when the maestro recovered. Laurie Nagel and H. Alexander of Victoria, and P.K. Lee of South Australia, were each tried once as bowlers. Nagel's 2 for 110 at Sydney in the First Test was better than Alexander's 1 for 154 at the same venue in the last, but Lee surpassed both of them with 4 for 163 in that last match. Lee also made 42 and 15, whereas Nagel's total was 21 and Alexander's only 17. Lee probably should have toured England in 1934, but his place went to Hans Ebeling, of Victoria, whose one Test at the Oval on that tour yielded 2 and 41, and 3 wickets for 89 runs. Australia won this game by 562 runs, but Ebeling never played again against England.

The rain-drenched Brisbane Test of 1936-7 against Gubby Allen's side provided a debut for Ray Robinson of New South Wales. He scored

2 and 3 (c. Hammond, b. Voce in both innings). How ironic to make one's only Test appearance — as a batsman — on a Brisbane gluepot . Robinson was only 22 and really should have been given another chance. Laurie Nash, a rough and ready Victorian, who played only once for his state, was introduced into the final Test at Melbourne in 1937. With the rubber poised 2-2, Nash was probably Australia's insurance against a return by the English to Bodyline tactics. Nash's 5 for 104 in the match was the next best contribution to O'Reilly's in bowling the Englishmen to an innings defeat. He ought in fact have been taken to England in 1938 when Australia sported its weakest bowling side of the century.

In the post World War II era, Australia rarely picked one-Test men, except when they were required to substitute for a temporarily injured regular player. Thus Fred Freer, a fast-medium bowler from Victoria, took the place of Ray Lindwall at Sydney in 1946. His 3 for 74 and 28 not out could not prevent Lindwall's return for the next match. The same series saw Mervyn Harvey — the great Neil's elder brother — open for Australia at Adelaide in the Fourth Test. Barnes was injured and Harvey scored 12 and 31 as partner to Arthur Morris. Barnes returned for the last Test, but Harvey could well have been worth a trip to England — though it might have been at his younger brother's expense. Finally Ronnie Hamence of South Australia took Ian Johnson's place at Sydney for the last game. He scored 30 in the first innings (batting at No.6) before running out of partners. Hamence did come to England in 1948 but played in no further Tests. Like Edgar Mayne in 1921, he lost out to fierce competition from a glut of talented players. (Yet a superb cover drive of his off Jim Sims at Lord's in 1948 remains firmly in the memory.) At Leeds in 1948 Ron Saggers, the New South Wales keeper, replaced the injured Don Tallon. Saggers made 3 catches and allowed only 6 byes in over 800 runs, but Tallon was just that vital bit better and resumed his place at the Oval.

In 1950-51 the Australians were in difficulties over an opening partner for Arthur Morris. Sid Barnes was in disgrace with the Board of Control and his mantle fell on Jack Moroney of New South Wales. Moroney had enjoyed a good tour of South Africa during the previous season, but his Test baptism was by fire. He lasted 4 balls in his first innings — c. Hutton b. Bailey from a leg glance — and only 3 in his second — l.b.w. Bailey. Thus Moroney's Ashes career lasted 7 balls and provided him with a pair, an even less impressive record than that of Dr. R.L. Park in 1920. The last Test of 1955 at Sydney saw the

dropping of Arthur Morris from Australia's Team. William Watson of
New South Wales was Morris' replacement. He scored 18 and 3. Jim
Burke promptly took over from him for the 1956 tour of England.
During that series Pat Crawford, of New South Wales, got his chance in
the Second Test at Lord's. Lindwall and Alan Davidson were both
injured and Crawford opened the bowling with Keith Miller — for 4.5
overs. Then he broke down and departed from Test Cricket with 0
wickets for 4 runs and 0 runs as a batsman. (He bagged a pair but the
first duck was 'not out'.) Crawford was the first of a succession of
quick bowlers who were introduced to Tests in the fifties and sixties
and then rapidly dropped. The Chucker series of 1958-9 had Keith
Slater (Western Australia) bowling at Sydney in the Third Test. He took
2 for 101, but his action — like that of many others — was suspect, and
he did not hold his place.

In 1961 Ron Gaunt of Victoria was chosen as partner for Alan
Davidson at the Oval. He took 3 for 53 and 0 for 33 — economical, but
not very impressive figures. C. Guest, also of Victoria, followed at
Sydney in 1963; his bag was an even less impressive 0 for 59. Peter
Allan (Queensland) took the injured Graham McKenzie's place at
Brisbane in 1965. He captured 2 for 83. Then in 1971, when McKenzie
finally dropped out, Duncan, of Victoria, and Dell, of Queensland, were
given one match each. Duncan's 0 for 30 at Melbourne was surpassed
by Dell's 5 for 97 at Sydney, but by that time Denis Lillee had been
discovered. Dell was probably unlucky to miss the 1972 tour of
England where he might well have been more effective than David
Colley.

Two more discarded debutants were Brian Taber, the New South
Wales stumper, who played at Edgbaston in 1968, and Ken Eastwood,
the Victorian opening bat. Taber scored 15, made a couple of catches
and conceded 4 byes in 550 runs. He then lost his place to Barry
Jarman and eventually to Rodney Marsh. Eastwood's 5 and 0 at Sydney
in the final Test in 1970-1 was no substitute for Bill Lawry's grafting,
though he owed his inclusion to his state captain's fall from favour.
Something of a veteran, Eastwood was out of his depth against Snow
and Peter Lever. Another bowler tried in the sixties was David Sincock,
a South Australian leg-spinner. Sincock conceded 98 runs in 10 overs in
Bob Barber's match at Sydney in 1966, without taking a wicket.
Innings of 29 and 27 were not sufficient to redeem him in the eyes of
the Aussie selectors.

The most recent loners in the Australian ranks have been Mick

Malone, Trevor Laughlin, Andrew Hilditch, Dirk Welham and Carl Rackemann — the last three still young enough to challenge for further honours. Malone made his debut at the Oval in 1977. With 6 wickets for 67 and an innings of 46, he seemed to have taken a long lease on a place in the side. Then he joined Kerry Packer's circus and later moved to Lancashire. He reappeared recently in state cricket and though now 32 may yet receive further caps. Laughlin, a Victorian, played at Brisbane in 1978. Innings of 2 and 5, plus 0 for 60, hardly established his credentials as a Test all-rounder. He was one of the early casualties of Graham Yallop's unsuccessful side. The second 1978-9 Anglo-Australian encounter at Sydney saw Andrew Hilditch make his debut as opening partner to Graham Wood. He was run out for 3, scored 1 in his second knock, and has not been called on since.

The Oval Test of 1981 saw 22 year old Dirk Welham of New South Wales make one of the most impressive debuts in the history of Anglo-Australian Tests. This bespectacled batsman made only 24 in his first knock, but then proceeded to claim his place in the record books by scoring a vital ton in his second. When he joined Alan Border, just before lunch on the fourth day, Australia were 104 for 4 — a lead of only 142. Welham, dropped when 18, helped Border to add 101, and then batted on to take Australia past 300. He was dropped again — on 99 — but then cover drove Botham for 4 to reach his century and apparently ensure his selection for further Tests. Inexplicably the Australians did not select him for any match in the 1982-3 rubber.

Carl Rackemann of Queensland had his opportunity at his home ground, Brisbane, in November 1982. Injuries to Denis Lillee and Terry Alderman in the previous Test paved the way for Rackemann and Jeff Thomson to stake their claims. Ironically, the veteran Thomson clinched his place, but new boy Rackemann broke down with a groin strain and blew his chances for the rest of the series. His 2 for 96 compared unfavourably with the returns of Thomson and Geoff Lawson.

The unluckiest of these abandoned Australians were Hartkopf, Lee, Nash, Hamence, Dell and Welham. All six played well enough at this first time of asking to have been honoured further. None of the rest could complain too bitterly, except Edgar Mayne whose career was ended almost before it began by a combination of Jupiter Pluvius and Kaiser Bill. Malone, of course, set himself back by joining Kerry Packer at a crucial stage of his development. Of these instant rejects 26 — just half — hailed from Victoria, a clear sign that the influence of Melbourne has too often played a major part in Australian team selection. The almost equal rejection rate of both countries (one in five players failing to survive their baptism) points to a consistency of sorts in the deliberations of the selectors. It cannot have provided much solace for the unfortunate rejects.

6

BRITISH BRACES

Seventy-eight cricketers have been given two chances to prove their ability in the Ashes Test arena. Most of them made their appearances in consecutive Tests of the same rubber and the vast majority failed to make good use of the opportunities granted to them. We have already seen that more than 100 of the players who appeared only once in these games did little to encourage the selectors to pick them again. Much the same applied to the majority of the 'two timers'. A fair proportion were of course temporary replacements for injured regulars. They more or less had to be selected because they were members of beleaguered touring sides. Nevertheless, a few performed with distinction and fully merited further honours which, alas, were not forthcoming.

Of the 45 Englishmen in this category only a handful showed exceptional potential. The first of these was Alan Hill of Yorkshire who, as a member of Lillywhite's pioneers, averaged 50 with the bat and captured 6 wickets at 21.66 each. Hill's career was brought to an untimely end by an injury – though, like most of his fellow pioneers, he had failed to gain the selectors' favour in home Tests. Six more of Lillywhite's side also missed further honours after that first tour. This was rightly so in the case of Armitage, Charlwood, Greenwood and Jupp for they were not of true Test Match stature. Lillywhite and Southerton, the round arm bowlers, probably had the requisite class in their prime – but they were veterans in 1877 and were no longer England's best bowlers.

During the rest of the nineteenth century, five more players turned out twice against Australia. Sir Timothy O'Brien of Middlesex had a flukey debut at Old Trafford in 1884 and was promptly dropped for the rest of the series. Four years later he reappeared at Lord's, was bowled in each innings by Charlie Turner and departed the Test scene with 24 runs in his 4 innings. O'Brien's 1888 replacement was Frank Sugg of Lancashire. Sugg began at the Oval with a streaky 31 which he followed with 24 at Old Trafford. England won both games by an innings, so Sugg could claim some status as a talisman even if his batting was only average. With competition for batting places from

Shrewsbury, Gunn and the two Reads, it is not surprising that Sugg failed to keep his place for the 1890 rubber.

In 1899 England's bowling was going through a transitional phase. Tom Richardson and Johnny Briggs were finished as Test bowlers and Wilfrid Rhodes was just beginning his international career. In this, the first five match series in England, the home side used 15 bowlers but they lost the rubber 1-0 with 4 drawn. Three of these bowlers played in two matches each. Charles Townsend of Gloucestershire was picked for the Second Test at Lord's and captured 3 for 50 with his leg breaks. Australia won by 10 wickets and Townsend was one of 5 players dropped. Recalled for the last game at the Oval, he contributed 38 to England's gigantic 576, but was only asked to bowl 13 overs in Australia's two innings. His captain, the autocratic Archie MacLaren, obviously did not esteem his bowling, despite Townsend's rating as one of Wisden's Players of the Year. 'Sailor' Young, Essex's medium-paced left hander, enjoying a great season, played at Leeds and Old Trafford, the third and fourth games. He bagged 6 wickets in each game and gave the redoubtable Victor Trumper a good deal of trouble, bowling particularly well at Old Trafford, where for good measure he hammered 43 useful runs. Inexplicably Young was dropped for the Oval game and was never recalled. His 12 wickets at 21.83 each constitute one of the better Test bowling records. MacLaren's third 'new' trundler was W.M. Bradley of Kent. This amateur fast bowler began with 5 for 67 at Old Trafford, forcing Australia to follow on. He was kept on for too long by his illustrious captain, bowling 33 overs in the first innings and 46 in the second. His return of 1 for 82 in the Aussies' second knock reflected this over-taxing of his powers. In the final game at the Oval, Bradley failed to get a wicket. This time he bowled 46 overs in the match for 84 runs and MacLaren promptly lost faith in him. When Archie selected his side for the 1901-2 tour of Australia, he opted for Sydney Barnes instead of the 'Old Cracks, Bradley and Richardson, who have gone stale'.

MacLaren's captaincy in this his first home rubber, displayed early signs of the fickleness which marred his leadership throughout his career. His reputation as a captain was tremendous but his performance was often sub-standard. In the cases of these three bowlers, he over-bowled Bradley, underused Townsend, and allowed Young, England's most effective bowler of the series, to be dropped for the final Test. At times MacLaren was a good twelfth man for Australia.

The 1901-2 tour provided a Test place for Charlie McGahey of

Essex. Joining the tour for the sake of his health, McGahey played in the 4th and 5th games at Sydney and Melbourne, as a replacement for the injured S.F. Barnes. MacLaren had only been able to take 13 players, so replacing his leading bowler with an average county bat was unavoidable. McGahey failed to contribute effectively and England lost both matches. Back in England Lionel Palairet, the Somerset stylist, was called up for the Fourth and Fifth Tests in 1902 (Tate's and Jessop's matches) as a replacement for C.B. Fry. His top score in 4 innings was 20, not a good return for an opening bat. England tried 4 different opening pairs in this rubber (MacLaren in charge again) and Palairet was partnered by Bobby Abel, in his last Test, and then by MacLaren. One of the many amateurs unable to tour abroad, Palairet had faded from the Test scene by the time the Aussies arrived again in 1905.

In the pre World War I era, three more cricketers were given a couple of games for England. Two of these came from Sussex. R.A. Young toured Australia in 1907-8 as reserve wicket-keeper to Humphries of Derbyshire. Bespectacled and scholarly-looking, Young was drafted into the First Test at Sydney to stiffen the batting. How often has England fallen into this trap. Young opened the 1st innings — with the youthful Jack Hobbs omitted from the side — and scored 13. Relegated to Number 7 in the second knock, he scored 3. As he also missed 3 vital catches, Young's debut was not a success. Humphries replaced him for the next 3 games, but, with the rubber lost, he returned for the final Test, scoring 0 and 11, taking 4 catches and allowing 30 byes. Australia won this game as well, so Young disappeared into Test history to ponder on two defeats on the same ground. It is unlikely that he would even have been considered for the side in England.

A more successful career was the lot of Joe Vine. Chosen for Plum Warner's 1911-12 side, Vine was something of a veteran. His batting for Sussex was still top-class, but his best days as a leg-break bowler were behind him. A place in this very strong England side was difficult to obtain, but an injury to fast bowler Hitch gave Vine a chance in the last two Tests of the series. At Melbourne he batted ninth — the strength of the batting was such that Woolley and Philip Mead were Nos. 7 and 8 — scoring 4 not out in a total of 589. England won by an innings. Promoted one place at Sydney, Vine scored 36 and 6 not out to finish his Test career with a batting average of 46 and, since England won this Test too, a 100% victory record.

In the Triangular Test rubber of 1912 Harry Dean, a left-arm bowler from Lancashire, played at Lord's where he took 2 for 49, and the Oval where his 4 for 19 in the second innings helped Frank Woolley to clinch the only win of the rubber. Curiously, he was omitted from the Second Test at Old Trafford, his home ground, Schofield Haigh of Yorkshire being preferred. The Great War effectively ended Dean's prospects of further recognition.

The Roaring Twenties erupted on the English cricket world in the shape of Warwick Armstrong's Australians. Abe Waddington, a Yorkshire pace bowler, toured in 1920-21, playing in the First Test at Sydney (1 for 88) and the Fourth at Melbourne (0 for 31). At least, Waddington had his second chance. The following season, back in England, no fewer than 10 players were discarded after just one appearance. Two men were a little luckier. Vallance Jupp, then of Sussex, later of Northants., and Donald Knight of Surrey played at Trent Bridge. Knight, whose early confidence had been impaired by a blow on the head while fielding in 1920, opened with Holmes in the absence of the injured Hobbs and scored 8 and 38. His second innings was just beginning to flower when he was disastrously run out by Hendren's change of mind, after he had fairly committed Knight to a run. Jupp succumbed to the pace of McDonald and Gregory in his two innings and was given a mere 5 overs by Johnny Douglas when Australia batted. Even so, he bowled Warwick Armstrong at a cost of only 14 runs. Knight was retained for the Lord's Test, where he failed with innings of 7 and 1. Jupp was dropped for this game, but was recalled for the next one at Leeds. Here he scored 14 and 28 and captured 4 wickets with his off breaks. Percy Fender then got his place for the remaining games. Since England lost all 3 matches, very few of the side survived, and Jupp and Knight were not among the fortunate.

Arthur Gilligan's tour, of 1924-5, provided the only opportunities for A.P. Freeman, of Kent, to play against Australia. 'Tich', one of the most prolific wicket-takers of all time, captured 5 wickets at 51 apiece in the First Test at Sydney. He was Maurice Tate's main support in this game, when, for good measure, he scored 50 not out in the second innings. England had pinned hopes on leg spin for this tour, and so Dick Tyldesley took Freeman's place for the Second Test . He failed to take a wicket and 'Tich' returned for the Adelaide game. In this match he injured a wrist while fielding and failed to do himself justice with the ball, but again did well with the bat. In a defiant rearguard action he helped his captain to bring England close to victory. A gallant effort ended 12 runs short. Freeman's finger-spinning style was not really suited to Australian conditions. His lack of success there seemed to influence the selectors against him for home Tests, yet he was selected for a second tour in 1928-29. At his peak in the late twenties and early thirties, Freeman would probably have done well in the home rubbers of 1926 and 1930.

Freeman, born in 1888, was knocking on a bit by then, so the selectors tried a couple of younger googly merchants instead. In the sodden 1926 series Greville Stevens of Middlesex played in the last two matches. At Old Trafford he captured 3 for 86 and scored 24; at the Oval, in the match which brought the Ashes back to England, he scored 17 and 22 but only managed 2 for 98 with his bowling. Certainly, Freeman would have been a better bet than Stevens. Ian Peebles, also of Middlesex, played in the corresponding games in 1930. At Manchester he bowled 55 overs, causing Bradman considerable trouble and taking 3 for 150 in a total of 345. In Australia's massive 695 at the Oval, Peebles claimed 6 victims for 204 in 71 overs of high class googly bowling. Unfortunately Peebles suffered an injury to his shoulder and though he continued in county cricket through the thirties, his great promise was never fulfilled at Test level.

1934 saw the aftermath of Bodyline. With Larwood and Voce unavailable , and Farnes injured after the Lord's Test, England tried 'Nobby' Clark of Northants. at Manchester for the Third Test. Clark, a left-arm quickie, took 1 for 116 in the match. He was replaced by Bowes at Leeds, only to be recalled at the Oval for the deciding game of the series. Australia scored 701 (Clark 2 for 110) and 327. In this latter innings Clark took five for 98 in 20 overs, bowling dangerously but erratically. Australia won by 562 runs and Clark dropped out of the Test picture. He was never in Farnes' class — nor Bowes' — and was probably lucky to survive his debut match. The same series saw the entry and exit of J. Hopwood (Lancashire). Ostensibly an all-rounder, Hopwood played at Old Trafford and Leeds, scoring 12 runs in 3 innings and taking 0 for 155 in 77 overs, one of the least glorious of Test careers. As he performed the Double for his county in 1934, Test selection seemed justified, but the step-up in class was beyond him.

The last 'two-timers' of the inter-war period were Arthur Fagg (Kent) and Jim Sims (Middlesex). These two visited Australia with Gubby Allen's side. Fagg played in the first two Tests — both of which were won — but did not contribute significantly to the successes. He fell ill, of rheumatic fever, later in the tour and had to return prematurely to England. His form immediately prior to World War II was impressive — though competition for the openers' positions in the early forties would have been very intense. (Hutton, Barnett, John Langridge, Washbrook, Gimblett to name a few). Like many, Fagg lost his best seasons to the War. Jim Sims played at Sydney and Melbourne, scoring 3 runs in 2 innings and taking 3 wickets for 244 runs with his leg breaks. A good county player, Sims was well past thirty when he made this tour and like Hopwood, he was not able to raise his game sufficiently.

Yet another in the succession of English leg spin failures was Peter Smith of Essex. In the first post-war tour Smith obtained a good haul of wickets in minor matches. He replaced Bill Voce for the Second Test at Sydney, took 2 for 172 and was dropped. After a bout of mid-tour illness, Smith returned for the final Test also at Sydney. This time, he bowled only 10 overs for 46 runs. Smith was 38 years old, had lost some of his best seasons to the war and had not been well. It was asking too much of him to be effective against one of Australia's strongest-ever teams.

The same all-conquering team arrived in England in 1948. England, searching for middle-order batsmen to replace the retired Walter Hammond tried Tom Dollery of Warwickshire at Lord's and Manchester. Three innings brought just 38 runs, Dollery being clean bowled each time by one of the Aussie pacemen. The extra speed of Lindwall & Co. was too much for him. In this same series England was also searching for a pace bowler to partner Alec Bedser. Dick Pollard, of Lancashire, had toured Australia in 1946-7 without making a Test appearance. He now made two in quick succession. 3 for 59 at Old Trafford was a good effort and at Leeds he began by dismissing Hassett and Bradman for next to nothing. After that his bowling declined and he finished the match with the poor analysis of 2 for 159. Like Sims and Dollery, Pollard was well into his thirties, too old to make a lasting impact as a pace-bowler.

A number of young players went to Australia under Freddie Brown's leadership in 1950-51. One of these was John Warr, the Middlesex pace bowler, who bowled 36 overs at Sydney and 37 at Adelaide to the tune of 281 runs and 1 wicket. Warr, a bad bat and, at that time, a worse field had only willingness and perseverance to offer. His selection was largely due to injuries to senior players. Another was Gilbert Parkhouse, the Glamorgan batsman, whose 77 runs in 4 innings in the Second and Third Tests disappointed the high hopes of the selectors. He was replaced by David Sheppard (not then Reverend) who achieved even less. By the end of the series Parkhouse was 4th in England's batting averages. The controversial Brian Close also made his debut in this series. He scored 0 and 1 and, despite his tender years – he was only 19 at the time – he incurred the censure of the Press for the crudity of his methods. It was 11 years before he played against Australia again. This second occasion was in Benaud's Match at Old Trafford in 1961. Close made a useful 33 in the first innings, but his slogging methods against the wily Australian captain failed to stem the tide in the last innings and once more the Press roundly condemned him. Having seen no less a batsman than Peter May bowled round his legs out of the rough on that occasion, one tends to question why Close should have been the scapegoat. (If May had got his leg in front of that ball he could not have been out as l.b.w. did not apply to leg breaks pitched outside the line of the stumps. I wonder why the Press didn't give May the same kind of roasting as they gave Close.) Although he appeared in Tests against other countries – and indeed captained England – Close's swan song against Australia was this Old Trafford debacle.

In between Close's two efforts, six more players made twin appearances for England. Don Kenyon, Worcester's opening bat, scored 29 in 4 innings in 1953; while Alan Oakman, of Sussex, scored 14 in 2 innings in 1956. Oakman's contribution in the field was much more important than his batting. He made seven fine catches at short leg to Jim Laker's off spinners – 5 of them in Laker's Match at Old Trafford. His batting and bowling were not up to standard however, and he had to make way for a fit Denis Compton at the Oval. The 1958-59 tour blooded a host of new players. Arthur Milton, Gloucester's opening bat, failed in the Brisbane and Sydney Tests with 38 in 4 innings; as did Roy Swetman, the reserve stumper, much overrated by the Press, who had to replace a suddenly injury-prone Godfrey Evans in the Third and Fifth Tests. Swetman did manage 41 in his first Test knock at Sydney but it took him 2½ hours and the injured Evans was much-missed behind the stumps. His performance at Melbourne was only average, yet the Press hastened Evans's premature retirement by an undue eulogising of Swetman's skills. Peter Loader, also of Surrey, won selection for the first two Tests over his pace-bowling rivals, Frank Tyson and Freddie Trueman. He bagged 7 wickets at 27 each, but tired noticeably in both games which resulted in defeats for England. An accident later in the tour ensured that he would not be recalled and Trueman established himself as Statham's partner in subsequent seasons.

The last of this group was John Mortimore of Gloucester. He was flown out as a replacement off-spinner towards the end of this tour and played at Melbourne in the last Test. He scored 44 not out and 11 and took 1 for 41. For the next 5 or 6 years Mortimore was overshadowed by his county colleague David Allen, but in 1964 at Old Trafford he was selected for England once again. This was Simpson's Match, when the Australian skipper scored 311, and Mortimore bowled 49 overs for 122 runs on one of the plumbest wickets of the post-war era. In that same game Tom Cartwright, Warwickshire's stock bowler, delivered 77 overs, 32 maidens, taking 2 wickets for 118, a wearying baptism. The next game at the Oval found Cartwright trundling a further 62 overs, 23 maidens, to take 3 for 110. Five wickets for 228, even with 55 maidens thrown in, was a dispiriting experience for one of county cricket's most consistent bowlers. Philip Sharpe, Yorkshire batsman, was given the number six place at Trent Bridge and Lord's in the 1964 rubber. He scored 71 in 3 innings for an average of 35.50, but was dropped once both Boycott and John Edrich were free of injury. Since his slip fielding was outstanding, Sharpe had every right to feel aggrieved about his exclusion from further Tests.

The Lancashire pace bowler Ken Higgs toured Australia in 1965-66. He played at Brisbane, taking 2 for 102, then was injured and missed the succeeding Tests. His next appearance was on his home patch at Old Trafford in 1968, where his haul was 2 for 121. David Brown of Warwickshire took over for the rest of the series. Another 1968 debutant was the ill-starred Colin Milburn. The genial Northants. opener gave a fireworks display at Lord's scoring 67 in 80 minutes on the second morning. He made 83 before holing out to Walters on the square leg boundary. Then he was injured and missed the next two Tests. Returning at the Oval, Milburn made 8 and 18, but most judges felt that he had ensured his place for years to come. Sometime later Milburn lost the sight of one eye in a motoring accident and retired, perforce, from Test cricket, in one of the saddest endings to a career.

Lancashire produced two Test pace bowlers in the early seventies: Ken Shuttleworth and Peter Lever. Both toured with Ray Illingworth in 1970-71. Shuttleworth appeared at Brisbane, where he took 5 for 47 in the second innings, and Perth. His total bag of 7 wickets cost 34 runs each and he was supplanted by Bob Willis for the rest of the series.

Wayne Larkins of Northamptonshire made his debut at Melbourne in the Third Test of the short tour of 1979-80. Batting at number 3 he managed only 25 and 3 and was not called on again until the Oval Test of 1981. There, Larkins was picked as an opener and he obliged with scores of 34 and 24. His future participation in these matches must be doubtful since his recent visit to South Africa.

The unlucky players in the above list were undoubtedly Milburn and Sharpe among the batsmen and 'Sailor' Young, Dean and Peebles among the bowlers. Vine, though a veteran, also merited further selection and Freeman was entitled to a chance to purvey his wares in his own country. The only other unfortunates were pace bowlers Alan Hill and Loader, both of whom suffered from hot competition. When one considers that injuries prematurely curtailed the careers of Milburn, Peebles and Hill; that Dean and Vine lost out to World War I; and that Freeman was pushing 40 and could not have been expected to achieve what he actually did in the thirties; then only Phil Sharpe and 'Sailor' Young were scurvily treated by the selectors. Two mistakes in forty five is not a bad record.

H. 'Sailor' Young (Essex) played twice in 1899, taking six wickets in each game (average 21.83); he also averaged 21.50 with the bat.

7

KANGAROO COUPLETS

Thirty three Australians have been given just two bites at the Test cherry. Four of these were among the 1877 pioneers. Nat Thompson, Tom Kendall, Kelly and Hodges have already been considered, Kendall being the really unlucky discard. His 14 wickets fully justified further recognition, especially as he outshone Spofforth in the Second Test.

In 1880 G. Alexander, the tour manager, was pressed into service at the Oval. Injury had deprived Australia of Spofforth and, with only 12 players available, Alexander had to fill the breach. He did so nobly, making 33 at number 10 in the second innings, actually outscoring the redoubtable Billy Murdoch in a stand of 52. Alexander and Moule — the No.11 — helped Murdoch to avert the innings defeat, and, though Australia lost by 5 wickets, the manager, with 2 for 69 (Barnes and Lord Harris) in England's first innings, plus a good catch to dismiss E.M. Grace, had reason to be satisfied with his efforts. Four years later Alexander again made up the number. The 1884 tourists, just returned from England, were picked 'en bloc' for the First Test at Adelaide. Spofforth and Midwinter were unavailable, so Alexander played. This time he failed to make an impact, Australia lost again, and his Test career was over.

In the same match W.H. Cooper — like Alexander, a Victorian — also ended a two match Test career. Cooper took up cricket on medical orders fairly late in life. He was all of twenty seven when he began bowling and within five years he was playing for Australia. At Melbourne in the First Test in 1881 Cooper took 9 wickets in the for 200 runs. This impressive return was earned with leg breaks of high quality and he seemed to be on the threshold of a successful career. Injury supervened however and Cooper disappeared temporarily from the scene. He reappeared in 1884 as a surprise selection for the tour of England. Unfortunately an accident to his bowling hand occurred on the voyage to England, and consequently he was only able to play a few of matches. The beleaguered state of the side when they returned to Australia made his services necessary at Adelaide. He failed with bat and ball, and decided to retire from the game altogether. Though a moderate batsman, he was a fine field at point and his retirement was a serious loss to Australia.

F.J. Burton, of New South Wales, was one of a queer conglomeration who played in the second Sydney Test of 1887. This was one of the periods when Australian selection was marred by inter-state squabbling. Burton replaced the great Jack Blackham as stumper, but did not distinguish himself. He batted number 11, scoring 0 and 2, both not out. The following year, again at Sydney, Burton somehow found his way into the batting order at number 4. He scored 1 in each innings, and did not even have the consolation of keeping wicket, for the mighty Blackham had returned. England won both games, so Burton derived little satisfaction from his Test appearances.

The 1890 tourists to England included several newcomers to Test cricket. Three of these — Barrett, Burn and Charlton — played in both Test matches; the third game at Old Trafford was rained off without a ball being bowled. Australia lost a low scoring game at Lord's and the left-handed Dr. Barrett became the first to carry his bat through a complete Test innings. A stonewaller, Barrett collected 67 out of Australia's second innings of 176 and made himself a special place in Test history. At the Oval, he was much less successful and his four Test innings produced a total of 80 runs at an average of 26.67. Barrett's medical duties restricted his cricket opportunities when he returned to Australia. He was not chosen for the Tests against W.G's. 1891-2 side, but he was considered for the 1893 tour of England. His slowness in the field was always a drawback and it probably cost him his place in that team.

The other two players were out of their depth in Test cricket. Ken Burn of Tasmania had been chosen for the 1890 tour on the misconception that he was a wicket-keeper. On the voyage to England it transpired that he had never kept in his life. Burn only made the Test side because Frank Walters was even less effective than he was, and because Sammy Jones, the smallpox victim of 1888, had never really recovered his form. The Tasmanian made 41 in his four innings. Percy Charlton of New South Wales, a 23 year old all-rounder, did little with the bat. The presence of the redoubtable Turner-Ferris combination in the side restricted the opportunities of the support bowlers and Charlton was not given a bowl at Lord's. At the Oval, however, he captured 3 for 18 in 6 overs, promising figures. Unfortunately Charlton was not blessed with good health and his subsequent first class performances were well below Test standard.

Another Tasmanian, the high-scoring Charles Eady, toured England in 1896. He was then 25 but much less experienced than most of his team-mates. With Jones, Trumble, Giffen and McKibbin taking 100 wickets each, Eady's quick bowling had little chance to shine, while his cramped batting style was found seriously wanting. His Tasmanian reputation probably gained him a place in the First Test at Lord's. He scored 10 not out and 2 and, even though he was Australia's best bowler in the 1st innings with 3 for 58, he was replaced by Frank Iredale for the rest of the series. Back at home, Eady was ignored for the next half a dozen seasons. Then in 1901-2 he amassed a colossal 566 for his club, Break O'Day, against Wellington and was recalled to the Test side for the final game against Archie MacLaren's side at Melbourne. Batting at No.10, Eady made 5 and 3 and, though his quick bowling accounted for 3 wickets at a cost of 10 runs each, he was obviously not a candidate for a permanent place in the side. Probably his remote situation away from the centres of Australian cricket adversely affected his prospects of regular selection.

D.R.A. (Algy) Gehrs, of South Australia, was twice picked as a substitute for Sid Gregory in the early years of the century. In the Fifth Test at Melbourne in 1904 he scored 3 and 5, making a couple of catches. Chosen for the 1905 tour, Gehrs found the competition for Test batting places far too hot. However, an injury to Gregory let him into the side at Old Trafford. He scored 0 and 11, Australia lost by an innings, and that was the end of Gehrs as a Test player.

The treatment of R.J. Hartigan, of Queensland, in 1908-9 left a good deal to be desired. For the Third Test at Adelaide Hartigan was given the place of G.R. Hazlitt whose wild throw had given England the winning run in the previous Test. Hartigan batted at No.8, scoring 48 in his first knock and helping Australia to a respectable 285. England replied with 363, then the Australians slumped to 180 for 7. At this point Hartigan was joined by Clem Hill suffering from influenza. Hill had not fielded, but he certainly batted effectively. Together these two put on 243, still the record Test partnership for the 8th wicket; and Hartigan scored 116 before falling to the mighty Barnes. Australia totalled 506 and ran out unexpected winners by 245. Hartigan's reward was to lose his place to the diminutive Sid Gregory. Gregory's lengthy Test career had almost ground to a halt in England in 1905 when injury forced him out of the final two Tests. The obvious man to make way for his recall in 1908 was Peter McAllister, whose six innings in the series to date totalled 114, 2 runs less than Hartigan's century knock. However, Hartigan, from unfashionable Queensland, was 'unavailable' and McAlister, a Victorian, perhaps because he had pull with the selectors, survived. Neither McAlister nor Gregory succeeded in the Fourth Test at Melbourne so Hartigan took the Victorian's place at Sydney. Hartigan, batting at number nine, failed this time, but he had done enough to book a place with the 1909 tourists. His performances on that tour were poor however. He appeared in barely half the matches, scoring a mere 400 runs at the mediocre average of 13 per innings. The indications are that he was not fully accepted by the players from the older states and lost interest as a result. He appeared in none of the Tests and was never considered again once he had returned to Australia. In view of his impressive debut, Hartigan merited a longer run of Test appearances. The 'Powers that be' failed to provide him with proper recognition and encouragement.

The 1912 Triangular team, led by Sid Gregory, comprised a handful of experienced players and a host of new boys. Two of the latter were D. Smith of Victoria and S.H. Emery of New South Wales. Smith, who was probably lucky to get a Test place at the expense of Edgar Mayne, played at Lord's and the Oval, collecting 30 runs in 3 innings, once not out. Emery, a dangerous but erratic leg-spin bowler, played in the rain-ruined games at Lord's and Old Trafford. He took 2 for 68. Though his best balls were well-nigh unplayable, his efficacy was impaired by the inaccuracy of his length, and he was outshone by the honest-to-goodness consistency of Jimmy Matthews.

Between the wars, a relatively stable period of Australian Test selection, only 3 players fell into this category of two-timers. The first of these was Ernie Bromley of Victoria, a tall, strong-wristed left hander. At Brisbane in 1933 Bromley played in place of Grimmett, scoring 26 and 7. He was supplanted for the last Test at Sydney by P.K. Lee of South Australia. Bromley however got the vote over Lee for the 1934 tour of England. He was chosen for the Lord's Test, made 5 runs in the match and was relegated to reserve status.

In 1936-37 the young Victorian Ross Gregory took over Len Darling's place for the last two Tests. At Adelaide Gregory collected 23 and 50, supporting his captain, Bradman, in a stand of 135 for the 5th wicket in the second innings. Australia squared the series in that game and at Melbourne clinched the rubber with an innings victory. Gregory contributed 80 to a stand of 161 with Badcock for the 5th wicket and seemed to have ensured his Test place for years to come. Eighteen months later however he was omitted from the 1938 touring side. Gregory's promising career came to a sad end during World War II when he was killed on air operations. That 1938 side included Mervyn Waite of South Australia, a medium-paced opening bowler. Waite was not called on for Test matches until the game at Leeds when he replaced Chipperfield. His 20 overs cost only 40 runs; Australia won and Waite retained his place for Hutton's Test at the Oval. There he bowled 72 overs for 150 runs and the wicket of Denis Compton. Then World War II came and Waite bowed out of Test cricket with 1 wicket for 190 to his credit.

The post-war years have seen a succession of short trials take place, mostly of bowlers, in the Australian ranks. Bruce Dooland, South Australia's leg spinner, who was later to play county cricket for Nottinghamshire with great success, turned out at Melbourne and Adelaide in 1947. He supplanted George Tribe of Victoria, but his 8 wickets for 43 runs each were hard earned, and Tribe regained his place for the final Test against Hammond's side. Dooland was Australia's best bowler at Melbourne, but he was expensive at Adelaide. If he had not moved into Lancashire League cricket, he would probably have been given Doug Ring's place on the 1948 tour. Ring, a burly Victorian leg spinner, was reserve member of Bradman's 1948 team. He gained a place in the Oval test because of an injury to Ernie Toshack, and bowled 28 tidy overs to take 1 for 44. His next appearance was at Lord's five years later. Replacing Jack Hill, Ring took 2 for 127 in the match, poor figures which confirmed his lack of true Test class. Jack Hill of Victoria, the man Ring replaced in 1953, bowled mainly top spinners. He acquitted himself well at Trent Bridge, taking 4 for 61 in the match, but was omitted at Lord's. Recalled at Old Trafford, he was the Australians' most effective bowler with 3 for 97 in England's only innings. Then he was dropped again, never to return. Australia would have been well advised to use him in all five Tests, for he was certainly a better bowler than either Ring or the raw youngster Richie Benaud.

Ian Craig was only 17 when he toured England in 1953. A right-handed batsman, he had an unfortunate tour and played no Tests. In 1956, at the ripe old age of 20, he toured again, and this time he was selected for the Manchester and Oval Tests. In Laker's match he scored 8 and 38. This latter innings took more than 4 hours, spread over 3 days because of interruptions by rain. Craig played Laker better than most in this game, but he failed at the Oval. His four innings brought him 55 runs and his combat with England ended before he was 21. He captained Australia in South Africa in 1957-8 and might have led against England in 1958-9, but hepatitis decreed otherwise. Richie Benaud took over and Craig's career was ended. He was clearly asked to do too much too soon.

The 1958-9 rubber was, like 1932-3, one of the more explosive ones. Australia unexpectedly won 4-0 and there was a good deal of acrimony about chucking. Two bowlers, Lindsay Kline and Gordon Rorke, were members of this successful side. Kline, a left-arm googly merchant from Victoria, made no impact at all in the first two Tests with his bowling, but his 'catch' of Cowdrey at a crucial point in the first match virtually decided that game. Most unbiased watchers thought the ball was not up. Kline's bowling showed the poor return of 0 for 77 in 25 overs and he was dropped for the remainder of the series. On the other hand, Rorke's bowling in the 4th and 5th games made much greater impact. Rorke, a massive pace bowler from New South Wales, collected 8 victims in the two games at 20 runs apiece, a better return than his illustrious team mates, Lindwall and Davidson, achieved. However, a suspect action, allied to a notorious drag on delivery, cast doubts on his real ability and he was among the many victims weeded out in the Australian Board's Chucker Hunt.

Both Rorke and Kline had Test batting averages of infinity (they scored 7 runs between them). Another New South Welshman of this period, Frank Misson, had the same average and gained the distinction of helping materially towards winning a Test match. Misson toured England in 1961 as a second string seam bowler. He appeared in the first two Tests at Edgbaston and Lord's and captured 7 wickets at 34 runs each. For the rest of the series the young Graham McKenzie took over the position of Davidson's opening partner, and Misson made way for Richie Benaud who had recovered from his shoulder injury. Misson's fame rests, however, on his batting not his bowling. At Lord's Misson batted last in Australia's 1st innings and scored an unbeaten 25 in a stand of 49 with Slasher Mackay, showing a surprising technique as he helped his side to a lead of 134. Australia won by 5 wickets and Misson had good reason to be satisfied with his efforts.

One of the poorly treated Australians was Barry Shepherd of Western Australia. This burly batsman took Peter Burge's place at Sydney in the Third Test of 1962-3. Australia won by 8 wickets, and Shepherd ran out of partners when he had made 71 in the first innings. England collapsed in their second knock, and Shepherd was not needed to bat again. The next Test at Adelaide was drawn. Shepherd contributed 10 and 13 and promptly gave way to Burge for the final

Test. His Test average at this stage was 47. Although he played 7 more Tests against other countries, Shepherd was never to oppose England again. He should have toured with Simpson's side in 1964.

In 1968 Eric Freeman, a useful all-rounder, made a likely-looking bowling debut. His 4 for 78 at Edgbaston included John Edrich, Cowdrey and Barrington as victims. In the next game at Leeds his haul was only 1 for 85. He was omitted for the Oval match in favour of Ashley Mallett. Ian Chappell's 1972 side gave an opportunity to Graeme Watson of Western Australia. He had a bad first match at Old Trafford, missed the next 3 Tests, and did little better at the Oval. 21 runs and 3 wickets for 92 were definitely not Test Match class.

Another two-match man was Gary Gilmour of New South Wales. Gilmour, a left-arm paceman and hard hitting bat, made his debut at Leeds in 1975. His bowling was impressive (9 for 157 in the match) and Gilmour seemed to be on the threshold of a fine career. A sore finger caused his omission from the Oval Test, but he was back in the Australian ranks for the Centenary Match at Melbourne in 1977. His form deserted him in this game, 20 runs and 0 for 33 being his contributions. This caused his omission from the 1977 tour to England, after which he took his talents into the camp of Kerry Packer. After the end of the Packer Circus, Gilmour did not regain his place, so his career had more potential than achievement.

During the 1978-79 series, K.J. Wright, the West Australian keeper and P. Carlson, a Queensland all-rounder, were picked for the last two tests against Mike Brearley's all-conquering team. Wright, replacing J. MacLean of Queensland, showed excellent form behind the sticks at Adelaide. 3 catches in each innings and only 2 byes conceded in a match total of 529 constituted an impressive debut. At Sydney his performance was less competent, and the return of Rodney Marsh from the Packer games prevented Wright from extending his tenure as Australia's stumper. He is young enough to come again though. Carlson was not in the least impressive. His batting realised a paltry 23 in 4 knocks, while his 2 wickets cost nearly 50 runs apiece. Carlson's career as a Test player began and ended with that series.

Julien Wiener of Victoria played twice during the 1979-80 rubber. He opened the batting, scoring a good 58 in the second innings at Perth. His four knocks realised 104 runs with an average of 26.00, but he was twice run out and lost his place for the final match at Melbourne. As he was not chosen for the Centenary tour of England, Wiener's chances of more Tests against the old enemy seem remote. In the 1981 series, injuries to Rodney Hogg and Geoff Lawson left Australia short of pace bowling for the last two Tests. Mike Whitney, a strongly built left-arm bowler from Sydney, was in England playing for Gloucestershire. Despite his lack of experience — he had only played in six first class matches — he was pressed into service for the last two Tests. Called in as a stop-gap, Whitney's main role was to provide stock-bowling relief for Dennis Lillee and Terry Alderman. His efforts, full of honest toil and sweat, went largely unrewarded; his 5 wickets costing 49.20 each. Whitney's prospects of a permanent Test place were certainly not enhanced by his premature baptism in this rubber.

The unfortunate batsmen in the above list were Ross Gregory and Barry Shepherd. Hartigan probably earned a further chance in 1909, though his form on that tour was mediocre. Of the bowlers, W.H. Cooper retired voluntarily, Gordon Rorke was a political discard, while Gilmour placed himself out of court. The really unlucky man was Tom Kendall whose performances in those first ever Tests at least entitled him to subsequent preference over Frank Allan. According to Spofforth, Kendall put on a lot of flesh, so his career was probably destined to be short-lived. Nevertheless, he should not have been passed over for Allan on the 1878 tour, nor should the 'Bowler of the Century' have been given preference against Lord Harris' Gentlemen's team at Melbourne in January 1879. The left-hander's bowling average (15.35) has been bettered by only Ferris and Iverson of Australia's first line bowlers.

Kendall, Hartigan, Gregory and Shepherd were four fine players, ill-served by fate and the selectors. Cooper and Gilmour made their own decisions, and most of the rest had little reason to feel aggrieved, but these four, with limited opportunities, made significant contributions to Australia's success. They deserved better treatment at the hands of their country's selectors.

THREE-TIME LOSERS – THE ENGLISH

Sixty cricketers – 29 English, 31 Australian – have appeared in 3 Tests apiece. These, at least, it can be argued, were given a fair trial before being consigned to the scrap-heap. After all, if a player has above average ability, he should be able to demonstrate it clearly at some stage during a period of 3 matches. Unfortunately, the majority of these men did just the opposite. Some 15 or 16 (about 25%) did establish a claim to further recognition, but the rest, to quote the American vernacular, quite properly became 'three-time losers'.

The English contingent includes four players who made their appearances in the most recent rubber. Graham Fowler (Lancashire) and Geoff Cook (Northants.) were accorded the honour of opening England's batting against Lillee, Lawson, Hogg & Co. Cook played in the First, Fourth and Fifth Tests, totalling 54 in his 6 innings. Fowler took Cook's place in the Second Test and remained for the Third and Fourth, scoring 207 runs at the useful average of 34.5. Cook, already well over thirty, is hardly likely to get another chance, but Fowler, whose absence from the Fifth Test was due to injury, will surely play more matches against the Aussies. Eddie Hemmings, Nottinghamshire's off-spinner, and Derek Pringle, the Essex all-rounder, made up the quartet. Hemmings' bowling produced 9 expensive wickets, but he surprised everyone with a very competent 95 in the last innings of the series. Pringle's batting average of 27.00 was encouraging, but his bowling lacked penetration, each of his 4 victims costing 53 runs. Like Cook, Hemmings is no chicken, so the possibility of further appearances for him is remote. Pringle may be luckier. Of the remainder, there were eight – 2 bowlers, 1 all-rounder and 5 batsmen – who could claim that they had done enough to justify their retention in the team.

First and foremost in this interesting group comes Walter Brearley, the Lancastrian fast bowler, who made an impressive start in 1905 at Old Trafford. Brearley took eight Australian wickets (4 in each innings) for 126 runs and was the chief architect of an innings victory which retained the Ashes for England. At the Oval, Brearley collected 6 more scalps (5 for 110 in the first innings). He was indisposed during much of

Australia's second knock — a handicap which prevented England from making a determined push for a third win in the series. Brearley, an amateur, was prevented by business commitments from accepting a place with the 1907-8 tourists. His only other Test against Australia came at Leeds in 1909. He had been invited at the last minute to join up at Lord's for the Second Test, but the tardiness of the summons irritated him and he declined the honour. (MacLaren was Captain again in this series and this whole episode smacks of his cavalier approach to team selection. Why, having won the First Test by 10 wickets, England should make wholesale changes at Lord's is a complete mystery. No doubt, MacLaren had a theory for it!) By the time Brearley did make himself available the rubber was all-square. At Leeds poor batting by England gave Australia the chance to take the lead in the series. Brearley's efforts as support bowler to Barnes and Hirst were not up to his previous standard, so he was dropped, never to be recalled. Brearley's 17 Australian wickets for 355 runs, (average 20.88) nevertheless compares favourably with the returns of all the regular Test fast bowlers. Probably his forthright attitude did not endear him to authority.

The all-rounder was Albert Relf of Sussex. Eight times a performer of the Double, Relf toured with Plum Warner's first M.C.C. side in 1903-4. He was given a place in the first two Tests but had little opportunity to shine. Batting number 10 at Sydney, Relf scored 31 in a 9th wicket stand with 'Tip' Foster which realised 115. (This, of course, was Foster's fantastic debut innings in which he scored 287.) England won by 5 wickets and Relf, brought on to bowl late in each innings, delivered 19 overs for 62 runs without getting a wicket. At Melbourne, his opportunities were even more limited. Still down in the tail, Relf had two not out knocks of 3 and 10 and his bowling was restricted this time to a mere 3 overs for 17 runs, mainly because Wilfrid Rhodes took 15 wickets and hardly gave anyone else a look-in. England won again, but with his bowling virtually untried, the Sussex all-rounder lost his place to Ted Arnold of Worcestershire. He was not called on again during that rubber. Five years later, at the age of 35, Relf was drafted in at Lord's as a replacement for George Thompson of Northants. This was the series where the selectors were so choosy that 25 players were used all told, 11 of them being allowed just one game each. One of these selectorial playthings was Relf. In a strange looking collection — no Blythe, no Barnes, no Rhodes, no Jessop — Relf was England's best bowler. He captured 5 for 85 in Australia's first innings 350, as well as the only wicket (for 9 runs) to fall in their second. The Australians' 9 wickets win was no fault of Relf's for his bag included Trumper, Noble, Armstrong, Syd Gregory and Bardsley (twice) — some haul! He was promptly discarded for Leeds along with five others and, though Barnes, Rhodes and Brearley all played, England lost that one too. Just deserts for the fickle selectors, but a raw deal for Relf.

The five cast-off batsmen were Jack Sharp (Everton and Lancashire), George Brown (Hampshire), the Nawab of Pataudi (Worcestershire), Graham Roope (Surrey), and David Steele (Northants.). Sharp, one of England's rare double internationals, was one of those six replacements summoned to Headingley for the Third Test in 1909. Batting number 4, he figured in a stand of 106 for the third wicket with his county colleague, J.T. Tyldesley. Sharp's 61 was England's top score and he was instrumental in steering his side to within 6 runs of Australia's first innings total. Unfortunately the redoubtable Jessop was injured and England, batting one short in both innings, collapsed against Cotter and Macartney on the last day. Sharp's second knock realised 11. He was, surprisingly in view of the selectors' record, retained for the Old Trafford match. England, batting second in a rain-affected contest, salvaged a comfortable draw, Sharp scoring 5 and 0 not out. Again he was retained (perhaps being a Lancastrian was insurance against harsh treatment in 1909) and his day of triumph arrived at the Oval in August. Australia made 325 and Sharp, who had bowled one over in each of his previous Tests, took 3 for 67. England batted confidently on the second day, none more so than the Evertonian. In 105 minutes after lunch he and Hutchings clouted 142, Sharp going on to score 105 in 165 minutes. England led by 27 but Australia, to make the rubber safe, played for a draw and Sharp's second innings contribution was another 0 not out. Sharp's was the only century recorded for England in the whole series and it placed him at the top of the English averages with the fine figures of 47.00 per innings. He should have toured Australia in 1911-12, probably in place of S.P. Kinneir.

George Brown, the mighty yeoman of Hampshire, was selected for England in 1921. (The way the selectors conscripted men to the front line against Armstrong's marauders was reminiscent of Kitchener's 'I want you' campaign of the war years.) England's batting had fallen before McDonald and Gregory like wheat before the sickle in the first two Tests. Casting around for ways to strengthen the order, the selectors dropped Strudwick and substituted Brown as stumper-batsman. Although his wicket-keeping proved well below Strudwick's standard, the Hampshire giant contributed significantly as a batsman. Brown, a hefty, fearless cricketer, batted number 7 in the first innings at Leeds. (He would probably have batted 9 but for an injury to the Hon. L. Tennyson and the sudden departure of Hobbs for an appendix operation.) A stand of 97 with J.W.H.T. Douglas, to which Brown's contribution was a sterling 57 was instrumental in saving the follow-on. Eventually the Australians set England 422 to win, a task well beyond their beleaguered powers. Brown, opening this time, top-scored with 46 to complete a highly impressive debut. The remaining Tests were drawn. Brown, retained as opening batsman, forged a useful partnership with A.C. Russell of Essex. At Old Trafford they began with 65 (Brown 31), England's best opening stand of the rubber. At the Oval their efforts were 27 and 158. The Hampshire man's share of the latter success was a hard-hitting 84, but a lot of it was gathered from sub-standard Australian bowling. The fiery fast attack bowled only 9 overs between them, while Pellew, Andrews, Taylor and Collins trundled down 31. In the circumstances, Brown's top score was perhaps a devalued effort, though it left him with a Test average against the Aussies of 50. Born in 1887 Brown was nearing 40 when Gilligan's team toured the Antipodes in 1924-5, though this did not deter the selectors from picking 'Dodge' Whysall of Notts., who was the same age as Brown, as reserve stumper to Strudwick. Brown's fighting temperament entitled him to a chance to try his luck overseas. Perhaps his unfashionable county told against him. It is significant that his three chances came when the Hampshire captain, Tennyson, was leading England.

The Nawab of Pataudi, the third of England's Indians and a prolific scorer at Oxford University, made his Test debut on Jardine's Bodyline tour. Like Ranji and Duleep, he began with a century innings. At Sydney in the First Test after Sutcliffe and Hammond had taken the score to 300 for 2, he completed a painstaking ton. England totalled 524 and won by 10 wickets. In the next game at Melbourne, the only match which England lost, the Nawab scored 15 and 5. He was dropped in favour of Eddie Paynter for the rest of the series. Paynter headed England's batting list for the rubber, so the switch was justified, but a significant factor in the Indian's omission must have been his brush with Jardine over the latter's leg-side field placing. Pataudi declined to field close in at short-leg and Jardine was not the kind of captain to countenance independence of mind in his ranks — even from a fellow amateur. Pataudi was restored to favour in 1934. With Jardine, Larwood and Voce missing, the England selectors included as much experience as they could at Trent Bridge. The Nawab, at number 4, supplied innings of 10 and 12. The propriety of putting overseas players into English sides was beginning to come under fire at this time, and, as Pataudi experienced particular difficulties against Grimmett, it was probably a convenient excuse to drop him for the rest of the series. Thus the Nawab, after his auspicious start, tailed off with an average of 28 for his 5 Test innings.

David Steele, of Northants., was the most recent 'success' to be discarded. In 1975 England returned from a chastening experience in Australia at the hands of Lillee and Thomson. With a return series imminent, new batting blood was urgently required, and not just by Lillee and Thomson. Steele, an experienced county cricketer, was drafted into the side for the last three Tests of a four match series. England had already lost by an innings at Edgbaston. Steele started at Lord's with 50 and 45. At Headingley, he continued the good work with 73 and 92. Finally he contributed 39 and 66 at the Oval. With 365 runs in 6 innings, Steele's average of 60.83 places him fifth in England's all time list against Australia (fourth if we ignore George Macaulay's freak average of 76.00). Indeed, Steele's lowest innings of 39 is superior to the averages achieved by such as W.G., MacLaren, Jessop and Colin Cowdrey, all of whom enjoyed much greater selectorial favour. Though retained for the complete series against the West Indies in 1976, Steele did not enjoy the selectors' confidence as a potential tourist. Omitted from Tony Greig's side to India in 1976-77, the Northants. bat also missed the chance of appearing in the Centenary Test. Then the Packer affair blew up and in the welter of dismissals, rejections and re-alignings resulting from that fracas, Steele was most unkindly forgotten. So with his Test career scarcely begun, and with an imposing array of scores to his credit, David Steele, at the age of 37, found himself finished with Test matches. The critics said that his forward defensive style of batting was not suited to overseas wickets; that he should not be allowed to occupy a Test place in England which was needed for a younger batsman. Steele's admirers countered these arguments by pointing out his phlegmatic temperament; his lengthy experience; and his excellent Test record. If a batting average of 60 didn't prove Steele worthy of a regular Test place, then it is difficult to say what would. Loyalty to faithful servants has never been a significant quality of selectorial panels.

Middlesex's Phil Edmonds made an impressive start at Leeds in 1975, when he captured 5 for 28 in Australia's first innings with his left-arm spinners. He was retained at the Oval but failed to take a wicket in 44 overs, while Ian Chappell's men amassed 532. Edmonds was not selected against Australia again until after the defection of Derek Underwood to Kerry Packer. In the First Test at Brisbane in December 1978, which England won comfortably, Mike Brearley relied mainly on his pace bowlers and Edmonds was again wicketless. He lost his place for the rest of the series and has not been called since. The Middlesex all-rounder has played in ten Tests against other countries with a fair degree of success. His experiences against Australia have not done justice to his undoubted all-round ability.

Surrey's Graham Roope, with 77 at the Oval in 1975 and a couple of thirties in 1977, is another contemporary player who enjoyed some success. He soon lost the selectors' favour, however, and recently departed from the county game with his Test potential hardly tapped.

The remaining English three-time losers consist of 1 captain, 2 stumpers, 6 batsmen and 8 bowlers. The captain was 'Monkey' Hornby of Lancashire. Hornby's claim to fame, apart from being the first to lose the Ashes, is that he has the worst batting record of all England's skippers. His Test average was a shaky 3.50. 'Monkey' had other qualities however. His first Test appearance was for Lord Harris' 'Gentlemen''s side in 1879. Hornby was twice bowled out by Spofforth, for 2 and 4, but he did bowl 7 overs, all maidens, and captured Frank Allan's wicket. His career bowling average of 0.00 is the lowest in Test history. Later on this tour Hornby starred as a muscle man. When roughs attacked Lord Harris on the Sydney ground — they had crowd trouble in those days too — Hornby manhandled the chief larrikin into the pavilion and gave him into custody. 'Monkey' lost his shirt and was somewhat pummelled in the process, but his determination triumphed over the odds. Perhaps it was this iron hand touch in his character that gave him the captaincy for the celebrated 'Ashes' match in 1882. In the first innings he batted number 10 and was bowled by Spofforth for 1. In the second knock he promoted himself to open the innings. This time Spofforth bowled him for 9. Two years later, on his Old Trafford home ground the Lancastrian played his last Test. He was stumped by Blackham in both innings, but at least he

Lord Harris (Kent) captained England in the first home Test, at the Oval in 1879. His batting average was a respectable 29.00.

R. Pilling, A. Watson, A.N. 'Monkey' Hornby, R.G. Barlow (all of Lancashir
Pilling played 8 Tests as wicket-keeper. Hornby has the worst batting average
any England captain (3.50), but his bowling figures (7 overs, 7 maidens,
wicket) give him the best bowling analysis.

E. Tyldesley, F. Watson, C. Hallows, R. Tyldesley, H. Makepeace.

David Steele (Northants.) played three times in England in 1975. His fine record of 365 runs in 6 innings (average 60.83) was insufficient to ensure his long-term selection. *(Northamptonshire Cricket Club)*

avoided adding himself to Spofforth's victims this time. Boyle got him for 0 in the first innings and Palmer for 4 in the second. 21 runs in 6 innings plumbed a record depth which no other Test captain, and precious few other players have reached.

The stumpers were both good players who, in other periods, might well have been given more opportunities. Contemporary competition was hot, and one or two extraneous circumstances also intruded. Mordecai Sherwin of Notts. was a burly rough-diamond of a man. He was rather overshadowed by Pilling, Hunter and Alfred Lyttleton in England, but he got his chance when his county colleague Arthur Shrewsbury led the 1886-7 side to Australia. Sherwin played in both Tests that season. He made 3 catches and 2 stumpings, allowing 27 byes out of 450 runs in the 4 innings. A natural No.11, Sherwin scored 30 runs for once out, and England won both games. In 1888 at Lord's, Sherwin made his lone Test appearance in England. A catch in each innings, 8 byes and a pair did not persuade the selectors to keep him. Harry Wood of Surrey and Pilling of Lancashire were chosen for the succeeding Tests at the Oval and Old Trafford, perhaps because of their local pull. Whatever the reason for replacing him, it is clear that Sherwin's ability was a little below top class. Like many other nineteenth-century players, he owed his Test appearances to his availability to tour when better men were unable to leave England.

J. Humphries, the Derbyshire stumper, played in 3 Tests in Australia in 1907-08. He should have played in all 5. England's batting, as periodically recurs, was suspect on this tour. The time-worn ploy of strengthening the batting at the expense of the stumping was trotted out before the First Test and Humphries lost his place to R.A. Young of Sussex. The experiment was a failure on both counts. For the next 3 Tests Humphries kept wicket. He snapped up 7 catches, conceded 43 byes (out of 2,053 runs) and recorded a better batting average (8.8) than his rival. Unfortunately, he was unfit for the last Test, so Young had a second chance to prove his worth. At the end of it Humphries was still ahead, by a wider margin. This series was won by Australia 4-1. Humphries' was one of several heads that rolled on the return to England. He had made the tour because Dick Lilley, England's foremost keeper, had not been available. With ordinary luck, Humphries might have kept the place, but England's sorry showing precipitated changes. Lilley was recalled for the 1909 rubber and with Strudwick and 'Tiger' Smith also in the offing, Humphries' Test career was over.

The six batsmen were a pretty sorry bunch. Between them they completed 32 innings, scoring 418 runs at the princely average of 13 runs per visit to the crease. Only twice did they manage a score of more than 50, and 22 times they failed to reach double figures. Not much room for blaming the selectors here. In chronological order, the six were: G. Bean (Sussex), A.E. Knight (Leicestershire), Andy Sandham (Surrey), Stan Worthington (Derby.), Jack Crapp (Gloucester) and John Dewes (Middlesex). Three of them got their chances because they were members of touring parties and injuries and lost form always limit the competition on tour; two of the others, Sandham and Dewes, also made overseas appearances. Jack Crapp was the home games only man. Bean toured with W.G's 1891-92 team. He played in all 3 Tests, starting auspiciously with 50 in his debut innings at Melbourne. A broadly-built, phlegmatic-looking character, Bean batted at No.3 or No.4, but he only averaged 18.40. He was obviously not of real Test class and had no chance of making the team at home when faced with the competition of batting's 'Golden Age'.

Albert Edward Knight was the first man from Leicestershire to be capped against Australia. He went to Australia as one of the reserve batsmen in Plum Warner's 1903-4 side. Injuries to Bosanquet and Arnold let Albert into the team for the Second Test at Melbourne. He scored 2 and 0 and, unsurprisingly, dropped out again. At Sydney for the Fourth Test, with England leading 2-1, Knight was recalled to strengthen the batting. England won the toss and collapsed to 66 for 4; then Albert batted through the rest of the total of 249. He prodded along for 4 hours 20 minutes to accumulate 70 not out, while 137 were added at the other end. Rhodes, Arnold and then Bosanquet bowled out the Aussies and England regained the Ashes. Knight's second innings yielded only 9, but that 70 laid the foundation of the victory. Knight, a local Methodist preacher much respected in Leicestershire circles, was better equipped than many to absorb the slings and arrows of outrageous fortune . His religious faith no doubt helped him to accept philosophically the swing of the pendulum that gave him a pair at Melbourne in the final game. His Test average was 16.20, but that one outstanding innings helped win the series. Knight never played for England again, but he had done his duty and was able to retire with a clear conscience.

Stan Worthington spent the 1936-37 season jumping in and out of the England side. An opening bat, he partnered Charlie Barnett at Brisbane in the First Test; he made 0 and 8, and England's opening stands were 0 and 17. Dropped at Sydney, Worthington returned at Melbourne, mainly because Arthur Fagg had fallen ill and departed for home. This time he made 0 and 16 and England started with 0 and 29. Hedley Verity was promoted to take his place at Adelaide. This worked after a fashion but England lost and, with the series all square, Worthington was recalled at Melbourne in a final attempt to stiffen the batting. After Australia had first scored 604, Worthington, seizing his last chance, laid about him brilliantly; he rattled up 44, then trod on his wicket. His second innings realised 6 and England lost by an innings. Worthington was one of several casualties. Indeed, it was only his fine fielding that had kept him under consideration for so long. Perhaps he was unlucky in that last Test, but, as Bradman is reported to have said, 'The batsman is not supposed to tread on his wicket'.

Andy Sandham, Hobbs' great opening partner for Surrey, never got going against Australia. He had to bat down the order in each of his matches, not a situation to which regular openers take kindly. He played at the Oval in the last match against Armstrong's side in 1921, scoring 21 coolly in bad light at the end of the first day. His subsequent form got him on the boat with Gilligan's men in 1924-5. At Sydney batting at number 6 he scored 7 and 2, falling to Mailey each time. He was left out of the next three Tests, returning for the last, again at Sydney, where he scored 4 and 1. A batting average of 9.8 did no justice at all to Sandham's batting skill, but, denied his proper place at No 2 by Herbert Sutcliffe's superior talents, he was probably destined to struggle at Test level.

The two left-handers, Crapp and Dewes, were among the straws clutched by the 1948 selectors to combat Bradman's all-conquering side. Jack Crapp, 36 years old, fought his way into the side by scoring a fine century for his county against the tourists just prior to the Third Test. Crapp, like many others whose careers were sliced in two by the Second War, received his opportunity too late. His prime years were taken from him, and he was faced with the strongest Australian side ever sent to England. It was asking too much. At Old Trafford Crapp made a workmanlike start by scoring 37 and 19 in the only match saved by England in the rubber. He also made a couple of slip catches. The Headingley game was different. Scores of 5 and 18 and some shaky slip fielding in the second innings hardly inspired confidence and at the Oval it was even worse. 0 and 9 from a man picked for his batting ended Crapp's long-term usefulness. He did tour South Africa and played in some Tests during the following winter, but the Australians never encountered him again.

John Dewes was at the opposite end of the spectrum from Crapp. A prolific opening bat at school and University, he had already played in a 'Victory' Test in 1945. He was regarded as a young hopeful in 1948, a star of the future. With the rubber lost, England gave Dewes the injured Washbrook's place at the Oval. The pace of Miller and Lindwall hustled him out for 1 and 10. Despite this, he was one of several tyros sent Down Under with Freddie Brown in 1950-51. The results were just as inglorious as his Oval debut. At Brisbane Miller got him twice for 1 and 9. At Melbourne, he scored 8 and 5. By that time it was clear that Dewes' cramped style, which had accumulated plenty of runs in University cricket, was not equal to dealing with Australian bowling. If he had arrived 10 years later, when Lindwall and Miller were past their best, he might have stood a better chance of success. Dewes was the first of several of England's post-war University players who were tried and found short of real Test class. England lost all three Tests in which he played.

The 8 bowlers like the 6 batsmen did not enjoy a great deal of success. Best of the lot was Fred Root of Worcestershire, with Jack Sharpe of Surrey running him close. The rest, Arthur Mold, Dick Tyldesley and Roy Tattersall of Lancs; Jack Young and John Price of Middlesex; and Tommy Mitchell (Derbyshire) achieved virtually nothing. Root was a bowling innovator. A medium-paced opening bowler, he aimed his short of a length stuff at the batsman's legs and was adept in pinning the striker down by packing the leg-side field. Between 1910 and 1933 he hauled in a catch of 1,500 wickets, 219 of them in 1925. He seemed just the lad to pitch in against 'Horseshoe' Collins' Australians in 1926. In the dreary, wet season of 1926 Root played a significant part. He introduced his in-swing leg-theory to the Australians by taking 7 for 42 for the North of England and was quickly drafted into the Test side. His first appearance at Trent Bridge was restricted to watching from the pavilion while Hobbs and Sutcliffe scored 32. Then it rained for the rest of the match. Retained at Lord's, Root dismissed Collins and Woodfull for 70 runs in 36 overs. England replied to Australia's 383 with 475 for 3 declared, and Root bagged 2 for 40 in Australia's unfinished second innings. Surprisingly George Geary took his place at Leeds where England salvaged another draw. At Old Trafford Fred got his place back from Geary. He bowled 52 overs, 27 maidens and captured 4 for 84 in Australia's only innings. Rain prevented England from completing their reply and the sides went to the

Oval with everything to play for. Root lost his place to Larwood this time and went out of Test cricket with 8 wickets for 194 from 107 overs. (Curiously Jupiter Pluvius had decreed that he would never wield the willow at international level.) He was, perhaps, helped by the unusually wretched weather in 1926. Certainly he was lucky to miss the Leeds Test, where Charlie Macartney rampaged in scoring 151 in less than 3 hours. Perhaps Root's accuracy and negative line of attack would have stemmed that onslaught, but I doubt it. A good bowler, Fred Root has had many imitators, but few of them with his skill for bowling tight.

Jack Sharpe of Surrey was a one-eyed fast bowler who had a short-lived career. In 1890 he captured 179 wickets and was chosen for 'Nutty' Martin's Test at the Oval. With Martin taking 12 wickets and George Lohmann 6, Sharpe had to be satisfied with a tail-ender in each innings for 18 runs all told. He maintained his form so well in the following season that he was named as one of the Players of the Year. In company with his Surrey colleagues, Lohmann, J.M. Read and Abel, Sharpe was invited to join W.G's 1891-2 tourists. At Melbourne in the First Test Sharpe had 6 for 84 and 2 for 81, but England lost. He was much less successful in the next game, which England also lost, taking 1 for 122. His place went to the reserve keeper Philipson for the final game. Sharpe, a short, slender individual, probably found Australian conditions unduly taxing. His county career was virtually over by 1894. He had a dangerous yorker in his armoury and his 11 Test wickets at a cost of 27 runs each showed a potential which his frail physique prevented from maturing.

The Lancashire trio were disappointing. Arthur Mold, a devastating fast bowler for Lancashire, albeit with a suspect action, played in all 3 Tests of 1893. England was particularly strong in bowling at that time and Mold, though starting at Lord's with 3 for 44, was overshadowed by Lockwood of Surrey. At the Oval Briggs took 10 wickets and Lockwood 8, while Mold's thunder was stolen at his home ground, Old Trafford, by Tom Richardson and Briggs. 7 Test wickets at 33 apiece was so far below the standard of the Surrey pair that Mold could hardly expect to be retained. When the suspicion surrounding his bowling action is also considered, it is not surprising that the Test selectors ignored him for subsequent rubbers.

Rotund, rubicund Richard Tyldesley bowled leg-spinners accurately for Lancashire between the Wars. He enjoyed a great deal of success in county cricket, but, like 'Tich' Freeman, he was unable to translate this success to the Test arena. The inroads made by Arthur Mailey into the English batting in 1920-21, convinced the M.C.C. that leg-break bowlers were of the essence for Gilligan's tour in 1924-25. Tyldesley and Freeman were chosen on the strength of their English successes, and the Lancastrian already had 4 Tests against South Africa under his belt. In the Second Test at Melbourne (Freeman had taken only 5 very expensive wickets in the first), Tyldesley bowled 37 eight ball overs for 136 runs and no victims at all. 'Young Jack' Hearne showed him how it should be done with 4 for 84 in the second innings. There was more wrist in Hearne's bowling than either Freeman's or Tyldesley's, and he was accordingly more successful on the hard Australian tracks. Tyldesley played no more Tests on that Tour. He went into discard for nearly 6 years and then was called up for duty in 1930. The prevailing theory was that Bradman was vulnerable to leg-spin. Tyldesley played in the First and Third Tests; Robins in the First and Second; Peebles in the Fourth and Fifth. They were, except for Maurice Tate, England's most successful bowlers, but each had a bowling average of more than 33. Bradman's 'vulnerability' left him with a batting average of 139. Dick's 56 overs at Trent Bridge cost only 130 runs and his 5 wickets helped England to gain her only win of the rubber. He was then left out at Lord's in favour of J.C. White, but returned at Leeds where his bag consisted of tail-enders Grimmett and Wall for 104 runs. He made no impression on Bradman, who scored 334. Tyldesley was the tightest but the least penetrative of the English leg-spinners and he lost his place to Peebles for the last two Tests.

Roy Tattersall, a tall off-spin bowler, briefly rivalled Jim Laker for a place in the England side of the early fifties. Laker, inexperienced at the time, had a rough passage with Bradman's '48 side and was out of favour when Freddie Brown's team was formed for the 1950-51 tour. Come to that, so was Tattersall and any other off-spinner. However, injuries to Trevor Bailey and Doug Wright during that tour necessitated reinforcements, and Tattersall (with county colleague, Brian Statham), was flown out in time to play in the Fourth Test at Adelaide. The heat was intense and Tattersall's tidy 3 for 95 in the first innings was followed by an expensive 1 for 116 in the second, but only Wright took more wickets in the match for England, and Tattersall kept his place for the final Test. At Melbourne England achieved her first post-war victory over Australia. Tattersall, the bowler, contributed 16 economical overs but didn't take a wicket. Tattersall, the batsman, however, played an unexpectedly vital role. Replying to the Australian

217 England reached 200 with only 2 men out. When Tattersall at number 11 arrived the side had collapsed to 246. The Lancastrian defended gamely while Reg Simpson looked for runs, and when he was eventually bowled by Keith Miller for 10, the total had risen to 320. The lead of 103 put the match firmly in England's control and Tattersall was one of the heroes. His only other Test against Australia was at Trent Bridge in 1953. England were placed in a position to win, mainly by Alec Bedser who took 14 wickets, but rain ruined the last two days' play. Tattersall, with 3 for 22 in the second innings, played his part reasonably well, but his 28 overs in the match cost 81 runs and Laker was given the off-spinner's place for the later games in the series.

The Middlesex pair — Young and Price — differed greatly in style and temperament. Jack Young, a very accurate slow left-hander, shuttled his way in and out of Yardley's sides in 1948. In the First Test he bowled 70 overs, 31 maidens, to take 1 for 107. Doug Wright took the Middlesex man's place at Lord's. Wright was not a success, so they changed places again at Old Trafford. This time Young bowled 35 overs, 17 maidens, and took 2 for 67. He was then omitted at Leeds, a decision which in retrospect probably cost England the match. Young's steadiness in Australia's first innings would have been invaluable, and the last day massacre by Morris and Bradman could well have been averted if another spinner had been available to help Laker use the dusty wicket. Too late Young was recalled at the Oval, where his 2 for 118 in 51 overs could not prevent an innings defeat. Like Jack Crapp, Young was 36 years old when he entered Test cricket. His stock bowling might have been a useful support to Bedser and Wright on the 1946-7 tour, for he certainly was a better bowler than Jim Langridge or Peter Smith. Young's failure to make a reasonable haul of wickets and the fact that he was knocking on a bit influenced the selectors to look elsewhere for the future.

Big John Price, a clod-hopping fast bowler with a crab-like run (he approached from deep mid off), was first asked to bowl against Australia in 1964. The venue selected was Old Trafford, at that time a bowlers' graveyard. Price delivered 45 overs while Bobby Simpson crept his way to 311. It took two and a half days before Price dismissed the Australian skipper to finish with 3 for 183. In another drawn match at the Oval Price took 1 for 67. Nearly a decade passed before the selectors remembered the Middlesex bowler again. In 1972 an injury to Geoff Arnold of Surrey led them to the horses for courses solution and Price played at Lord's (Bob Massie's match). 3 for 115 on a wicket helpful to pace and seam was disappointing. Like Jack Young's and Dick Tyldesley's, Price's Australian wickets cost him well over 50 runs each.

I have saved Tommy Mitchell till last. Though a regular taker of 100 wickets for Derbyshire, Mitchell's average fielding and non-existent batting required his leg-spin bowling to be far superior to any rival's to justify his selection for Tests. In county games it often appeared so, but in Tests sadly it was not. There was probably some logic in sending him to Australia with Jardine's side. Walter Robins was unable to tour, Ian Peebles was injured, and Australian conditions favoured leg-spinners. Mitchell was eventually given Bill Voce's place for the Fourth Test at Brisbane. England won thanks to Larwood and the batsmen; Mitchell's haul was a useful 3 for 60. He picked up 53 wickets on the tour, so he worked his passage. Back in England in 1934 Mitchell played in the First and Fourth Tests. At Trent Bridge he was unable to spin the ball on that placid wicket. He bowled 34 overs for 108 runs and 1 scalp. That would probably have been the end of him, but just before the Fourth Test, Mitchell took 7 Australian wickets for 105 when they played Derbyshire at Chesterfield. He was summoned to Leeds and cost England 5 runs an over while Bradman plundered 304. Apart from delivering frequent full-tosses, Mitchell also contrived to drop Ponsford (who scored 181) off a straightforward catch in the covers when he had scored 70. In all the Derbyshire bowler's 4 Australian wickets cost the exorbitant sum of 71.25 apiece.

The selectors, in fairness to them, were not far wrong in discarding this collection of trundlers. All of them had done sufficient to justify their initial selection, and most of them were given adequate opportunity to shine. Root and Jack Young were, possibly, hard done by, but the rest were clearly short of the requisite class .

9

THREE TIME LOSERS – THE AUSSIES

The 31 Australians in this group are made up of 1 captain (David Gregory), 1 keeper (W. Carkeek), 4 all rounders, 7 bowlers and 18 batsmen. Gregory, as we have already seen, won two of his three matches as captain, but his prowess as a batsman was only moderate and he soon gave way to Billy Murdoch. His fame rests on his position as the Australians' first leader, and a successful one at that, who gained victory in two of his three matches.

Carkeek, Victoria's wicket-keeper, toured England in 1909 as reserve to Sammy Carter. In 1912, Sammy, along with Trumper, Hill, Armstrong, Ransford and Cotter, was in revolt against the Australian Board of Control. Consequently Carkeek became number one stumper for the Triangular series in England. He played in all three Tests, scoring 5 runs in two innings, grabbing a couple of catches, allowing 41 byes and generally proving that, as a keeper, he was a genuine reserve.

The all rounders comprised two run-of-the-mill players. Edward A'Beckett and Maurice Sievers of Victoria, and two outstanding figures: Sammy Woods and Albert Trott. The main interest in A'Beckett centred around his descent from the illustrious archbishop. In 1928 the Australian selectors, casting around desperately for successors to Jack Gregory and Charlie Kelleway, called on A'Beckett to fill the breach with his fast-medium bowling. At Melbourne and Adelaide in 1929 he toiled for 117 overs to take 3 wickets at 94 each. Not the form of a Test shock-bowler. A'Beckett's competent batting and fielding temporarily redeemed him. He was sent to England with the 1930 side, played at Leeds, scored 29, then was dropped. His poor tour figures (397 runs and 20 wickets) virtually finished him as a potential Test player.

Maurice Sievers played in the first three Tests against Gubby Allen's side in 1936-37. His batting contributions were negligible, but he had one purple patch with the ball. Heavy rain on the first night of the Melbourne Test influenced Bradman to declare at 200 for 9, giving Sievers a gluepot on which to operate. Sievers, a burly medium-pacer, took 5 for 21, setting up Australia's first win of the series. If Australia's fast bowler, McCormick, had not been injured, Sievers would not have played at Melbourne. For the next Test at Adelaide McCormick had recovered and Sievers was dropped. His 9 Test wickets at 17.88 place him well up in the list of Australian bowlers. He could hardly have been less effective as an opening bowler than Mervyn Waite was in 1938. As he also held 4 catches in his 3 Tests, Sievers had definite claims to a place on that tour. Perhaps the selectors listened too much to the views of Waite's state captain, D.G. Bradman.

Sammy Woods (New South Wales and Somerset) played for Australia almost by accident. In 1888 Woods was an undergraduate at Cambridge when Percy McDonnell's side arrived with only 13 players for a full tour. Despite the presence of Turner and Ferris, the Australians were the weakest side to visit England up to that time and, like all weak sides, they did not have the best of luck. The other Sammy — Jones — contracted smallpox after 7 games, Boyle proved to be a spent force, and Lyons did not begin to play well until late in the tour. Hence a summons to Woods to assist the side. Woods, an ebullient character, was Australian born, but spent most of his cricketing years in England. During the succeeding two decades he became a fine all-rounder and an inspiring leader for Somerset. In 1888 however his development had hardly begun and, though he appeared in all 3 Tests, his performances were mediocre: 32 runs in 6 innings and 5 wickets for 121. Australia won the First Test and lost the other two. Perhaps, if Sammy had returned to his native land, he might have been given further opportunities but, like Gubby Allen at a later date, Woods threw in his lot with England. He played for England against South Africa in 1895.

The last of these all-rounders was among the top ten Australians of all time. Albert Edwin Trott of Victoria, younger brother of Harry Trott, was chosen at the age of 21 for the last three Tests against A.E. Stoddart's powerful 1894 tourists. At the age of 22 he was discarded. By the time he was 23 Albert had quit the Antipodes for good and thrown in his lot with Middlesex. In January 1895 Australia was in the parlous state of two Tests down with three to play. To add to their difficulties Charlie Turner was ill and unable to play at Adelaide. On top of that, the 'Terror''s support bowlers, Coningham of Queensland and the young Hugh Trumble, had not been successful and were dropped. This left Australia with only the veteran captain, George Giffen (14 wickets in the first two Tests), and the rather erratic Harry Trott to bowl. To fill the breach, the selectors drafted S.T. Callaway of New South Wales and Albert Trott. Even then this gave them only 4 trundlers, plus some change bowling assistance from another new cap, Jack Harry, with whom to gain the vital victory to keep the series alive. The rubber really looked a good thing for Stoddart.

At Adelaide the heat was intense. Giffen won the toss and batted first. When young Albert arrived at number ten Australia had succumbed once again to the redoubtable Tom Richardson. 157 for 8 was not particularly healthy-looking even allowing for the under-prepared state of the wicket and two run outs, which had contributed to their downfall. Then almost immediately Albert lost his partner. He was joined, at this critical juncture, by Callaway. 157 for 9 became 238 all out, as the pair took risks against an English attack exhausted by the heat. Trott got the odd 38 and was undefeated. When England replied Trott opened the attack with his fast medium off-breaks. He bowled 3 overs for 9 runs; then George Giffen and Callaway, with 5 wickets each and backed by superb fielding, dismissed England for 124. The Aussies replied with a century from Frank Iredale and 80 from Bruce. When Trott came in at the fall of the 8th wicket the score was 283. The last two wickets added another 128 and Albert's share was an undefeated 72. It was at this stage that Trott turned a highly exhilarating batting performance into the most impressive all-round debut in Test history. (Only Keith Miller's 79 and 9 for 77 in the Brisbane match of 1946 comes near it.) The wicket was wearing, England faced a deficit of 525, and they were soon floundering against Albert's high-bouncing off-breaks. The Victorian captured 8 for 43 in 27 overs; Stoddart's team tumbled to defeat by the massive margin of 382. He hit the stumps 4 times, made 2 caught and bowleds and, for good measure, caught last man Tom Richardson off George Giffen. With 110 runs, 8 wickets, and a catch, Trott had made his mark in no uncertain manner.

In the following game at Sydney Albert kept his place, even though Charlie Turner was fit again. Callaway was the unlucky bowler who had to make way for the 'Terror'. The wicket was soft and Stoddart, who won the toss, seemed fully vindicated in putting Australia in when they collapsed to 51 for 6. Graham and Darling then doubled the score, but when Albert Trott, promoted one place in the order, joined Graham prospects did not look rosy. Vigorous hitting soon altered that and 112 runs were added before Graham was out for a splendid 105. Trott continued attacking and when he ran out of partners his tally was 85. He had now scored 195 Test runs without being dismissed. England lost MacLaren on the first evening; it then rained for two days. Harry Trott,

Giffen and Turner bowled England out for 65; then the latter two bowled unchanged to dismiss them for 72. Australia won by an innings and Albert didn't get a bowl. The last Test at Melbourne burst the bubble. Albert scored 10 and 0, took 1 for 84 and 0 for 56, made 1 catch, and the Australians lost the rubber. They should have won, but Giffen over-bowled himself, some catches were dropped, and J.T. Brown batted magnificently in England's second innings. And with this match Albert Trott's Test career for Australia ended. It is difficult to understand why. Albert finished on top of the batting averages: 5 innings, 3 times not out, 205 runs, highest score 85 n.o., average 102.50. (He is the only man on either side in these matches to average more than a century.) His bowling placed him third (average 21.33) behind Callaway and Turner. Brother Harry was chosen to succeed Giffen as captain for the 1896 tour of England. Yet. with all these things in his favour, the younger Trott didn't make the side. Of all selectorial blunders, and there have been a few in choosing Australian teams, this must surely rank as the worst. Albert should have had the vote over the untried and, as it was to prove, unsuccessful Charles Eady of Tasmania. I wonder if the mental instability of the Trotts manifested itself sometime in 1895-96 and deterred the selectors from choosing him?

The 7 bowlers given three chances to prove themselves for Australia were in chronological order McShane, Callaway, Oxenham, Blackie, Tribe, Philpott, and Colley. Only two or three of them showed good returns.

P.G. McShane, of Victoria, was one of the stop-gaps used in profusion by Australia in the mid-eighties. He was first selected for the last, and deciding, Test of the 1884-5 rubber. This had been a disputatious season; the Australians used no fewer than 28 players in 5 Tests and McShane was one of 14 who appeared only once (a foreshadowing of England in 1921). At Melbourne McShane bowled 3 overs for 3 runs in an innings where Australia used 8 bowlers and delivered 221 overs. Horan, his captain, really should have given him a longer spell, especially since Australia lost by an innings. Two years later McShane bowled another 3 overs at Sydney, for 6 runs this time, and again Australia lost. With Turner, Ferris, Spofforth and Garrett ahead of him in the queue, McShane, substituting for a sick George Palmer, could not have reasonably expected much bowling. He did make one contribution: a fine catch at square leg off a difficult high chance from Arthur Shrewsbury. In the following year McShane's last appearance at Sydney allowed him the luxury of 21 overs; and this time he took a wicket, inducing Johnny Briggs to give a catch to Jack Worrall. Thus McShane, despite pouching a grand running catch to get rid of A.E. Stoddart, finished with a career record of 1 for 48 from 27 overs. Australia lost all 3 games in which he played.

Sydney Callaway, the bowler who was called up with Albert Trott at Adelaide in 1895, had participated in two earlier Tests. He played in the first two matches against W.G's 1891-92 side. At Melbourne, Callaway, a right-hand pace bowler and a fair bat, began with 21 and 13 not out and 0 for 39 plus 1 for 7. The next game at Sydney found him bowling 27 overs for 40 runs, but he claimed no victims and scored only 1 run in his two innings. He lost his place to Donnan for the last game of that series. Callaway's recall in 1895 was purely as a stop-gap; Charlie Turner, as we have seen, being incapacitated. This time Callaway shone. He outscored Albert Trott in the stand for the last wicket in the first innings, and then shared the wickets with George Giffen when England batted. Indeed his 5 wickets cost less than half of those of his captain's (37 runs against 76). In the second innings, Callaway again figured in a last wicket stand with Trott, but this time he scored only 11 out of 64. Trott's devastating bowling, which settled the match, left precious little for anyone else in England's final knock, and Callaway only had 7 overs which cost 19 runs. Once Turner was fit, Callaway dropped out of the side; a harsh reward for a very useful contribution to Australia's victory. At least Callaway could look back on the day when he outshone George Giffen.

Thirty years after Trott and Callaway, another two bowlers trod the triple trail for Australia. In 1928-29 Percy Chapman's team was pillaging its way round the Antipodes and the Australian bowling cupboard was looking like Old Mother Hubbard's. With Jack Gregory and Charles Kelleway retired by illness, the Aussies were left with only Clarrie Grimmett as a Test class bowler. Still somebody had to be found to bowl, and, after casting their net wide, the selectors came up with Don Blackie of Victoria. Blackie, an off-spinner, was 46 years old, pushing 47 when he made his debut at Sydney. (He joined 45 year old 'Dainty' Ironmonger who had made his debut at Brisbane in the previous game. With Grimmett rising 37, the Australian attack was well into the sere and yellow in this series. In Blackie's 3 Tests, England made 636, 417, 332 for 7, 334 and 383, and won all the matches. The off-spinner began well with 4 for 148 (out of the 636), then did even better with 6 for 94 in the first innings at Melbourne. In the second innings he had 1 for 75, and at Adelaide his match figures were 3 for 127. Unfortunately his batting was negligible and he showed signs of becoming a liability in the field; not surprising considering the amount of work he was asked to do. Blackie bowled 210 overs in 3 games and his bag of 14 wickets at 31 each was, in view of the disparity in the strength of the sides, useful. However by the time of the Fifth Test Australia had decided on a policy of youth and Blackie was dropped. Still he has his place in the record books as Australia's oldest debutant. In Blackie's second Test (Australia's third), Ron Oxenham, a medium paced bowler with gifts of flight and swerve, was given Ironmonger's place. Oxenham, a Queenslander, had little success with the ball, but he did make scores of 15 and 39. At Adelaide he managed 4 for 67 in the second innings, but 3 of those were tail-enders, and, when he played in the last game at Melbourne his efforts were undistinguished. Oxenham's main virtue was economy — he bowled 72 maidens in 200 overs in his 3 Tests — but he lacked the penetration to reap a harvest of wickets at this level. 7 victims at nearly 50 runs each was not true Test class. He did however manage to finish on the winning side in his last game.

One of the few failures in Don Bradman's invincible sides of 1946-48 was George Tribe of Victoria. Tribe, a slow left-arm googly bowler, was given 3 Tests in 1946-47. He took 2 wickets for 330! Tribe later pursued a highly successful all-round career with Northamptonshire. In 1946 however Tribe's spin bowling was over-shadowed by Colin McCool and Ian Johnson; a disastrous last match at Sydney, when he bowled 42 overs (more than anyone else) for 153 runs, finished his Test prospects. Nearly twenty years later the Australians thought they had discovered a successor to Richie Benaud when Peter Philpott of New South Wales captured 5 for 90 on his debut at Brisbane. He flattered to deceive. 1 for 62 in the second innings, deteriorated to 0 for 133 at Melbourne, and, though he took 2 for 86 at Sydney, Australia lost there by an innings. Philpott was dropped with his bowling average at 46.37. In 1972 David Colley of New South Wales toured England as a reserve pace-bowler to Lillee and Massie. In 3 games he took only 6 wickets, and his main claim to Test fame was a fighting 54 in the Third Test at Trent Bridge. His bowling lacked bite; his total haul for the tour was a mere 33 wickets, and he was not called on again for Test matches.

Of the eighteen batsmen chosen to make a trinity of appearances for Australia, four of them, Charles Bannerman, Walter Giffen, J. Edwards and C.B. Jennings, belong to the pre-1914 period. Two more, Leo O'Brien and Keith Rigg played in the thirties; another two, Ken Archer and Jim DeCourcy, belonged to the fifties; Graeme Thomas to the sixties; the remainder are of a more recent vintage.

Charles Bannerman, as already demonstrated in the chapter on Pioneers, was Australia's first great batsman. Ill health, which according to W.H. Cooper resulted from burning the candle at both ends caused his early retirement, with a batting average (59.75), inferior only to Sid Barnes, the 'Don' and, of course, Albert Trott. If Charles had endured like his younger brother Alec, who stonewalled his way through 28 Tests, he might well have set records that would have taxed the best efforts of Australia's strongest batsmen to match. In those early games Bannerman was the only batsman who could claim parity with England's best.

The others in this group were pretty small beer. Walter Giffen, brother of South Australia's mighty George, scored 2 and 0 at Sydney in 1887. This inglorious start was not what the selectors expected from an opening batsman, so Giffen disappeared from the Test scene. However he was recalled for two Tests against W.G's. 1891-92 tourists; appearances for which he was indebted (so ugly rumour has it) to the influence of brother George. Walter repaid his brother's confidence with scores of 1, 3, 3 and 2. Even this startling exhibition of Walter's limitations did not prevent his selection for the 1893 touring side. George Giffen in his autobiography *With Bat and Ball* categorically denied that Walter's place was the result of his influence, but one wonders. No other batsman has been selected for an England tour on the strength of a Test average of 1.83.

In between Walter Giffen's Test appearances, J.D. Edwards of Victoria toured England in 1888. He played in all three Tests of that rubber, scoring 21 not out at Lord's, 26 at the Oval, three ducks' eggs and a single. It is not surprising that Edwards was not called on again after his return to Australia. C.B. Jennings, an opening batsman from South Australia, was another 'tourist only'. In 1912 he joined Syd Gregory's Triangular Team (largely a collection of unknowns), playing in all the Tests and averaging 14 against England. A sharp fieldsman, Jennings made 4 catches in the final Test at the Oval. World War I interrupted his career and Test opportunities never recurred.

The Bodyline series created havoc with some of Australia's batting regulars. Bill Ponsford was dropped after the First Test in 1932 to make way for the left-handed Leo O'Brien of Victoria. One of Australia's many 'Irishmen', O'Brien was unlucky to be run out by Fingleton when he had scored 10 at Melbourne. In his second knock Larwood bowled him for 11. Though Australia won the game, Ponsford was promptly recalled for the Adelaide match. By the time of the Fifth Test at Sydney, Ponsford was out of favour again. O'Brien returned and scored 61, partnering McCabe in a stand of 99. Australia lost and O'Brien was again discarded. He missed the 1934 tour of England but went to South Africa with Victor Richardson's 1935-36 team. When Gubby Allen's side arrived at Sydney for the Second Test of 1936-7, there was O'Brien as an opening bat replacement for the unsuccessful Ray Robinson. He scored 0 and 17; and that was the end of him as a Test batsman. O'Brien might have developed into a regular player if he had been given an extended run in the side, though he probably lacked that essential touch of class.

Another honest workman, Keith Rigg also from Victoria, was given a place for the last three games of the 1936-37 series. 118 runs in 5 innings with a top score of 47 was nothing very exceptional, but Rigg did claim the distinction of being on the winning side in each of his three matches.

World War II came and went. During the first post-war tour, Ken Archer played for Queensland against Wally Hammond's team. Four years later, he opened for Australia in 3 Tests against Freddie Brown & Co. 152 runs in 5 innings gave him an average of 30 and he included a couple of forties in his tally. Post-war Australia had however been accustomed to the prolific solidity of Sidney Barnes as Arthur Morris' partner and Archer had not measured up to the Barnes standard. He was dropped and the opening problem remained until Morris himself retired five years later. Archer deserved a touring chance in 1953; an effective opener would have taken the pressure from skipper Lindsay Hassett and could well have altered the outcome of that series.

On that very tour, Jim De Courcy, of New South Wales, played at Old Trafford, Leeds and the Oval. The poor form of all-rounder Richie Benaud in that series led Australia to strengthen the batting at his expense. De Courcy, who scored 1,200 runs on the tour, was the obvious replacement. When De Courcy began with 41 at Manchester that object seemed to have been achieved, but he tailed off badly with scores of 8, 10, 13 not out, 5 and 4. Australia's loss of the rubber sounded the death knell for the future Test hopes of a number of that side. De Courcy was one of the casualties.

In the middle sixties Graeme Thomas (New South Wales) was called to the Australian ranks. A good opening bat, Thomas had toured the West Indies in the previous season, but hot competition kept him out of the fray against Mike Smith's side until the Third Test. An injury to Bobby Simpson provided the opportunity for Thomas to partner Bill Lawry and the New South Welshman scored 51 and 25 in a match which Australia lost by an innings. Thomas retained his place at Adelaide and Melbourne at the expense of Simpson's unsuccessful deputy captain Brian Booth. He hit another fifty at Adelaide (Australia won this one by an innings) and finished with 19 in Australia's only knock at Melbourne. 4 innings for 147 runs at 36.75 was a useful beginning, yet Thomas was omitted from Bill Lawry's 1968 team. Australia could have done with another useful batsman on that tour. Certainly young Joslin of Victoria did little to justify his selection ahead of Thomas.

The seventies presented Australia with opening batsmen problems. The inability of Ian Redpath to go on tour meant that a partner had to be found for Ken Stackpole in 1972. Then by 1974-75, when Redpath was available again, Stackpole had retired. Rick McCosker was discovered during that series, but Redpath could not tour England in 1975; so Australia were short of a partner for McCosker. The same problem arose in 1977, with the added difficulty that McCosker lost his form after his jaw was broken in the Centenary Test. A number of second-line Australian batsmen were tried as openers during this period. The first of these was Bruce Francis of New South Wales. In 1972 it was hoped that his county experience with Essex would help him to make the advance to Test stature; it didn't. Francis made 52 in five innings and was dropped from the Leeds and Oval Tests. The next man tried was Wally Edwards of Western Australia. He played at Brisbane, Perth and Melbourne in 1974-75, scoring 68 in 6 innings; not much better than Francis's efforts. He was replaced by McCosker for the rest of that rubber. When Ian Chappell's second Australians arrived in England in 1975, Alan Turner of New South Wales was in the ranks. He was selected for 3 of the 4 Tests. Contributions totalling 77 runs in 5 innings placed him like his predecessors near the foot of the Test averages.

Another experiment involved Richie Robinson of Victoria. Robinson was chosen for the 1977 tour as reserve stumper to Rodney Marsh. A series of prolific innings in Australia during their 1976-77 season encouraged Greg Chappell to try him as a batsman in the Tests in England. At Lord's as a stop-gap opener Robinson scored 11 and 4.

He was dropped at Old Trafford, returned at Trent Bridge and Leeds as a middle order batsman, then was omitted at the Oval. Six innings for 100 runs, top score 34, placed Robinson squarely in the Francis, Edwards, Turner class. His association with the Packer group probably ended a Test career that was already in jeopardy.

Five other Australians have played only 3 times against England. Craig Serjeant of Western Australia top-scored with 81 on his debut at Lord's in 1977. 3 in the second innings and 14 and 8 at Manchester led to omission from the Third and Fourth Tests; at the Oval he made a duck. Nevertheless his form was useful enough to make further selection likely. Chosen as vice-captain to Bobby Simpson for the party which toured the West Indies in 1977-78, Serjeant had every opportunity to line himself up for more appearances against England. He was not included in the sides which opposed Mike Brearley however. Subsequently his career seemed to lose direction. He was one of the few members of Greg Chappell's team who did not defect to Kerry Packer. This seemed to have the effect of estranging him from the side in the later stages of the 1977 tour. Then he went to the West Indies as Simpson's heir apparent, but obviously failed to impress. His Test career fizzled out and, though he has continued to play for his state, his form since 1980 has been inconsistent. Another in and outer was Gary Cosier of South Australia and Queensland. Cosier made his debut at Melbourne in the Centenary Test. Batting at number 3 he scored 10 and 4, poor efforts; but he did grab a couple of smart close catches off leg spinner Kerry O'Keeffe. The two victims were Tony Greig and Derek Randall, who were well on the way towards winning the game for England when Cosier chipped in. Cosier next turned up in England in 1977 as a member of Greg Chappell's team. He was not a Packer man; he did not play in the Tests; his tour batting record was not outstanding. After the Packer rumpus Cosier was again picked for Australia as Graham Yallop's vice-captain at Brisbane against Brearley's team. He was run out for 1 in the first innings, then he scored 19 in the second. Retained at Perth he made 4 and 47, the third best contribution of runs to the Aussie cause. The selectors, stricken by two successive defeats, promptly dropped him. He never returned. Next in this batch comes Bruce Laird of Western Australia. Laird played twice against Brearley's 1979-80 team and averaged 33.00. His 74 in the first innings at Melbourne virtually ensured his place as a member of the Centenary Tour squad. In the Lord's match he scored only 24 and 6, reducing his overall average to 27.00. However, with Australia short of top-class openers, he could gain a few more caps in future series.

The remaining two appeared in their three Tests in the 1981 rubber. Martin Kent of Queensland distinguished himself by coming third, behind Dirk Welham and Alan Border, in the batting averages for that series. He scored a couple of fifties in averaging 28.50 and looked a promising recruit for future rubbers. However, like Welham, he was surprisingly ignored for the most recent series; I suppose somebody had to make way for the return of Greg Chappell and David Hookes. Less successful was the youngest of the Chappell brothers, Trevor. In six innings he managed only 79 runs and was omitted from the last three matches of that six Test series. The success of Kent and Welham makes the possibility of further chances for Chappell remote.

The real losers among these 31 Aussies were Bannerman, Trott, Sievers, Archer and Thomas. Bannerman's frailty cut him off in his prime and, though he survived until 1930, his Test career never blossomed as it should have done. The others should have toured in 1896, 1938, 1953 and 1968 respectively. Trott was particularly badly treated and he departed from Australian cricket in high dudgeon. His all-round play could have made the vital difference to the narrow defeat of his brother's 1896 side. I wonder that Harry Trott did not press for Albert's inclusion. Perhaps brotherly love was not highly developed in the Trott tribe, or perhaps the genial Harry wished to avoid charges of favouritism and didn't push his brother's claims sufficiently. Whatever the reasons, Albert had every right to be aggrieved.

Sievers could not have done worse than people like Waite and White of the 1938 side. Conceivably he could have done a lot better. (Those selectors also managed to omit Grimmett and Tallon; they were obviously very idiosyncratic in their thinking.) In view of the poor form shown by Colin McDonald and Ian Craig in 1953, both were very lucky to get the selectors' nod over Ken Archer (or, indeed, over Jim Burke, who was left languishing in New South Wales after making a century on his Test debut). As Ron Archer and Tallon were already in the side, perhaps Queensland was considered to have received her share of places. Or perhaps Victoria, with only Hassett and Bill Johnston certain of Test places, was determined to maintain her usual quota; hence the inclusion of McDonald. Something similar may have occurred in 1968. Bill Lawry (Victoria) was skipper and 7 of the party were Victorians. Joslin was the untried youngster of whom great things were expected — much like Ian Craig in the fifties, but with much less reason, for Craig had a successful Test series against South Africa under his belt. The experience of Thomas would have proved much more effective than the untried Joslin. The most recent discard, Martin Kent also has reason to feel aggrieved, though Australia still has time to make use of his talents as batsman and fielder. Thirty one men were given a reasonable trial and twenty five were found more or less wanting. Perhaps the Australian selectors could be forgiven for discarding Sievers, Archer and Thomas; but never for Albert Trott!

10

ENGLAND'S NEARLY MEN

The four Test men fall into one of three categories. Either they were tourists who managed their appearances because there were few alternative choices; or they were men whose skills were considered only suitable to home wickets; or they were budding stars who, for reasons other than cricket, were unable to pursue their career. A few, of course, shuttled in and out of Test teams making the odd appearance over a number of series, but the majority should have secured a permanent place. For one reason or another they didn't quite make it. They are the 'Nearly Men'.

Twenty three Englishmen almost made the big time. So did 12 Australians. 12 of them were tourists; 13 played only at home; the other 10 managed a bit of each. Sickness curtailed the careers of 4 or 5; World War II finished one; one was 'chucked' out; commitments outside cricket claimed 6 more; and 7 of them are still currently playing. At least 12 of the rest performed well enough to merit further games without managing to convince the selectors.

The English contingent is sprinkled with aristocrats: Lord Harris, the Hon. Alfred Lyttleton, the Hon. Ivo Bligh, the Hon. L.H. Tennyson; it sounds like the Debrett's 1st XI. There was also Prince Duleepsinhji. The Kentish autocrat Lord Harris played, as we have seen, a vital role in establishing the Tests on a home and away basis. His 'Gentlemen of England' were perhaps a little too high-hat for the general Australian public, which probably made his 10 wicket defeat in 1879 that much sweeter to the Diggers. Nevertheless his Lordship, with scores of 33 and 36, made 25% of the Gentlemen's runs against a rampaging Spofforth who bagged 13 wickets in the match. In true British style, he went down with all guns blazing. In 1880, at the Oval, Lord Harris had his revenge. A measure of the esteem in which he was held, and the place which he occupied in the higher levels of the M.C.C. can be gauged from his appointment as England's first home captain, despite the presence of the three Graces and Alfred Lyttleton in the ranks of his team. It required an unusual man to make E.M. and W.G. knuckle down. England's first innings of 420 contained not only W.G's. 152 and A.P. Lucas' 55, but also an excellent 52 from Harris himself.

His Lordship missed the 'Ashes' match of 1882, but returned for the last two Tests of 1884. He led England to an innings win at Lord's, but had the worst of a high scoring draw at the Oval. In the latter game he achieved a certain notoriety by using 11 bowlers. Mind you, since Australia totalled 551, he needed them. England, weak in bowling at this time, had a team full of batsmen (only Ted Peate was a rabbit) and Lord Harris' arrangement of the batting order was fraught with difficulties. Almost inevitably this array of batting talent faltered in replying to Australia's mammoth score, but a much disgruntled Walter Read, coming in at number 10, saved his Lordship's bacon. Determined to show his captain the error of his judgment, Read scored 117 in less than two hours and made the game safe. Lord Harris' own contributions in this rubber totalled 24 runs in two completed innings. Nevertheless his Test career average was a useful 29.00. A good player, his Lordship, if not quite in the highest class. He certainly gave tone to England's early Test ventures.

The best of Lord Harris's eleven bowlers in that Oval Match was the Hon. Alfred Lyttleton, who had been selected as stumper! After Peate, Ulyett, Steel, Billy Barnes, Barlow, W.G., and Read had bowled 286 overs for 6 wickets between them at a cost of 494, the Hon. Alfred, still wearing his pads, polished off the remaining 4 in 12 overs for a mere 19. And he did it by bowling under-arm lobs! Granted his victims were the Australian tail, he emerged with one of the best bowling averages in Test history. The ironic part of this spectacular feat is that Lyttleton's keeping, is more often than not forgotten. For example, in that colossal Australian total he allowed only 7 byes. He was, undoubtedly, the best amateur keeper of his day, though whether he was better than Pilling of Lancashire is open to question. Lyttleton actually started his Test career in the first match in England in 1880. He allowed 16 byes and claimed no victims in the game, and in the low-scoring 'Ashes' encounter of 1882 he did little better. Pilling played at Old Trafford in the First Test of 1884 (hometown choice again) but Lyttleton returned for the two London matches. At Lord's he had no victims and, apart from his 4 bowling scalps, only one at the Oval. Just two catches in 4 Tests does not indicate exceptional ability. As the requirements of his legal career prevented him from touring, the Hon. Alfred was not really a good investment as a permanent Test player in a key position. Dick Pilling toured Australia in 1881-82 and was in good form at home throughout the early eighties. He really should have had Lyttleton's place in these four home Tests. Even though Alfred had a definite edge as a batsman — he averaged 15 in Tests as opposed to the Lancastrian's 7 — he probably owed his selection to his contacts in high places at Lord's. Still, those lobs have provided one of the perpetual talking points of Test history.

In between Lyttleton's Test appearances, the Hon. Ivo Bligh set forth to retrieve the Ashes. Considering that his 1882-83 tourists were only 12 strong and that Morley, his only fast bowler, was badly injured on the way out to Australia, 'St. Ivo' did wonderfully well in achieving his object. He was the skipper who actually received the 'Ashes' when some Melbourne ladies ceremoniously burned a bail, sealed it in an urn and presented it to him. Ivo showed his appreciation by marrying one of the ladies. Bligh's own performances left something to be desired though. In 7 innings his top score was 19, nowhere near good enough to ensure him of a place in the side back home in England. He was however a safe field, holding 7 catches during the rubber, so he certainly did his bit for England.

Lionel Tennyson was an aristocrat of a later, more democratic, age than his predecessors. Harris, Lyttleton and Bligh partly owed their inclusion in Test teams to their exalted positions in the Victorian class system. By the time Tennyson came to the fore, World War I had swept the Victorian and Edwardian ages away and, though his title may have opened the door to selection, Tennyson's playing prowess had to be exceptional for him to be invited through it. Tennyson had all the flamboyance of a Regency Buck. He was the extrovert captain of Hampshire from 1919-1933 and with his rumbustious batting he caught the selectorial eyes in 1921. (Hardly surprising, for who didn't in that traumatic season?) Belatedly invited to join the side at Lord's, he was stumped by Carter off Mailey for 5 in his first knock. He arrived at number 7 (why he was sent in after A.J. Evans is incomprehensible), in the second innings, with England on the run, at 165 for 5. After a little early luck, the Hon. Lionel drove Gregory, McDonald and Mailey for a little matter of 74 out of the 118 added by the English tail. Undefeated at the end, Tennyson came from his first match with honours second only to those of Frank Woolley, whose two nineties had earlier defied the rampant Australians. The 1921 selectors had further surprises in store. Before the Third Test Tennyson received a telegram. He read it, rolled it into a ball, shied it at the ceiling, caught it, and exclaimed 'Good Heavens, they've asked me to captain England!' (I'm not sure about the 'Good Heavens'; the Hon. Lionel may have used a stronger term).

And captain England he did, for the remainder of the series. As a strategic captain, Tennyson had limitations, not least a shaky knowledge of the more abstruse Laws. But as a leader by example he stands with F.S. Jackson and Freddie Brown. In the Headingley game, Tennyson split his left hand fielding a slashing cover drive by Macartney. With Hobbs already absent with appendicitis, which had developed on the first day, the English batting was thus lamentably reduced. Tennyson's answer was typical. Coming in 9th in the first innings, he set about Gregory and McDonald one-handed in a superb burst of attacking cricket. 94 were added for the last two wickets, 63 of them to Tennyson in 80 glorious minutes. He was last out and was cheered off the ground after an epic knock which required his illustrious grandfather's pen to do it justice. England still lost, but not before the Hon. Captain added 36 more to his tally in the second innings. Rain ruined the Manchester Test. The first day was lost. Tennyson, forgetting that the rules for two day games should now apply, declared England's innings too late on the second day and Armstrong insisted that England should bat on. The crowd became rowdy and Lionel – with help from the umpires – had to explain the situation to them before play could continue. England eventually led on the first innings for the first time in the series, but it was barely possible to commence their second knock before time expired. At the Oval Tennyson played his final knock against Australia. He had not batted at Old Trafford, but this time he hammered a truculent but disciplined 51. This positive lead from his skipper stirred the obdurate Philip Mead to add 70 at the other end, just at a time when he seemed to have become bogged down against Armstrong and Mailey. The 121 gathered for the 6th wicket was England's best stand of the series until Russell and Brown beat it in the second innings with an opening 158. England led again and looked capable of better things in both of these matches.

Tennyson was not a lucky player. Injuries lost him his first match as skipper, while the weather deprived him of the opportunity to cash in on superior positions in his other two games. His forthright character probably cost him support at Headquarters and he disappeared from the English Test Match scene very rapidly. Although he captained a number of touring sides, the Hon. Lionel never played in another official Test. Scant reward for a fighting skipper whose 57.25 batting average places him 8th in England's all-time list against the Aussies.

Having dealt with the aristocracy, the 'tourists only must now be considered. This group includes old-time amateurs C.F. Leslie, G.B. Studd, F.L. Fane; professionals Harry Makepeace, A.C. Smith, I. Jones and D. Lloyd; and the ubiquitous William Midwinter. Leslie and Studd were Middlesex members of Ivo Bligh's party. They hardly set the world on fire. Leslie caused a slight stir at Melbourne by taking 3 for 31 with his fastish bowling. He scored a rapid 54 in the next game (also at Melbourne) but then his efforts fizzled out. 4 wickets at 11 apiece for the series were a better contribution than his 15 runs an innings batting average, but Leslie was not of real Test class. The same remark applies even more emphatically to G.B. Studd. One of three cricketing brothers, all of whom captained Cambridge, G.B. sports one of the worst records of a recognised batsman in Test matches. In seven starts on Bligh's tour, Studd scored just 31 runs with a highest score of 9 and an average of 4.42. The redeeming feature was his fine fielding which brought him 8 catches at mid off during the series. Neither of these two cricketers could aspire to play for England in England.

In 1907-8 F.L. Fane of Essex travelled out to Australia as vice-captain to A.O. Jones. A fine, forward-style batsman, he played in 4 of the 5 Tests, captaining England in the first 3 because of Jones' illness. England won the second of these by the skin of their teeth but generally speaking they were outclassed by the Australians. Fane, an opening bat, made some steady contributions. He only scored one 50 — at Melbourne in the Second Test — and his average of 24 was nothing to write home about, but he did considerably better than his unfortunate captain. For many seasons he was a stalwart batsman for Essex and in 1905-06 showed himself adept in dealing with South Africa googly bowling on matting wickets. With home competition from Jackson, Fry, Jessop and others it is not surprising that Fane's only opportunity to play against Australia came on this tour. Perhaps with less responsibility thrust upon him, he would have done more justice to his batting ability.

The Lancastrian Harry Makepeace went on the ill-fated 1920-21 trip to the Antipodes. Harry made his first appearance for Lancashire in 1906 and he was pushing 40 when called on by England for this tour. Like Jack Sharp he played Soccer for Everton, with whom he gained F.A. Cup Winners and League Championship medals in the pre-World I days. He also collected 4 International Caps. In the immediate post-war years he established his position as the Lancastrians' soundest bat and fully deserved his tour place. In Australia Makepeace was not chosen for the First Test at Sydney, but he played in the remaining four. His debut at Melbourne was a failure: a brace of 4s. He came good at Adelaide with 60 and 30 and, back at Melbourne, topped that with 117 and 54. The century took nearly four hours, but it was a fine sheet-anchor effort compiled at a time when the leading English bats were succumbing for twenties and thirties. His second innings fifty helped Rhodes to clear the Australians' lead with only 1 wicket down, but Mailey got both of them — plus 7 others — to set up another Australian win. In the final match at Sydney Makepeace failed with scores of 3 and 7, understandable at the end of a long and arduous tour. Only the great Hobbs had an appreciably better Test average than Makepeace at the end of this series, so no doubt Harry expected further calls to the colours in the home series of 1921. With practically everyone else in the country having a run, it is astounding that Makepeace lost out, especially since he totalled 2,000 runs for the season. He had seemed a pretty good player of fast bowling too, for his wicket fell 3 times each to spinners Armstrong and Mailey during his 8 innings in Australia. The 1921 selection processes appear more bizarre at each fresh appraisal. Makepeace probably lost his best years to the First War. He was 33 and an established player in 1914. His dogged batting was highly effective for Lancashire throughout the twenties and he was a potent factor in their successive Championships of 1926-28. Not a pretty bat, Harry Makepeace was technically far better equipped than most of the dashers selected by England during his period.

Modern Times have thrown up three more 'tourists only'. Ted Dexter's 1962-63 side included Alan Smith, of Warwickshire, as reserve stumper to John Murray. The events reversed their roles. Ostensibly Smith's batting was superior and this persuaded the tour selectors to favour him. He played in 4 Tests, though his presence in the last two was due to an injury sustained by his rival during the Third Test. Smith's batting proved a spurious asset. His average was only 11.75 with a best score of 21. Behind the stumps his work was often untidy, but he did snap up 13 catches; he failed to demonstrate any clear superiority over Murray and both of them were later discarded in favour of Jim Parks in 1964. Smith did, at least, achieve the distinction of going through his Australian Test career unbeaten; one win and three draws to be precise.

I.J. 'Jeff' Jones, of Glamorgan, was an unlucky cricketer. (Two other unfortunates in this group were Fred Morley and Duleep — of whom more anon). Jones, a left arm quickie, toured in 1965-66 with Mike Smith's team. Injuries to Brown and Higgs opened the way to his selection for the Second Test and he retained his place until the end of the rubber. Jones' long-striding approach and unusual delivery angle presented problems to the Australians. In addition he found the hard pitches much to his liking, and he was England's best wicket-taker with 15 victims in the series, though at the high cost of 35 apiece. Jones' best Test performance was at Adelaide. After Simpson and Lawry had launched the Australian innings with an opening stand of 244, Jones weighed in with 6 wickets. Australia totalled 516 and the Welshman's 6 for 118 represented fine bowling. Unfortunately England's supine batting failed to take advantage of a chance to retrieve a first innings deficit of 275. All out for 266, they lost by an innings and the Australians squared the series. By the time of the next rubber in 1968 Jones' Test career was virtually over. That zip possessed by the best fast bowlers did not come readily to Jones and a recurring elbow-injury reduced his effectiveness. He was never the same again after 1966, though he clung on in county cricket until 1970 before giving up.

David Lloyd of Lancashire was a member of Mike Denness' ill-fated 1974-75 side. Like most other bats in that team he found Lillee and Thomson a rare handful and his best score in 4 Tests was 49 on his debut at Perth. Although reaching double figures in 6 of his 8 knocks, Lloyd never really showed signs of coping efficiently with the fast bowlers; but then, who did? The Lancastrian's top-class close fielding reaped him 6 catches, but, in common with several others of that side, Lloyd lost his place before the next rubber.

The ubiquitous William Midwinter's career has already been outlined in the chapter on the pioneers. With 14 Tests altogether, he does not really belong among the Nearly Men. One way or the other, Midwinter made it. The curiosity of his appearances for England is that they all took place in Australia.

Apart from Lionel Tennyson, five men played all of their four Tests in England. The first of these was Schofield Haigh of Yorkshire. 'Scofie' made his debut in 1905, playing at Lord's and Headingley. His medium paced off-breaks were only moderately effective and he dropped out until 1909. In that rubber he played at Lord's without success and disappeared again until 1912, when he failed to get a wicket in the rain-ruined Old Trafford match. Despite his excellent record for Yorkshire, Haigh's bowling was not equal to the demands of Test cricket. 4 wickets for 139 runs in 4 matches was a very disappointing contribution.

In 1926 Arthur Carr, the forthright captain of Nottinghamshire, led

England to four successive draws. That sodden series prevented Carr from displaying his batting talents. He managed only one trip to the wicket, for 13 runs, in what must have been a series of depressing experiences. To make matters worse he made a name for himself in Test history by putting Australia in at Leeds and dropping their century-maker, Macartney, when he had scored 2. Carr must have been glad to see the back of 1926, and perhaps the selectors were glad to see the back of Carr. Certainly, his period of tenure produced no glories. He made way for the ebullient Percy Chapman to begin one of England's most fruitful eras.

Four years later, K.S. Duleepsinhji followed his illustrious uncle 'Ranji' into the English ranks. England's second Indian Prince began with a scintillating 173 at Lord's, plus a second-innings 48. He had been called in as a replacement for the injured Herbert Sutcliffe, but this fine start ensured his place for the rest of the series. Despite his fine batting, England lost by seven wickets at Lord's (Bradman 254). They drew at Leeds (Duleep 35 and 10, Bradman 334); and at Old Trafford (Duleep 54). The Oval Test saw Australia (Bradman 232) clinch the rubber, but Duleep with 50 and 46 maintained his form. He averaged 59.42 for his 7 innings, better than anyone except Sutcliffe (87.20) and Bradman (139.14), on either side. Duleep was a certainty to tour Australia with Jardine's side, but he was laid low in the summer of 1932 by tuberculosis. He never played top-class cricket again. Like Colin Milburn at a later period, the crowd-pleasing Indian was tragically taken from the game which he graced so well.

Jack Flavell, Worcestershire's speedy bowler of the sixties, played twice against Benaud's team in 1961 and twice more in 1964. At no time did he look capable of spear-heading England's attack. 7 paltry wickets, less than 1 per innings, for 52 runs each demonstrated clearly that Flavell was no adequate successor to Statham or Trueman. England would have done better to persevere with Derby's Les Jackson. The last of the home games only group is Barry Wood of Lancashire. Wood, a competent player of pace-bowling, made an impressive start at the Oval in 1972, scoring 26 and 90 against the might of Lillee and Massie. It was certainly not his fault that England lost and Australia squared the rubber. Wood missed the 1974-75 tour. His sturdy skill against pace might well have been a lot more useful then than the dubious abilities of a number of others who did make the trip. When Ian Chappell's men visited England in 1975, Wood was quickly recalled after the debacle at Birmingham had put the Australians in the driving seat. He played in the remaining games, but, apart from a fifty in the second innings at Lord's, made little impression on the series. England really missed the boat by failing to persevere with the Lancastrian after his initial success.

Six players remain. These were all selected for tours; all, save one, also made the side in England. Four of them come into the category of pace bowlers; the other two were batsmen; one was ill-fated; one is still playing and available for more Tests; the rest were rather less than successful. The ill-fated one was Fred Morley. In 1880 Morley was the finest bowler in the land. He bowled left-handed, round arm and very fast, with the ability to turn the ball either way — a formidable attacker. At the Oval in the first Test in England, Morley captured 8 wickets at less than 20 each, and played an important part in England's victory. Four years later, at the age of 33, he was dead. Selected to tour with Ivo Bligh in 1882-83, poor Fred broke a rib when the tourists' ship, the *Peshawar*, was involved in a collision out of Colombo. The injury was not diagnosed, and, as the only fast bowler in the party, Morley felt obliged to play in 3 of the 4 Tests. He performed creditably (8 for 150 altogether) but he must have aggravated the injury. He developed lung congestion, declined gradually during 1883 and died in 1884. Morley was one of the worst batsmen ever to appear in Tests, but he more than made up for that with his 16 scalps at 18.50 apiece. 124 of his 243 overs were maidens; one of the most economical records in Test history. His analysis places him in the top flight of English bowlers and England won three of the Tests in which he played. Certainly no bowler of comparable pace and accuracy appeared in English cricket for another decade.

Another pace bowler was Harry Howell of Warwickshire. In the years immediately after World War I Howell was probably England's paciest bowler. He had strength, pluck and good control, but he was not a lucky bowler. In Australia in 1920-21 Howell played in 3 Tests. His first appearance at Melbourne yielded 3 wickets and a plague of dropped catches. Australia won by an innings. The next game at Adelaide was a repeat performance. Collins, dropped twice off Howell, at 53 and 60, went on to score 162. Kelleway, in the second innings, made 147 after being missed in the slips off the Warwickshire man before he had opened his account. Howell's 4 wickets in the game cost over 200 runs. Back at Melbourne Howell bowled poorly. 27 overs yielded 122 runs (nearly 5 runs an over) and no wickets. He missed the final match through injury. The return rubber in 1921 found Howell back in the side at Trent Bridge. England lost by ten wickets, and

Howell's 9 overs cost 22 runs. That was the end of his Test career versus Australia. The selectors dropped him, along with five others, and his Test record of 7 wickets at the astronomic cost of 70 runs each, for once fully justified them. Howell shares the distinction with Harry Makepeace of having been on the losing side in all of his Tests against the Australians. Bad luck or no, he was a resounding flop.

Gilligan's team of 1924-25 included Walter Whysall of Nottinghamshire. Whysall's batting was a definite asset and he also took on the duties of reserve stumper to Strudwick. He was not included in the first two Tests, but gained a place at Adelaide for the Third. A long Australian innings came to an end shortly before the close of the second day and Whysall found himself opening the innings for England with Maurice Tate. He was bowled by Gregory for 9, but redeemed himself by top-scoring in the second innings. England lost by only 11 runs and Whysall's 75 − batting fifth this time − was a sound, hard-hitting knock. The Notts. man kept his place for the remaining Tests. At Melbourne he went one better with an excellent 76, sharing a stand of 133 with Roy Kilner for the 7th wicket. England totalled 548 and won by an innings. In the final Test Whysall failed, falling in both innings to the debutant Grimmett. During this tour Whysall attained his 36th birthday, so it was perhaps not too surprising that he was passed over on his return to England. He faded from the Australian Test scene until 1930, when, rising 42, he was summoned to the Oval for the last Test. His solid style was expected to be useful in a play to a finish, but his contributions were paltry. (Four years later, the selectors committed the same error when Frank Woolley was called up for the corresponding match.) England lost the game and the Ashes and Walter Whysall ended his Test career with a batting average just under 30. If he had been retained in 1926 (though it is difficult to guess at whose expense), Whysall could well have provided middle order solidity for a number of years.

Jumping nearly 40 years we find Len Coldwell, a Worcestershire seam bowler, making two appearances in each country. In 1962-3 he went out to Australia with Tex Dexter. It was anticipated that his style, reminiscent of Tate and Bedser would prove effective on Australian wickets. The selectors were sadly deceived. His two Tests yielded 3 wickets at over 50 each and he was dropped. In 1964 Coldwell played at Trent Bridge and Lord's. 3 for 48 in the first game promised well but 1 for 110 at Headquarters ended the experiment. 7 wickets in 4 matches almost exactly matched his Worcester contemporary, Flavell's record. There was little reminiscent of Tate or Bedser about the results of Coldwell's bowling.

John Hampshire of Yorkshire is one of the modern era's less fortunate batsmen. His Test appearances were spasmodic. He showed promise when he first appeared and visited Australia with Illingworth's triumphant 1970-71 team. On that tour Hampshire was regarded as a reserve batsman, but he was selected for the last two games of that six match series. At Adelaide he began with a useful 55, but 10 and 24 at Sydney were not enough to clinch a permanent place. Consequently Hampshire's next appearance was delayed until the Oval match of 1972. He replaced the unsuccessful Keith Fletcher at number four and again made useful contributions of 42 and 20. Despite his steady scoring, the selectors were not inclined to persevere with him: number fours are expected to make tons, not just thirties and forties. Hampshire's remaining Test took place at Leeds in 1975 (the 'George Davis' match). He scored 14 and 0. In view of the selectors' persistence in sticking to inconsistent batsmen like Keith Fletcher, Hampshire's in and out career hardly gave him a chance to do himself justice. He was too often regarded as a stop-gap replacement instead of a class batsman in his own right.

Last, but hopefully not least, of these Nearly Men is Norman Cowans, the current Middlesex fast bowler. Cowans began the 1982-83 series as England's third pace-man, but, with Willis and Botham using the new ball, he bowled only 31 overs in the first two matches and captured only one wicket. Dropped for the Third Test, which was lost, Cowans returned for the last two and picked up 10 wickets for 260. His 6 for 77 in the second innings at Melbourne was the main factor in England's narrow victory. With more positive handling from his captain, Cowans may prove a thorn in Australia's flesh for some time to come.

A summing-up of these English discards leads one to the conclusion that Duleep and Fred Morley would certainly have been picked more frequently but for illness; that the Lancastrians, Makepeace and Wood, and Whysall of Notts., had earned further chances; and that the redoubtable Lionel Tennyson's bluff approach and brave defiance were not to the selectors' taste. Even if the poet's grandson was no great shakes as a skipper, his courageous batting was a commodity in short supply in the twenties and he should have played in many more Tests.

A respectable Test side could be assembled from these one to four Tests men. A batting order of. George Brown, Milburn, Steele, Duleep, Jack Sharp, Tennyson, Albert Relf, 'Sailor' Young, Walter Brearley, Morley and 'Nutty' Martin, would surely give a good account of itself. Perhaps the tail is rather long, though the varied attack of Brearley and Morley, followed by Martin and Young, does not look at all bad, while Relf, Steele and Milburn would supply the change bowling. George Brown would keep wicket and the Hon. Lionel would be skipper. Fielding looks suspect, but one can't have everything. That batting order is impressive — the brave Brown, mercurial Milburn, solid Steele, dashing Duleep, steady Sharp and turbulent Tennyson — what problems they would present if they were all on song together. A match between these and the colonial Nearly Men would be worth seeing.

One hundred and sixty eight Englishmen have now been considered, approximately half of the total Test roll. Nearly 130 of them failed to justify their selection; a fact which vindicates the selectors' decisions to discard them. But one does wonder why a lot of them were picked in the first place.

11

AUSTRALIAN ALMOSTS

If an Australian manages to appear in four Tests against England, he generally goes on to appear in more. There are only twelve instances of Australians who played just four times against England, and a couple of those could receive further honours. First of these almosts was the South Australian, J. O'Connor. He replaced the injured 'Tibby' Cotter, at Adelaide in 1908 and made an impressive debut in front of his home crowd. O'Connor, a left-hand bat, was a medium-paced right-hand bowler; it was his bowling that took the eye. He captured 3 for 110 in England's first innings, bowling 40 overs and sharing the main burden of the attack with Saunders. In the second innings after Australia, thanks to Hill and Hartigan, had made 506, these two bowlers shared the wickets in bowling Australia to victory by the generous margin of 245 runs. O'Connor's 5 wickets cost him only 40 runs, so that he finished the match with 8 for 150. As he also made a couple of double figure scores his debut was decidedly useful. Two Tests remained in the series. O'Connor kept his place but failed to maintain the form which marked his debut. Only 4 wickets at Melbourne and none at all at Sydney made many feel that his Adelaide form was misleading.

The South Australian was however chosen to tour England in 1909. With 77 wickets on the tour it would seem that he was a success, but he was slow to find his form. Chosen for the First Test, he bowled only 8 overs to take 1 for 40. Australia lost by 10 wickets and that was the end of his participation in Tests. Curiously all of O'Connor's best performances on this tour occurred after he had been dropped from the Test team. Frank Laver took his place and topped the Test bowling averages, so poor O'Connor never obtained a second chance. O'Connor's 13 Test wickets cost 26.15 each, mainly because of that successful Adelaide debut. He eventually mastered English conditions well, so perhaps he should have been tried again.

When Don Bradman began astonishing the natives in the late twenties, there was another young New South Welshman whom many considered to be a better bat than 'the Don'; this was Archie Jackson. Jackson was only 19 when he made his first appearance at Adelaide in 1929. An opening batsman, he played beautifully, indulging in fluent square and late cuts as well as elegant forcing shots on the leg-side. He reached his century in just over 4 hours and went on to 164, the highest Australian debut innings since Charles Bannerman's. This match was very evenly contested. Australia thanks to Archie led by 35, after losing their first three men for 19. England, with Hammond and Jardine in fine form, set Australia 348 to win. Jackson made 36 in his second knock before giving a catch to Duckworth, so that his first Test yielded exactly 200 runs. Despite 58 from Bradman and 87 from Jack Ryder, the Aussies failed by 12 runs. With one game left of the rubber, Australia faced a whitewash . At Melbourne, they replied to England's 519 with 491 (Bradman 123, Woodfull 102) and eventually ran out winners by 5 wickets. Jackson's 30 and 46 were compiled in the same elegant way as his debut century and he finished the series at the top of the Australian batting list with an average of 69.00.

After this auspicious beginning, Jackson's Test career seemed assured. Yet by the time Woodfull's side arrived in England just over a year later his star was on the wane. Struggling against ill-health he missed the first two Tests; scored a paltry single at Leeds (Bradman 334); dropped out at Old Trafford; but was recalled for the final game at the Oval. This was Jackson's swan song. Dropped to number 5 in the order, he supported Bradman in a stand of 243 for the 4th wicket. This took place in wet conditions on the fourth day, and though Jackson's share was 73 against twice as many from 'the Don', he played an important role in regaining the Ashes for Australia. It was his last major innings. Tuberculosis, which had been plaguing him throughout this tour, tightened its grip and within two years, when Bodyline was at its height, Australia's 'second Victor Trumper' died. His passing was sad, but he left an indelible mark on Anglo-Australian Tests. Jackson's batting average against England of 58.33 has been bettered only by Bradman, Charles Bannerman, Sid Barnes and Albert Trott. But it is not the figures that are remembered. It is the style, the elegance and the youthful promise unfulfilled that linger in the memory. Amid a long line of Australian Ironsides , Jackson stands out as a dashing Cavalier.

In the late thirties two more Nearly Men arrived in the Australian ranks. For Frank Ward, of South Australia, Fortune first smiled, then frowned. The smiles began when Ward was preferred to his illustrious state colleague Grimmett for the first Three Tests of 1936-37. At Brisbane he began unpropitiously with 2 for 138 in England's first innings. The absence of McCormick (injured) and the faith of his captain (Bradman) gave him the bulk of the bowling in the second innings. Seizing his chance, Ward captured 6 for 102 in 46 overs, but Australia, caught on a gluepot, lost heavily. On the strength of this effort Ward was retained at Sydney and Melbourne. His total bag in those Tests was 3 for 192. He was completely outshone at Melbourne by Fleetwood-Smith who had missed the first two games through injury, and was quite rightly dropped for the rest of the rubber.

Surprisingly Ward gained a place in Bradman's 1938 team. In retrospect the Australian selectors discarded Grimmett too hastily and Ward was the lucky gainer. In England he captured 92 wickets on the tour, second to the great O'Reilly, but his lone Test appearance at Trent Bridge was a complete failure. With no batting credentials at all, Ward's 11 Test wickets at 52 apiece were an expensive luxury for Australia at a time when the sides were very evenly matched. Indeed Australia's heavy dependence on Bradman probably indicated that England was the better all-round team. Ward was elevated by woolly thinking at selectorial level into a role which he only once looked capable of filling adequately. World War II terminated his Test career.

Another war-time casualty was Ben Barnett, Victoria's stumper. Selected as Oldfield's replacement for the 1938 tour − another controversial decision − Barnett kept very efficiently in all the Tests of this series. England scored 2,643 runs in the rubber while Barnett conceded just 36 byes. He contributed a sterling 57 to Australia's victory at Leeds and looked set for a prolonged Test career. Then came the War, and for Barnett a Japanese P.O.W. camp. When he returned to big cricket after the hostilities had ceased, he was unable to withstand the challenge of the mighty and younger Don Tallon. Barnett, like Jackson, never had the chance to fulfill his potential.

The next four Test Aussie was an extremely controversial figure. Ian Meckiff, a fast, left-handed bowler from Victoria, played in four matches against Peter May's Englishmen in 1958-59. His record in that series was most impressive. Despite competition from Benaud and Davidson, Meckiff headed the averages with 17 wickets at 17 apiece. Meckiff began fairly modestly with 5 scalps at Brisbane, a match won comfortably by Australia. Three weeks later on his home ground at Melbourne Meckiff bowled Australia to a second victory. His 6 for 38 in England's disastrous second innings gave him a match return of 9 for 107. The Englishmen had no answer to his jerky, erratic style of bowling. The next match, on a Sydney pitch which favoured spin-bowling, was not a success for Meckiff. He bagged the first wicket of the game, but later he strained a tendon which forced him to miss the Adelaide Test. He returned for the last match at Melbourne, but only managed two more wickets. A promising beginning had tailed off. On the other hand the controversy surrounding Meckiff's bowling mushroomed as the series progressed. At this period several Australian bowlers had suspect actions. The most suspect of all was Meckiff's. There was certainly a good deal of jerk in his delivery, sufficient to contravene Law 26 in the eyes of many independent observers. Australian umpires did not apparently subscribe to these opinions; they certainly did not call the Victorian. The English journalists, possibly subjectively, were convinced that not only Meckiff, but also Gordon Rorke, Jim Burke and Keith Slater, all of whom bowled during the series, were chuckers. England had lost the series 4-0 and many Australians said it was a case of sour grapes.

Not so Sir Donald Bradman. Once this acrimonious season was over, he and his colleagues set to work to root out the chuckers and draggers. By the time of the next tour to England (1961) most of the offending bowlers had gone from the first class game. Meckiff was still playing and had indeed taken part in nine further Tests against other countries during the interim. However diplomacy dictated that he should be omitted from a tour where he was virtually certain to be no-balled by the stricter English umpires. (When the South Africans had toured Britain in 1960, their Meckiff, Geoff Griffin, had been driven out of the Test bowling ranks by determined application of Law 26.) Meckiff never toured England and he was not called to the colours when Ted Dexter led the next trip to Australia. Finally he was called in his own country when he played against the South Africans in 1963, and his chequered Test career was effectively over. Meckiff achieved the distinction of never being on the losing side against England, but the cloud surrounding his performances in 1958-59 has impaired the esteem due to Benaud and Davidson, who were the chief architects of a sweeping Australian success. Meckiff, despite his fine figures, was really a support bowler to the big two. He has sadly a claim to notoriety rather than fame.

In 1970 Australia was seeking a fast bowler. Graham McKenzie's powers were declining and a new spearhead to the attack was needed. Alan 'Froggie' Thomson of Victoria, was thought to be the answer. A good effort for his home state against M.C.C. got Thomson into the Test side against Ray Illingworth's team. He played in the first, second, fourth and fifth games of that rubber (the first six Test series) and achieved virtually nothing of note. Thomson bowled over 1,500 balls in capturing 12 wickets, a striking rate of 1 wicket every 15 or so overs. In addition, each wicket cost him the expensive sum of 54 runs. Although Australia drew the games in which Thomson played and lost the two which he missed, his wrong foot style of bowling was obviously not the answer to selectorial prayers. The advent of Dennis Lillee in the last game of the series put paid to Thomson as a Test bowler. He was lucky to survive so long.

While Thomson was being tried as the answer to the pace bowling problem, the Australian selectors were also experimenting with leg-spin. A top-class successor to Richie Benaud had yet to be found, and in 1970-71 the man in possession, Johnny Gleeson, found himself under challenge from Kerry O'Keeffe (New South Wales) and Terry Jenner (South Australia). Throughout the seventies these two googly bowlers were in and out of the Australian side. O'Keeffe was the more favoured, particularly for overseas tours, while Jenner's total of caps against the Old Enemy was four, all of these appearances occurring in Australia. Against Illingworth's team, Jenner played in the first and last of the six Tests. His debut at Brisbane was not a success (2 for 95), but at Sydney he captured 4 for 81, bowling a lot of the time in harness with O'Keeffe. When batting in this match, Jenner was the passive cause of the row which developed when John Snow of England was warned for bowling persistent bumpers. He hit the unfortunate Jenner in the face and was warned; Illingworth took exception to the warning and led the England players from the field. In the circumstances Jenner's innings of 30 was a courageous effort. His bowling, however, did not get him a place on the plane to England in 1972. He reappeared for the Brisbane Test in 1974, took 2 for 69 and was promptly dropped. The selectors smiled on him again for the Adelaide match (Fifth Test of the rubber) and Jenner must have relished the prospect of playing on his home pitch. He began in fine style with a first innings contribution of 74. Going in at 84 for 5, Jenner played a leading part in rescuing Australia and lifting the total to 304. Sadly that was the end of his success, twenty overs yielding only one wicket for 67 runs. Jenner was not selected for the 1975 and 1977 tours, and he subsequently lost his place in his state side.

A very different prospect was Bob Massie. A West Australian with experience of English conditions (he played a fair amount of cricket for Kilmarnock in the early seventies), Massie had fine control of swing and swerve — both in and out. Chosen for Ian Chappell's 1972 tourists,

Massie missed the opening Test at Old Trafford through injury. Coming into the side at Lord's, the West Australian proceeded to write his name large in Test history. Australia, already one down in the series, needed a victory. Massie made sure they got it. In 60 overs of superb medium-paced bowling Massie captured 16 wickets for 137 runs. This *tour de force* was the best piece of Test bowling ever for Australia, and indeed only Jim Laker and Sidney Barnes have exceeded Massie's figures. Having eclipsed the mighty Spofforth, and on his Test debut at that, Massie seemed set for an illustrious career. Unfortunately that career did not work out as expected. Massie played in the rest of the 1972 Tests capturing 5 wickets at Nottingham, none at Leeds, and only 2 at the Oval. This gave him 23 for the rubber (in 4 games) as against Dennis Lillee's 31 (in 5). Both of them averaged less than 18 runs for each victim, the best double effort in a series since Miller and Iverson in 1950-51. Nevertheless the signs were that the English had rumbled Massie by the end of the 1972 season, though Lillee, with his extra pace, was still posing serious problems. When Mike Denness' side visited Australia two years later, Massie was conspicuous by his absence. He had been missing from his state side since December 1973; though he made an appearance against South Australia in November 1974, his 3 wickets were not sufficient to help him regain a permanent place. The advent of Jeff Thomson as Lillee's Test partner certainly compensated the selectors for any concern over Massie's lost form. Massie's meteoric progress as a bowler, like Archie Jackson's as a batsman, soon burned itself out and already he is just a name in the record books.

Ian Davis of New South Wales crammed his four match Test career into five months of 1977. Like Gary Cosier and David Hookes he made his debut in the Centenary Test at Melbourne. An opening bat, Davis scored a very useful 68 in the second innings, materially assisting his country to a 45 run victory. He was an obvious choice for the 1977 tour. In England Davis failed to make his mark. His first 6 innings yielded less than 100 runs all told and the reserve stumper, Robinson, was given his place for the Lord's Test. A couple of useful knocks against Notts. and Derby got him into the side at Old Trafford and he kept his place at Trent Bridge and Headingley. 6 Test innings realised 107 runs and Australia lost all three matches. Davis was dropped at the Oval. After returning to Australia Davis threw in his lot with Kerry Packer. His future as a Test player, already problematic, was irretrievably lost as a result.

During the 1978-9 rubber two more Australians made four

appearances. Rick Darling of South Australia may gain further favour, but John MacLean of Queensland has come and gone. MacLean, the Queensland captain and stumper, played in the first 4 games against Brearley's side. His keeping to the fast bowling of Hogg, Hurst and Dymock reaped 18 catches, a fine harvest. His batting was poor however, particularly against the spinners, and he was replaced by the younger Keith Wright for the rest of the series. W.M. (Rick) Darling enjoyed some success as an opening bat against Brearley's England. 8 innings produced 221 runs, with 91 in the Fourth Test at Sydney as the highlight. He was dropped for the final Test of the rubber in favour of Andrew Hilditch, but his subsequent record is good enough to make it possible that England has not seen the last of this descendant of the great Joe Darling.

Most recently Keppler Wessels of Queensland (formerly of South Africa) played the last four tests against Bob Willis' team. He proceeded to make the finest batting debut since Archie Jackson's, scoring 162 and 46 and collecting the man of the match award. By the end of the rubber his eight innings had yielded 386 runs for an average of 48.25; figures which should assure his place as an opening bat for some time to come.

The unlucky players in this small group have been Jackson, Massie, Barnett and, possibly, O'Connor. Bringing the one, two and three Test men into consideration, Australia could assemble a very effective side. Charles Bannerman and Archie Jackson would open followed by Graeme Thomas, Ross Gregory, Barry Shepherd, Roger Hartigan, Albert Trott, Ben Barnett, Mick Malone, Tom Kendall and Bob Massie. Perhaps another bowler would be needed to back up Kendall, Massie, Malone and Trott, in which case Maurice Sievers could be brought in instead of Graeme Thomas. It is significant that Dave Gregory is the only regular Australian captain who played in less than 5 Tests. The Australians seem to pick better in the first place, and allow their skippers to retain their confidence a good deal longer than their English counterparts do. Anyway Ben Barnett, a fine stumper, could captain the team, or maybe Barry Shepherd of West Australia.

One hundred and twenty seven Australians have played in less than 5 Tests. In considering their records it is fairly apparent that nearly a hundred of them did little to justify their inclusion. Australian selectors have been perhaps fractionally better than the English in choosing the right players, but in both cases about 40% of the total choice has proved dud.

PART TWO

THE LESSER LIGHTS

Of the 330 cricketers who have made 5 or more appearances in these Test matches, 217 (roughly two thirds) distinguished themselves sufficiently to be regarded as stars or, at least, featured players. The batsmen among them scored more than 500 runs and, with only one or two exceptions, averaged more than 25 per innings. The bowlers captured 25 wickets, generally at a cost lower than 30 apiece, and almost always at the rate of 3 or 4 victims per game. The stumpers dismissed at least 20 victims. All of these leading lights have been considered and appraised time and again in cricket literature. Our concern here is with the 113 players who, often because of their own shortcomings, sometimes because of limited opportunities, occasionally because of the whims and inconsistencies of selectors failed to achieve those standards.

These lesser lights have been divided into Bankrupt Batsmen, who did not score enough; Bountiful Bowlers, who gave away too much for too little return; Assorted All Rounders, who were considered to have batting and bowling skill, but who failed with one and sometimes both; and Second Choice Stumpers. There are two other groups: those who did an adequate job, the Solid Workmen; and those who performed exceptionally well, but for one reason or another were unable to play in more Tests – the Shooting Stars. All these lesser lights made their mark in the Anglo-Australian series.

The Australian Team of 1884: (Back row) Percy MacDonnell, George Alexander (manager), George Giffen, G.E. Palmer. (Middle row) F.R. Spofforth, J. M. Blackham, W.L. Murdoch (capt.), G. Bonnor, W. Midwinter, A.C. Bannerman, H.F. Boyle. (Front row) W.H. Cooper, H.J.H. Scott.

12

BANKRUPT BATSMEN

Most of the one hundred and forty nine batsmen who have represented their countries in 5 or more of these Test matches achieved good solid results. Thirty-two however failed to justify their selectors' confidence, their impact on the Tests ranging between the negligible and the fleeting. It is reasonable to contend that if a man is chosen for his batting alone, and then averages less than 25 runs per innings, he has failed to come up to expectation. After all at a level where fifties are hoped for from each front line batsman, an average of less than half that figure is just not good enough. 20 Englishmen and 12 Australians failed to achieve that reasonable standard.

Fourteen of the Englishmen made most of their appearances during overseas tours, probably because there was no one else to pick. First of these was John Selby, the Notts. batsman, whose limited opportunities have already been mentioned in the account of the Lillywhite Boys . Selby, by the lower batting standards of his day, was more of a success than a failure. In his 6 Tests, all in Australia, he scored 256 runs at an average of 23.27; not bad for the early eighties. His best efforts were 55 and 70 in the first match of the 1881-2 rubber at Melbourne. He finished his Test Career on the same ground with 48 not out two months later. Probably he deserved a chance to represent England at home, but the amateur competition − and influence − was too fierce.

Next on the list comes Charles Studd. In the first innings of that original Ashes debacle at the Oval, Studd was bowled by Spofforth for a duck. A combination of mismanagement by his skipper 'Monkey' Hornby, who relegated him to number ten and fool-hardiness by Ted Peate, who failed to give him the strike, ensured that C.T did not bother the scorers in the second knock either. Consequently in 1882-3 he went a-touring with Ivo Bligh's side with no runs in his Test bank at all. He may as well have not bothered. Seven innings yielded just 160 runs and only in the last Test did Studd make significant contributions: 48 and 31. The reputation built up in his Cambridge years was definitely not maintained Down Under and Test cricket saw him no more after his return from the tour. He went evangelising instead.

A decade later Francis Ford of Middlesex toured with Stoddart's first side in 1894-5. Ford, a legendary hitter, was unable to cope with George Giffen's slows and made only 168 in 9 innings for Stoddart. His best efforts were 30 and 48 in his first Test at Sydney. Another batting passenger on this tour was Surrey's Billy Brockwell. Brockwell had played one Test in England in 1893, scoring 11 in his only innings. Like Ford, he scored well in the First Test, 49 and 37, but his 8 remaining efforts combined failed to double his tally. Brockwell made one further appearance at Old Trafford in 1899 when he scored 20. 202 runs in 12 innings plus 5 very expensive wickets was the sum total of Billy Brockwell's Test career.

Stoddart's next tour — he certainly seemed to pick'em — included two more passengers. J.R. Mason of Kent opened the innings in the first three Tests with the redoubtable Archie MacLaren. While MacLaren scored 370 in his six knocks, Mason amassed 55. He was relegated to number eight for the two final games where he did only marginally better. Mason's average of 12.90 for 129 runs is the lowest of any Englishman chosen for his batting form alone. The Kent man's replacement was Yorkshire's Ted Wainwright. Like Brockwell, Wainwright had played one Test in 1893 and had done nothing to establish himself. In the first two Tests of 1897-8 Wainwright did as well at number 8 as Mason was doing at number 1. His promotion to opener yielded 63 runs in 4 innings, though 49 of them assisted MacLaren in a stand of 111 at Sydney in the last match. Wainwright Brockwell were clearly nothing more than solid county pros operating out of their class.

Another touring flop around the turn of the century was Warwickshire's Willy Quaife. This diminutive bat went to the Antipodes as a member of MacLaren's 1901-2 team. In the previous home rubber Quaife had played at Leeds and Manchester, scoring 44 in 3 completed innings — another case of flimsy credentials. His efforts on tour with the exception of the Third Test at Adelaide were feeble. At Adelaide, he and Len Braund added 108 for the 6th wicket (Quaife 68) after a middle order collapse. Willy also scored 44 in the second innings, but England still lost. Quaife's real trouble was Monty Noble who dismissed him in half of his 12 Test innings. 228 runs for an average of 19.00, with nearly half the tally coming in one Test, made it clear that Quaife was not a Test player.

A colleague of Quaife's on this tour was the ill-fated Arthur Jones of Nottinghamshire. 'A.O.' made his Test debut at the Oval in 1899. He enjoyed some success in this game scoring 31 and dismissing Trumper, Trumble and Kelly with his slows. When his prehensile slip-fielding is added to his talents with bat and ball it can be seen that Jones had the makings of a formidable all-rounder. Jones, however, was not blessed with good health and the 1901-2 series was the only one of four rubbers in which he played throughout. He scored less than 100 runs, with a top score of 28, and the selectors reasonably enough forgot about him for the next 10 Tests. He reappeared in 1905 scoring 40 runs in 4 innings and then was honoured with the 1907-8 captaincy, probably because he was the only amateur available. Illness laid him low on that tour and he was unable to play until the Fourth Test. 68 runs in 4 innings was all he could manage and it was surprising that he retained his place (though not the captaincy) for the first two matches of 1909. 3 innings then produced 62 runs, by which time it was clear that he lacked the strength and, perhaps, the ability ever to succeed at Test level. Jones' main contribution to England during his decade of in and out Test cricket was probably his 15 slip catches. In view of the talent available in Edwardian times it is amazing that he was given so many chances. Was he somebody's blue-eyed boy?

Plum Warner has long been honoured as one of England's great captains. True his 1903-4 team regained the Ashes; true his 1911-12 side did likewise; true also that Plum spent most of this latter tour recovering from illness and the credit for the team's success must be given largely to his deputy, Johnny Douglas. Despite his 'greatness', Warner was never asked to lead against the Aussies in England and the reason may well have been that his batting prowess was not quite good enough. In 1903-4 Warner averaged 28, after beginning his Test career with a duck. His best innings were a 68 out of an opening 122 at Melbourne, and 48 plus 79 (out of an opening 148) at Adelaide. At this stage of his career, with the Ashes regained, Warner looked well set for further honours. They did not materialise. There can be little doubt that Warner's weak health and the hot amateur competition of the era made it difficult for him to obtain and hold a place on batting merit. It is a moot point whether Warner's flair for captaincy was more valuable to England than MacLaren's undoubted superiority as a batsman. Stanley Jackson was a better man than either in both respects, but his public duties rendered him unavailable for regular cricket. Unfortunately for Plum, Jackson *was* available for the 1905 home series that followed Warner's triumphant tour of Australia. The selectors plumped for the better man and Plum went into limbo.

Between 1904 and 1911 he played in just one Test (at Old Trafford in 1909) before being recalled to the captaincy for the 1911-12 tour. His illness on the way out to Australia virtually ended Warner's Test career. He made a consolation appearance in the Triangular rubber of 1912 and vacated the scene with a batting average of 23.91 for 287 Test runs.

Nearly half a century went by before the next tourist only appeared. Jack Ikin of Lancashire went to Australia as a virtually untried member of Hammond's post-war side. He played in all the Tests, batting 10 times and averaging 18.40. His best effort was a 60 at Sydney in the Second Test; his worst was a pair at the same ground in the last. Ikin also made 48 at Melbourne in the third match, when he helped Norman Yardley in a stand of 113 for the 6th wicket. Probably he is best remembered for his controversial 'catch' at Brisbane which would have dismissed Bradman for about 160 less than he eventually made. The catch was disallowed and the resulting acrimony established the atmosphere of no quarter which has marred so much Anglo-Australian cricket since the end of the Second World War.

Twenty years later M.J.K. Smith led a lively side for the 1965-6 tour. Smith had been given one Test chance, at Edgbaston in 1961, prior to this tour. His captaincy was sound and enterprising; unfortunately his batting did not match it. In 7 innings he only managed 107 runs, with 41 at Melbourne as his best contribution. On return to England he dropped out of the Test scene for the next five years. Then in 1972 he was recalled as number four batsman in Illingworth's team. 6 innings in the first 3 Tests yielded 140 runs. All his knocks reached double figures; none exceeded 34. Pace bowling generally undid him; Denis Lillee dismissed him four times. Perhaps if the selectors had persevered with him in 1961, Smith might have become a Test batsman. As it turned out, his most prolific county years were spent on the fringe of the Test team.

The disastrous tour of 1974-5 virtually put paid to the long term Test aspirations of Denis Amiss. The Warwickshire batsman had suffered a traumatic Test baptism in 1968. At Old Trafford he had bagged a pair and it took six long years before the selectors were ready to pitch him into the Aussie cauldron again. During the rehabilitation period Amiss had converted himself into an opening bat of merit. Sadly his debut down under coincided with the advent of Jeff Thomson as Lillee's bowling partner. The pacemen dismissed him 7 times out of 9 and the best he could produce was a very fine 90 in the second innings at Melbourne. Amiss finished that tour in the doldrums with 3 successive ciphers (including another pair), a state of affairs which continued at home in the first two matches of 1975. 19 runs in 4 innings, three times out to Lillee, once to 'Thommo', settled Amiss' immediate future. By 1977 he had worked his way back into the side and he scored a good 64 in the Melbourne Centenary Match. He was helping Derek Randall to win that game, when he allowed Greg Chappell to terminate their third wicket stand of 166 by bowling him; the vital wicket of the match. Two home Tests against Chappell s 1977 tourists realised a paltry 43 runs and Amiss' chequered career against Australia, spread over 9 years and 5 rubbers, came to an end with a total of 305 runs in 20 completed innings. Half of his total had been accumulated during his two best knocks and, bravely though he tried, he was clearly not equal to coping successfully with the pace bowlers. 13 of his innings were nipped in the bud by either Lillee or Thomson.

A parallel may be drawn between Denis Amiss and Graham Gooch. Gooch, currently at the height of his powers but banned from Test cricket following the Breweries XI tour of South Africa in 1982, has hardly advanced beyond the White Hope stage against Australia. The Essex player began like Amiss with a pair at Edgbaston in 1975. He was given a second chance at Lord's where he scored 6 and 31. Then he disappeared from the side for three years. His next appearances were in Australia. He played throughout the 1978-9 rubber with limited success. Tried as opening partner to Boycott, his first 4 innings realised 48 runs. He reverted to number 4 for the rest of the series, but his only notable effort was 74 at Sydney in the final Test. Gooch returned a year later for the post-Packer tour, Omitted from the First Test he was recalled as an opener for the last two. After a mediocre game at Sydney, he came good at Melbourne with 99 (run out) and 51. England lost this series as thoroughly as they had won the previous one, but Gooch had the consolation of heading the averages with 172 runs at 43.00 per innings. It had taken him 5 years and 10 Tests to make his first real impact on Australia. When the Centenary match was played at Lord's, Gooch, enjoying fine form in a dank and dismal summer was expected to lead England's bid for victory. He played some dashing strokes but succumbed to fine bowling by Denis Lillee before he was properly set. Scores of 8 and 16 were disappointing contributions and the Essex man still had leeway to make up when the 1981 rubber took place. He failed, scoring only 139 in his 10 innings and was dropped from the final Test. Gooch with an average of 19.93 for his 618 Test runs has been a sad disappointment against Australia.

The remaining failed tourist is J. Maurice Read of Surrey whose career was as disjointed as that of Arthur Jones. Read was a middle order batsman who made the side for the 1882 Oval game, possibly as a home town selection. Batting at number 7 he scored 19 not out and 0. Read's next 8 appearances were on tour. He went 3 times to Australia as a member of the all-professional sides of 1884-5, 1886-7 and 1887-8. Apart from 56 and 47 in successive games at Sydney in 1885 he achieved nothing of note. It was consequently surprising that he was selected for the home Tests of 1890. Four innings produced 90 runs, and he sustained his form well enough for W.G. to invite him to join his 1891-2 tourists. Read scored a useful 57 in the innings victory at Adelaide and he averaged 26 for that rubber. At home in 1893 he retained his place for the first match, scored 6 and 1 and was then abandoned by the selectors. He had played 15 Tests, spread over 7 rubbers, for the mediocre total of 447 runs at an average of 18.62. Read's chief consolation must have been that he was on the victorious side in 9 of his 15 Tests.

Five batsman in this category played most of their Tests against the Australians at home in England. Contemporary with Maurice Read was the amateur A.P. Lucas. Like some of the other amateur batsmen, Lucas' career was restricted by his unavailability for overseas tours. He did make one trip, with Lord Harris' 'Gentlemen' in 1878-9, but four of his five Test appearances took place in England. His only achievement was a solid 55 in a stand of 120 with W.G. at the Oval in 1880. He was a participant in the 'Ashes' game — where he achieved the distinction of dropping Hugh Massie during his vital second innings, and he made two more appearances in 1884. Like Hornby, Studd, O'Brien, Christopherson and Lyttleton, Lucas was one of the privileged amateurs who deprived better professionals of Test places in the eighties. His final average of 19.62 was as much as could be expected in the circumstances.

Around the time that Lucas faded out of Tests, the Notts. professional, William Gunn, came to the fore. Tall, strong and dour of temperament, he toured with Shrewsbury's side in 1886-7 and made no impression whatever in either Test. In 1888 and 1890 he appeared in 4 more Tests again without distinction. In the nineties however his county role as a support to the batting genius of Arthur Shrewsbury helped him to acquire a reputation for soundness which made him an automatic choice for the 1893 home rubber. At that stage Gunn had batted 11 times in Tests and scored 129 runs, poor going for a number 3 batsman. Obviously 1893 was crucial, for Gunn could not expect on his record to keep out his amateur rivals much longer. At Lord's he supported Shrewsbury in a second wicket stand of 152 (Gunn's share was 77) in a drawn match. He flopped at the Oval where England won by an innings, but at Old Trafford he came in at 43 for 2 and was still there when the innings ended 200 runs later. Gunn's 102 not out was his only Test ton. It occupied him for 4 hours 10 minutes — professional bats were cautious even in those days — and he carried England to a useful 39 run lead on a difficult wicket. The weather prevented a finish. In 1896 Gunn played at Lord's, but lost his place at Old Trafford to the new star Ranjitsinhji. He was invited to play at the Oval, but led a group of five professionals who demanded a double fee for appearing in the deciding match of the rubber. In the event, Hayward, Abel and Richardson — all Surrey players — withdrew their request, but George Lohmann and Gunn stuck to their principle. They were both replaced in the side. Billy Gunn's last Test in 1889 was the first ever played on his Trent Bridge home pitch. His scores of 14 and 3, bowled by Ernest Jones each time, brought his Test career, during which he was only once on the losing side, to an end. There is no doubt that Billy Gunn was a fine county bat. His return for Nottinghamshire and the Players during the nineties was impressive, but his Test record was poor for a bat of his reputation: 392 runs at an average of 21.77 (his bosom pal, Shrewsbury, averaged 35) is very much at the lower end of the scale. Indeed if the 1893 rubber is ignored, Gunn's figures diminish to 184 runs at 13 per innings. It does seem that his county reputation got him selection more often than he deserved. Billy Gunn was an elegant, safe bat but was generally vulnerable to the pacier Aussie bowlers, particularly the redoubtable Turner and Ferris.

An even better stylist than William Gunn was R.H. Spooner of Lancashire. Neville Cardus' lyrical appreciations of Reggie Spooner and his style have left a reputation which the subject's limited appearances in Test matches did little to substantiate. Spooner was one of those amateurs whose personal commitments prevented him from regular first class play. He never toured and his home Tests amounted to 2 in 1905; 2 in 1909; and all 3 in the dreary Triangular series of 1912. The Lancastrian, an opening bat, was sent in at number six in the Fourth Test of 1905. He played a lovely innings of 52 before giving a return catch to Charlie McLeod. His support of his skipper F.S. Jackson produced a stand of 125 which set England well on the way to an innings win. Retained for the Oval game, Spooner was bowled by Cotter for a duck. England, thanks to Fry and Jackson, were already in strong position at 283 for 4, so Spooner's loss was not crucial. The Aussies replied strongly and, when England batted again, Spooner, at number seven this time, joined his Lancastrian team mate Johnny Tyldesley in a rousing partnership of 158 for the 6th wicket. At one stage they added 127 in 80 minutes. Spooner's share was 79, and when he was out Jackson declared. The game was drawn however.

Spooner's career should have developed further from this highly promising start, but he could not tour in 1907-8. In 1909 he came into a losing side for the last two matches. At Old Trafford, his scores were 25 and 58. His stand with Plum Warner in the second innings made sure that England would not be defeated, despite their poor first innings of 119 all out. At the Oval Spooner failed and went into cold storage again until the next Aussie visit in 1912. This was a disastrous rubber for Spooner. He batted at number 3 — Hobbs and Rhodes opened — in all three Tests. His 4 innings produced just 3 runs: three singles and a duck. Spooner's previously respectable average of 33 declined to a sorry-looking 21.18. World War I intervened at this point and when it was over Spooner was one of those considered for the captaincy of the 1920-21 tour of Australia. He had to forgo the opportunity, again because of private commitments, so his career was effectively terminated by the War.

Two more modern batsmen followed career paths similar to Spooner's. One of them, the left-handed Willie Watson of Yorkshire and Leicestershire, enjoyed a famous debut in 1953. The First Test at Trent Bridge had been drawn and Watson was drafted into the Lord's side as a replacement for Reg Simpson. Watson began inauspiciously with only 4 in his first knock, but his second innings was an epic. Australia, leading by 342, tumbled out England's first 3 batsmen for 20. On the last day Watson helped Compton take the score to 73. Compton then fell and, with five hours left, Watson was joined by Trevor Bailey. In an historic stand they added 163 match-saving runs. When Watson succumbed at last to a googly from Doug Ring, he had batted for 5¾ hours and had joined the illustrious ranks of Grace, Ranji, R.E. Foster, George Gunn, Duleep, Sutcliffe, Leyland, Pataudi, Hutton and Compton with a century (109) on his debut. He seemed set to make England's problem No. 5 position his own. The rest of Watson's career was anti-climax. He failed to keep his place even for the rest of the rubber. After two unproductive games, he was dropped at the Oval to make room for

Peter May. He was out of favour when Hutton's side went Down Under a year later and his reappearance in 1956 was not successful. 32 runs in 4 innings quickly consigned Watson to the wilderness again. Somewhat surprisingly he was selected, at the age of 38, for the 1958-9 tour. By that time Watson had transferred to Leicestershire, for whom he had an outstanding season in 1958. On the strength of that Watson was given a tour which he should really have had four years earlier. It was ill-starred from the start. On the voyage out the Leicestershire man damaged a knee. He missed the First Test, made 0 and 7 in the Second, was dropped for the Third, returned with 25 and 40 in the Fourth, then pulled a muscle and missed the Fifth. After that heady debut century, Watson's final record of 272 runs in 7 matches was extremely disappointing.

Another middling performer was Peter Parfitt of Middlesex. Left-handed like Watson, Parfitt began with a dogged innings when England was up against it. At Brisbane in 1962-3 Australia started with 404. England was in difficulties at 220 for 5, when Parfitt, batting four hours for 80, helped Ken Barrington and the tail to lift the score to 389. The match, despite a snorter of a second innings by Ted Dexter, ended in a draw. Parfitt played once more in that series, scoring 0 and 28 at Sydney. In 1964 he appeared 4 times, making a very disappointing 73 in 5 innings. (He managed to fail at Manchester where England replied to Australia's 656 for 8 with 611.) He then disappeared from the England-Australia clashes for 8 years.

His return in 1972 was not unsuccessful. Playing in the last 3 Tests, Parfitt scored 46 in a stand of 117 with Luckhurst for the second wicket at Trent Bridge. He failed at Headingley, but finished in some style with 51 and 18 at the Oval. His 15 innings, spread over 10 years, realised 302 runs for an average of 21.57; and he never surpassed that initial 80. He did make a useful contribution of 12 close catches.

Last on this list of bankrupt bats comes Peter Willey of Northamptonshire. Willey, who has been in and out of the Test side for some years, played in the three Tests in Australia in 1979-80 and the Lord's Centenary game later that year. His 7 innings realised just 40 runs. Surprisingly he was retained for four of the 1981 matches. This series yielded better results (179 runs) but only once did he exceed 50. With an average of 14.60 from 15 innings against Australia, Willey, with the exception of J.R. Mason and A.O. Jones, proved the most bankrupt of all these English batsmen. Like his contemporary, Gooch, Willey was dropped from the final matches of this rubber.

Not surprisingly 12 of this 20 were associated with losing sides. Lucas and Smith achieved parity of wins and losses; Ford, Warner and Gooch are just ahead of par; J.M. Read was victorious in 4 of his 7 series; while Billy Gunn only lost once and Spooner not at all. Amiss in 1977, Jones in 1905, and Willey in 1981 were partially involved with successful teams, but nearly all the rest were members of badly beaten outfits. All in all they should have scored more runs.

The 13 Australian batsmen who failed to average 25 per innings contain some well-known names — and some surprising performances. Bottom of the list however comes Harry Donnan, an obscure New South Welshman, who played 5 Tests in the nineties. His fielding according to George Giffen 'not very smart', and this may have militated against his selection for the 1890 and 1893 tours of England. Donnan did play against W.G.'s side in 1892, scoring 29 runs in 3 completed innings. After a spell in the wilderness he was selected for the 1896 trip to the Old Country. An injury spoiled his play in the first Test, but subsequently he failed to reproduce the form which brought him 1000 runs for the tour. His 6 Test innings yielded only 46. Donnan thus holds the unenviable record of the lowest average (8.33) by a player solely picked for his batting.

Another batsman who flattered to deceive was South Australia's Tasmanian immigrant, C.L. Badcock. Known as 'Musso' because of his dark, Italian looks, Badcock began badly in 1936-7. Two Tests for only 10 runs (though he was ill during the second game) led to his replacement for the next two. An injury to Chipperfield allowed him back into the side for the last Test, the decider of that rubber. Australia won the toss and Badcock went to the wicket with the score at 303 for 3; Bradman and McCabe had been enjoying themselves. He soon lost Bradman, but then embarked on a long partnership with the other youngster of the side, Ross Gregory. They added 161 for the fifth wicket and Badcock's final tally was 118, an innings which ensured the victory set up by Bradman and McCabe. It also booked his passage for the 1938 trip to England. 1938 proved disastrous for 'Musso'. He played in all four Tests (Old Trafford was deluged and play never started) and scored just 32 runs. He bagged a pair of spectacles at Lord's of all places, and finished his Test career with an average of 14.54 for 160 runs, four-fifths scored in his one big innings. In the county matches Badcock helped himself to more than 1500 runs, but he failed to raise his game at Test level.

Peter McAllister of Victoria played in eight matches during the first decade of this century. His chief claim to fame now is that his nose was punched by the Australian skipper, Clem Hill, at a selectors' meeting in 1912. Prior to that fracas McAlister had been in bad odour with some of the leading players. Probably this dated back to the 1909 tour of England when McAlister was appointed vice-captain and treasurer of the first touring party to be officially sponsored by the Australian Board of Control. Certainly McAlister's place in that touring squad could not have been due to his Test playing record. His appointment ahead of such stalwarts as Trumper, Sid Gregory and Armstrong undoubtedly sowed the seeds of future trouble. In 1903-4 McAlister had opened the innings in the last two Tests and scored 48 runs. That was not enough to get him on the 1905 boat, though McAlister himself attributed his omission to the influence of Frank Laver. He then played 4 times in 1907-8 scoring 155 in 8 innings.

His selection for the 1909 tour brought him into direct confrontation with Frank Laver who had been appointed tour manager by the players, not by the Board. The tour proceeded in an uneasy atmosphere which festered on after the team returned home until it crystallised into a power struggle between the Board and the players in 1912. With his attention largely distracted by his friction with Laver, it is not surprising that McAlister failed to improve his Test record. He played in the Tests at Lord's and Leeds, scoring 49 in 3 completed innings. His only consolation was that Australia won both games. By 1911-12 McAlister had dropped out of the Test running and was working on the administrative side of the game. His physical clash with Clem Hill was the direct result of a selectorial dispute when McAlister suggested that Hill, the current Australian captain, should be dropped to make room for Charlie Macartney. (Hill favoured Macartney's selection, but obviously not at his own expense.) The captain took umbrage and punched McAlister. A brawl ensued and the resultant publicity did no credit to anyone. When McAlister's 252 Test runs at the paltry average of 16.80 are considered, it seems clear that he sought to make an impact at selectorial level to compensate for his failure as a player. Impact was certainly achieved, but only on McAlister's nose and I doubt whether he was any the better pleased for it.

In the eighteen eighties Harry Moses, a left hander from New South Wales, enjoyed a reputation for defensive batting. He was invited to join several tours to England but he always found it impossible to accept. In

Australia, he played in the short series of 1886-7 and 1887-8 with limited success, and he also appeared in two games against W.G. Grace's side in 1891-2. His final appearance came in the fourth match against Stoddart's side at Sydney in 1895. All told Moses batted 10 times against England for 198 runs and a top score of 33. On that kind of form he was no loss at all to the tourists of 1888, 1890 and 1893.

Eighty years later John Inverarity of Western Australia reversed Moses' experience. Twice he was picked to tour England, but failed to gain the selectors' favour for home games. Inverarity was pitched into the final two Tests of 1968 as an opening bat. He performed quite well at Leeds, and top scored with 56 out of a last innings 125 at the Oval. Most of this knock took place on a murky afternoon, during which many spectators had given active help to the ground staff in mopping up the saturated ground. Australia found Underwood almost irresistible on the drying wicket, but Inverarity nearly saw them safely to a draw. England won with six minutes to spare. Despite this effort Inverarity was not picked for the 1970-1 series. He returned to England with Ian Chappell's side in 1972 and played in 3 Tests. No longer required as an opener, Inverarity found runs hard to come by batting at number 8. Five innings produced only 61 runs. Inverarity's final tally of 160 runs in 8 completed innings is not impressive, but, in view of that 56 at the Oval, Australia probably missed a trick by not persevering with him as an opener.

Len Darling of Victoria played in 7 Tests during the Thirties. He was selected as a middle order batsman for the last two games of the Bodyline series. A competent start with 17 and 39 at Brisbane was followed by a top scoring 85 at Sydney. Though Australia lost both matches, Darling looked a useful future prospect, particularly as he was a fine close fieldsman. The promise was not fulfilled. Darling came to England in 1934. He played in 4 of the Tests, but 6 innings produced only 77 runs. By 1936-7 he was something of a back number, though, having lost the first two games of that rubber, the selectors recalled him for the Third Test on his Melbourne home ground. Darling made 20 and 0 and that was the end of him. 245 runs at an average of 20.41 was far too low for a Test bat in the heavy-scoring thirties.

Twenty years later Les Favell, a hard-hitting South Australian opener, hovered on the fringe of the Test team for a number of seasons. He never came to England, though why Jack Rutherford of Western Australia was preferred to him in 1956 is hard to fathom. Favell made 6 appearances during the 1954-5 and 1958-9 series. During Tyson's tour, he opened the innings with Arthur Morris in the first 3 matches. A top score of 30 in five knocks led to his replacement by Colin McDonald. He regained his place for the last Test but failed again. In 1958-9, Favell played at Sydney and Adelaide as a number five batsman. He shared a fine stand of 110 with Norman O'Neill (Favell 54) at Sydney, but flopped at Adelaide, his home ground. 203 runs at 22.55 per innings was Favell's final record; one that does scant justice to a bat who, on his day, could hit brilliantly.

The latest Aussie to fail to live up to expectations was Peter Toohey of New South Wales. A lot was hoped of him when he played against Mike Brearley's team in 1978-9. Toohey appeared in 5 of the 6 Tests, but his only worthwhile effort was 81 not out at Perth. That innings was a splendid rearguard action which saved Australia from following on. England, 119 ahead, consolidated their lead and Australia was unable to avoid going two down in the rubber. Toohey's remaining innings revealed a vulnerability to off-spin. He survived in the side for the First Test of 1979-80, but two more poor scores cost him his place. His career tally of 171 runs at an average of 15.54 is sadly disappointing. Toohey is young enough to come again, but he will have to show outstanding improvement to make it.

The remaining 'failures' comprise an interesting quartet. The reputations of Hugh Massie, George Bonnor, Sammy Jones and Tom Horan — particularly the first two — are far greater than their records apparently deserve. Even after allowing for the lower scoring by batsmen in general in the seventies and eighties, the averages recorded by these first line batsmen are not really defensible. Massie and Bonnor, both hitters, probably wasted too many opportunities through rashness. The former's reputation is founded almost entirely on one innings, a knock that lasted three quarters of an hour. This took place in the second innings of the 'Ashes' match at the Oval in 1882. Massie, an opener, set about the English bowlers while the ground was wet and the ball was soggy. After a fireworks display, he was bowled by Steel for 55 out of the 66 put on for the first wicket. Then, as the wicket deteriorated, Australia collapsed to 122 all out. Though Spofforth then bowled the Australians to a sensational win, his feat would not have been possible but for Massie's great attacking innings. Prior to this game, Massie had played throughout the rubber of 1881-2. He already had a reputation for impetuosity and his only effort of note was a top scoring 49 at Sydney in the Second Test. Subsequently Massie played in four more Tests. Apart from a 43 at Melbourne in 1883, he achieved nothing and was relegated from his position as opener. His final Test, in 1885 at Sydney, found him skippering the side to a win by 6 runs. This was the season when the captaincy changed hands for each of the five matches. Not surprisingly England won the rubber. Despite his victory, Massie, with a batting record of 249 from 16 innings, was not called upon again. In half of his knocks he failed to reach double figures; not what is expected from a number one bat. Still he did lay the foundations of Australia's first victory in England, an achievement in itself.

Contemporary with Massie was George Bonnor, the Victorian giant. A born hitter, Bonnor stood six feet six and relied on his reach to slam at the ball fast-footed. This often caused his downfall at the hands of wily bowlers. Bonnor toured England five times, but only appeared in two series in Australia. His initial claim to fame came in the 1880 Test at the Oval when his colossal skier was pouched by Fred Grace. The hit carried 115 yards from the wicket and the batsmen were turning for their third when Fred put himself into the history books. Curiously, Bonnor failed in all his Tests in England. 1884 yielded 43 runs; 1886 brought 9; while 1888 provided twenty four. 97 runs from 18 innings proved that the English bowlers had the giant's measure. He was not the luckiest of hitters. Apart from the Fred Grace catch, he was dismissed by a superb caught-and-bowled by Ulyett at Lord's in 1884, a catch described by W.G. as 'foolhardy'. Bonnor's highest Test score in England was a mere 25; his last 10 innings failed to rise beyond single figures. In Australia the story was rather different. He made his debut there in the series against Ivo Bligh's side. He top-scored with 85 in the first innings at Melbourne, twice hitting A.G. Steel into the crowd, clouting Bates into the elm trees and being dropped − for once − by Walter Read off a soaring straight hit. Altogether Bonnor made four hits for 5 during his knock and thanks to him Australia won comfortably. The extra match of this series found Bonnor opening the innings. He again top-scored, despite being unwell. His 87 kept Australia in the game and made possible the victory which tied the rubber. The Fourth Test of 1884-5 (at Sydney) was the occasion of the giant's greatest innings. Coming in at number 8, with the score 119 for 6 in reply to England's 269, Bonnor was confronted with a wicket inclined to lift at one end. He began streakily, but, using his reach to smother the lifters, he was soon middling the ball. In 115 minutes he hammered 128 runs, and gave no chance until the stroke which brought his hundred was missed in the slips; the finest display of hitting seen in a Test prior to Ian Botham. The eighth wicket stand with Sammy Jones realised 154 of which Jones' share was 40. After tea Bonnor clouted 113, the record number of runs scored in a single session of play in Australia. During that innings, Bonnor hit 3 fives and proved that fortune favours the brave. As a *tour de force* on a bowler's wicket this knock remains unsurpassed. Bonnor never played for Australia 'Down Under' again. The disputes which were rife during the 1884-5 season caused his omission from the final Test and his poor form on the 1886 tour ensured that he was never recalled. His total of 512 runs from 30 innings for the poor average of 17 hardly indicates his real value as a Test hitter. In Australia he batted 12 times and scored 415; an average of 34.57, which on its own would place him ahead of all his contemporaries. Certainly Bonnor played three match-winning innings during that time. His Test career lasted two rubbers too long and he never learned to cope with English conditions.

Thomas Horan, who later wrote for *The Australasian* under the pen name of 'Felix', has already been considered in the account of the Australian Pioneers. His bowling record, 11 wickets at 13 apiece, is much more impressive than his mediocre batting performances. At Sydney in 1885, having handed the captaincy over to Hugh Massie, Horan out-bowled Spofforth in the first innings. He captured 6 for 40 in 37 overs of fastish bowling, making good use of a spot churned up by Spofforth's follow-through. England fell 48 behind and never quite recovered. Horan's presence in 15 of the first 21 Tests was due however to his reputation as a batsman. Consequently 471 runs in 25 completed innings constituted a poor return for a man who was rated second only to Charles Bannerman in the late seventies and early eighties. His one century, at Melbourne in 1882, was distinguished by some fine straight driving, but his only other noteworthy knock was a fighting 63 at Melbourne again in the first of his two Tests as skipper in 1885. Like Massie, Horan disappeared from Tests after that series.

The only member of this ancient quartet to emerge with a career average over 20 was S.P. 'Sammy' Jones. This New South Welshman had a chequered career. He started young, appearing in two games of the 1881-2 series when he was barely 20 years old. At that time he was a tail-end batsman and probably owed his place to his lively fielding rather than his batting prowess. He managed to remain undefeated in 3 of his 4 knocks which realised 67 runs. Jones came to England in 1882. He did little to distinguish himself, but inadvertently contributed to the 'Ashes' victory. Batting number 8 in the second innings, Jones went gardening after completing a single and W.G. Grace, taking a rather mean advantage of a callow youth, ran him out. This so incensed

Spofforth that 'The Demon' set about bowling England out for 77. Perhaps if Jones had not been 'victimised' the Aussies would never have found the determination to whip the English. Jones, with scores of 0 and 6, had little to write home about. He missed the next eight Tests, but reappeared for 4 of the games in 1884-5 as an opening batsman. Success was again limited and after two matches he dropped down the order. Nevertheless he was selected for a second tour of England in 1886. Again Jones opened the innings and this time he achieved solid results, topping the averages in Harry Scott's weak side. His best score was a fine 87 in the first innings of the first game at Old Trafford, his only score above fifty in his Test career. On returning home, Jones played in one Test that winter and in one more in 1887-8. That was the end of Sammy's international career for he was struck down by smallpox when touring England again in 1888. Though he recovered well enough to visit England with the 1890 side he never regained sufficient form to play in another Test. Jones' final record of 21.60 per innings from 432 runs could well have been improved, for he was still a young man (26) when illness struck him down.

The success rate of the Australian teams which included these batting 'failures' was surprisingly good. Bonnor, Jones, Donnan, Darling, Badcock, Inverarity and Toohey were involved with more defeats than victories, but Moses and Favell broke even; and the other three were well in credit. Massie was victorious 5 times in 9 starts, Horan had a very impressive 9 wins out of 15, while McAlister notched 6 successes out of 8. Their personal contributions may have been generally sub-standard, but the effect on their teams was by no means calamitous.

13

BOUNTIFUL BOWLERS

It is more difficult to decide what constitutes a bowling flop than a batting failure. Bowlers, because of the vagaries of pitches and the whims of their captains, may not be given sufficient work to do themselves justice. They may even be directed to keep down the runs rather than to bowl down the wickets. Many have suffered because of poor fielding and wicket-keeping. Estimating a bowler's true worth is not an easy matter. Nevertheless a yardstick must be set. The principal aim of bowling must be to take wickets. A good bowler should be able to pick up 3 or 4 wickets per match. The next aim must be to keep the cost in runs down to a minimum. The average cost of each wicket to fall in 246 Anglo-Australian Tests is 29 runs. Therefore it would seem reasonable to expect a man chosen for his bowling ability to capture 3 victims a match at less than 30 runs apiece. Any bowler falling short of those minimum requirements has not done his job.

Using these criteria there are fifteen trundlers who have been over-bountiful, indeed profligate, in the exercise of their bowling skills. For England these consisted of fast bowlers Tom Emmett, Bill Hitch and Arthur Gilligan; medium pacers Barry Knight and David Brown; and left-hander Norman Gifford. The Australians were 'quickies' Evans, Bob McLeod, McCormick and Corling; left-handers Whitty, Hornibrook, Ironmonger and Bright; and leg-spinner Jimmy Matthews. Fifteen bowlers who captured less than 25 wickets, each of which cost more than 30 runs. The shortcomings of Tom Emmett have already been touched on in the account of the Lillywhite Boys. Emmett's 7 Tests, all in Australia, brought him just 9 scalps and, as we have seen, 7 of those came in one innings. The left hander's 'Sostenutor' apparently didn't work in Australia. That solitary *tour de force* on behalf of Lord Harris, who had precious little bowling at his disposal anyway, was Emmett's sole claim to Test fame, and a flash in the pan.

In 1911-12 a quick bowler, playing a minor support role to Foster and Barnes, was Surrey's William Hitch. 'Billitch' had some pretensions to classification as an all-rounder. Certainly he was an enthusiastic cricketer, hard-hitting with the bat, brave and prehensile at short-leg, energetic as a bowler, with a bizarre run-up. His 6 Tests yielded only 7 victims and, though he made two trips to Australia, he was not really top class. World War I divided Bill's career. He was 25 when he made his first tour in 1911-12. Though he played in 3 Tests, Barnes and Foster made sure that his pace-bowling opportunities were very limited. Nine years later, when Anglo-Australian hostilities were resumed, Hitch was over the hill as a bowler. His only achievement of note against the Australians came at the Oval in 1921. In what proved to be his last Test, Hitch had an unlucky opening spell. He removed Collins and Bardsley, but dropped catches prevented him from increasing his bag and he had to console himself with a hard-hit half century in England's second innings. Hitch, promoted to No.4, scored his runs in an exhilarating, unbroken stand of 71 with Jack Russell against Australia's occasional bowlers. Bill's knock was of no great significance but it must have pleased his Surrey supporters. Undoubtedly his best years were lost to that other Bill, the Kaiser.

Shortly after Bill Hitch's departure, Arthur Gilligan of Cambridge University and Sussex appeared in the Test team. Gilligan, one of England's fast-bowling captains, was an unlucky cricketer. In the early twenties, with all England searching desperately for fast bowlers, he bowled fast and well for Sussex and England. In partnership with the mighty Maurice Tate, Gilligan was expected to provide the riposte to Australia's Gregory and McDonald. For a season or two prior to the 1924-5 tour these expectations looked like being realised. Then unkind fate struck. During the Gentlemen *v.* Players match at the Oval in 1924, Gilligan received a heavy blow over the heart when batting against Dick Pearson, Worcestershire's medium-pacer. He was advised to retire from the match, but resumed his innings and scored a fine century. The blow exacted a terrible toll however. Gilligan never fully recovered from it and his fast-bowling lost its vital edge. That winter he was chosen to lead England in Australia. It was hoped that the cruise and the sunshine would restore his pristine fitness. Unfortunately this did not happen and the Gilligan who took 10 Australian wickets in 5 matches at the heavy cost of 51 apiece, was but a pale imitation of the potentially great fast-bowler of six months before. His batting also deteriorated and he retired from the game after his return from the tour. Fully fit, Gilligan could well have helped Tate to bring back the Ashes, for, though 'Horseshoe' Collins beat him 4-1, the Third Test was very close and England won the Fourth by an innings. If Gilligan could have entered the last match all-square with his fast-bowling powers undiminished, then the rubber might well have gone England's way.

Instead Gilligan— later an amusing and intelligent radio commentator — never fulfilled his early promise.

In the sixties and early seventies, the English selectors cast their net wide for pace bowling successors to Trueman and Statham. John Snow of Sussex eventually filled one half of the requirement admirably, but the other place was occupied by a procession of generally ineffective medium pacers. Two such bowlers enjoyed extensive trials, though in one case the trial was intermittent. Barry Knight of Essex went on successive tours to Australia. In 1962-3 under Ted Dexter he played at Brisbane taking 3 for 128 but was dropped for the rest of the series. He went one better in 1965-6 appearing in both of the Melbourne Tests, but his return was of a similar calibre: 8 for 250. (Knight did bag 4 for 84 in the first innings of the first Melbourne game, but three of them were tail-enders.) In 1968 the Essex man made his two home appearances — at Lord's and Edgbaston. In the first game he and David Brown caught Australia on a damp pitch in a humid atmosphere and skittled them for 78. Knight's share was 3 for 16 in 10 overs, plus a superb gully catch to dismiss the top-scoring Doug Walters. Unfortunately the weather intervened to reduce Australia's follow-on time, so that the match was drawn. The next game was also unfinished, Knight's solitary scalp costing 34. Fifteen Test wickets at 30 apiece, as well as a poor batting average, indicate that Knight was out of his class. Perhaps he would have done himself more justice if he had been selected regularly; intermittent appearances militate against consistent results.

In Knight's last two series, Warwickshire's David Brown played in 8 Tests as an opening bowler. His 11 wickets in 4 games on the 1965-6 tour cost 37 runs each; figures which he hardly bettered at home in 1968. Brown's first vital contribution came at Sydney in 1966 when he capitalised on Bob Barber's superb 185 by dismissing 5 Australians for 63 runs and forcing a follow-on which culminated in England's sole victory of the rubber. At Lord's in 1968 Brown (in harness with Knight) nearly repeated the performance. 5 for 42 in Australia's first innings of 78 set up the follow-on, but rain on the final day enabled Bill Lawry's side to scramble a draw. These two efforts were Brown's best. He suffered to an extent from the pedestrian English fielding of the time, but his bowling lacked the consistency required for regular sucess at Test level. His final figures against the Aussies of 23 wickets for more than 800 runs — and requiring 75 deliveries to claim each victim — are those of a good county bowler operating somewhat out of his depth.

The 1964 series provided 2 appearances for Norman Gifford of Worcestershire. Gifford, a left hand bowler, was regarded as a possible successor to Tony Lock. He performed very tidily at Lord's; 3 for 31 in the match from 29 overs, and less impressively at Leeds (2 for 109 from 54 overs). Then he went into the wilderness for 8 years. In the latter four of those years Gifford was overshadowed by Kent's Derek Underwood. He was then recalled for the first three Tests of 1972, but his haul was a solitary wicket for 116 runs. This was the period when pace bowlers began to do virtually all the bowling and spinners came to be regarded as change bowlers only. Even so Gifford's meagre returns provided no threat to Underwood, who soon resumed his place as a regular member of the team. The Worcestershire bowler's 6 wickets in 5 appearances is the smallest haul of any Englishman picked primarily for his bowling.

These six bowlers had a combined haul of 70 wickets for 2657 runs from 5875 deliveries. In other words they required 84 balls (14 six-ball overs) to capture each victim and gave away 38 runs in the process. The nine Australians who are next to be considered conceded 37 runs for each wicket, but they required 103 deliveries to get their man.

Between 1881 and 1886 Edwin Evans of New South Wales played in 6 Test matches. Born in 1849, he was over thirty when he started his international career and, though he relied on medium-pace, good length stuff, his best days were already behind him. His 7 victims were all captured in his first two Tests during 1881-2. Certainly it was a mistake to take him on the 1886 tour to England where he managed only 28 wickets in as many games. Evans' Test wickets cost 332 runs and he bowled nearly 45 overs to claim each one.

Bob McLeod, of Victoria, played in two complete rubbers in the nineties. In Australia against W.G. Grace's side his fast-medium length bowling yielded 10 wickets for 227 runs, figures which led Australians to believe that a permanent successor to J.J. Ferris as Charlie Turner's opening partner had been found. On his bowling debut McLeod got rid of Grace, Abel and Stoddart in 12 balls, after the first two had opened with a stand of 84. The Victorian's final tally of 5 for 55 in 29 overs represented fine bowling. After that however the Englishmen realised that he was chiefly a straight up-and-downer and his successes became less frequent. In 1893 McLeod came to England. He bowled 85 overs in the three Tests, but only claimed 2 wickets. He finished at the foot of the tour averages with only 43 victims (Turner, Trumble and Giffen got over 100 each); and he dropped out of the Test reckoning on his return to Australia. McLeod's 12 Test wickets cost 32 runs apiece.

Bill Whitty of South Australia also made 6 Test appearances. His matches were spread over three rubbers between 1909 and 1912. Whitty, left-handed and medium paced, toured England in 1909. He opened the bowling in the First Test, the only one Australia lost, and did not take a wicket. He lost his place to Frank Laver for the rest of that series. In 1911-12 Whitty turned out in the first two games. 3 wickets for 185 sent him back to the wilderness for the remaining matches. The South Australian was fortunate to make his second trip to England in 1912. The battle between the Board of Control and the top players no doubt helped his recall. As things turned out Whitty justified his place by collecting 12 wickets in the three games at 21 runs each. His best match was the last, which Australia lost, when he bowled 71 overs for 140 runs and 7 wickets in the two innings. World War I broke out before Whitty could consolidate his hard-won position. By the time that Tests were resumed, Gregory and McDonald had appeared and 34 year old medium-paced left handers didn't have a look in. Whitty was probably pitched into Tests too early, though he did bag 75 wickets on that 1909 tour. By 1912 he had developed into a fine bowler. His 109 wickets at 18 each during that tour were well in keeping with those of the Trumbles, Nobles and Lavers of previous tours.

The unenviable title of Australia's least effective bowler in the history of these Tests falls to T.J. (Jimmy) Matthews of Victoria. Matthews, a slow leg-break bowler and contemporary of Bill Whitty, played 5 times just before World War I. He bowled 680 balls and took ('bought exorbitantly' might better describe it) 3 wickets for 277 runs. Matthews had two games against Johnny Douglas' side, bowling 64 overs for 1 wicket and 164 runs. Despite that he made the side for the 1912 tour; another cricketer made lucky by the defection of the players in dispute with the Australian Board. The strange feature of this tour was that Matthews, away from Tests with England, bowled pretty well. He performed 2 hat-tricks in the same Test match against South Africa and he also captured 85 wickets during the tour at less than 20 apiece. Yet against England Matthews was a complete flop. His most significant feat was a valuable 53 in the second innings of his debut at Adelaide in January 1912. He helped to save Australia from an innings defeat, but that apart his batting was as negligible as his bowling.

The 1928-9 series saw the introduction of two left-handed bowlers to the Australian side. Both were run savers who required helpful conditions to take wickets quickly, but the Australian bowling cupboard was pretty bare during that series and new blood was badly needed. First one into the side was Bert 'Dainty' Ironmonger of Victoria. Ironmonger, slow-medium with excellent control, was rising 46 (maybe 47) when he made his debut at Brisbane. Born in 1883(?), 'Dainty' had already established himself as a Sheffield Shield bowler before World War I. Indeed by 1920 Ironmonger was already a veteran, and he missed selection for Armstrong's and Collins' sides because there were better bowlers around in the early twenties. Now, very belatedly, he had his opportunity. Unfortunately he had to battle with England's strongest ever batting side. Chapman's men rattled up 521 in their first knock and 342 for 8 in the second. 'Dainty' toiled and spun through 94 overs in the match and his reward was 4 wickets for 164. Retained at Sydney, Ironmonger bowled 68 more overs in England's single innings of 636. He took 2 more wickets for 142. Ironmonger had delivered 59 maidens in the three innings and conceded less than 2 runs per over, but Australia needed a wicket-taker to support Grimmett, rather than a run saver. 'Dainty' disappeared for the rest of the series.

Apart from his age, Ironmonger had several other handicaps. He was a poor fielder and worse batsman (the original of the story about the groundsman's perspicacious horse which used to place itself between the shafts of the roller when a certain number 11 went out to bat). Additionally, 'Dainty' was minus the index finger of his bowling hand, so it was a wonder that he made the grade at all. Finally his bowling action was held by some to be suspect. Whether this suspicion was well founded is a moot point, but, since the Australian selectors never sent him to England, there must have been some risk of his being no-balled away from his own midden. Despite all these problems Ironmonger was recalled to the side to face Jardine's team in 1932. He had enjoyed two excellent home rubbers against the West Indies and South Africa during the intervening seasons between the English tours. After missing the First Test Ironmonger bowled tidily in the remaining games. His haul was 15 wickets at 27 each — and again he conceded less than two runs an over. The left-hander's best effort was 4 for 26 in the second innings at Melbourne, the only match Australia won. Australia lost a home series for the second time running by a 4-1 margin. Heads had to roll and Ironmonger — now nearly 50 (or 51) — was an obvious victim. All told, Dainty's 21 English wickets cost 711 runs and he bowled nearly

2,500 balls to get them. World War I robbed him of his prime years and he would not have got much bowling in Armstrong's 1921 side. Perhaps the selectors should have taken a chance with him in 1926 though. Ironmonger could be lethal on rain-affected pitches and English conditions in that dreary season might have proved tailor-made for him. He would certainly have been a more effective attacker than Everett turned out to be.

The other slow-medium left hander introduced in 1928-9 was Percy Hornibrook of Queensland. Hornibrook made his debut in the final match against Chapman's side. His 4 wickets cost 193, but Australia won and the Queenslander had done enough to book his ticket to England in 1930. Hornibrook's efforts on tour were an invaluable support to Grimmett — the Queenslander picked up 96 wickets — but he failed to come off in the first four Tests. When the Australians arrived at the Oval the series was all square, and Hornibrook had taken 6 wickets for 325 runs in 150 overs; 25 overs to claim a victim. His place must have been in some jeopardy, but the Australians had even less effective bowlers in reserve. Fortunately the batting, with Bradman rampant, was picking up enough runs to give their limited bowling a chance. Hornibrook's first innings effort of 0 for 54 was in keeping with earlier matches. Australia replied to England's 405 with 695 and then rain gave the Queenslander his chance. In 31.2 overs he dismissed 7 batsmen for 92 runs and bowled Australia to an innings victory and the recovery of the Ashes . This match apart, Hornibrook had never quite attained the standard expected at Test level. Consequently it was no great surprise to find Ironmonger replacing him for the next home series. When England arrived in 1932 for the Bodyline tour, the Queenslander was a back number as far as Tests were concerned.

In 1936 Australia brought Ernie McCormick into the side. This Victorian fast bowler looked promising and had already toured South Africa. He failed to come up to expectations. 11 wickets fell to McCormick in 4 games of the 1936-7 rubber. The cost was only 28 apiece, so McCormick was a fairly automatic choice for the 1938 tour. Then his troubles began. McCormick had great difficulty with his run-up and was frequently no-balled in the early games of this tour. He was also prone to injury and he could only manage an unimpressive 34 wickets in 18 matches during the tour. 10 of his scalps were Test victims, but they cost 34 each. It is unlikely that McCormick would have kept his place for the 1940-41 rubber, but anyway Adolf Hitler soon made sure that the question was an academic one.

Another unsuccessful paceman was Graham Corling of New South Wales. In 1964 Corling turned up as a support bowler in Bobby Simpson's side. A lively medium pacer, Corling's best Test effort was 4 for 60 in the drawn match at Lord's, but 3 of his victims were tail-enders. He toiled without reward on the Old Trafford graveyard where, like McLeod, he found that up and down stuff was a mug's game at Test level. That one series saw both Corling's debut and swansong, but he was never in a defeated Australian side.

Ray Bright of Victoria has been in and out of Australia's side during the past few seasons. A left-hand bowler of the flattish type, Bright first appeared in 1977; his bag from 3 Tests on that tour was 5 for 147. Then he joined Kerry Packer. After two years away from official Test cricket, Bright returned against Brearley's 1979-80 tourists. 1 for 36 was insufficient to hold his place after the first match, but he made the Centenary trip to England. At Lord's Bright toiled for 46 overs without taking a wicket, though he conceded no more than 2 runs an over. In the 1981 rubber Bright played in 5 of the 6 Tests. Used again as a relief stock bowler, the Victorian sent down 1,150 balls and captured 12 wickets, nearly 100 deliveries per victim. He was economical, conceding only 2 runs per over, but only once did he look capable of running through a side. At Edgbaston in the Fourth Test Bright dismissed 5 of England's first 6 in the second innings. He nearly set up an Australian win, but his batsmen let him down. The Victorian's 18 Test scalps have cost 37 runs apiece as well as needing 114 deliveries to lift each one. His usefulness to Australia must be highly suspect.

Like the bankrupt batsmen, these bountiful bowlers were rarely members of winning sides. Ironmonger, Matthews, Whitty, Bright and McLeod of Australia, and Gifford, Emmett and Gilligan of England were all involved with more defeats than victories. Barry Knight broke even as all his 5 games were draws; while Evans, McCormick and David Brown's successes just outweighed their reverses. Bill Hitch, mainly because he was a member of the great 1911-12 team, was victorious 3 times in his 6 starts, as was Percy Hornibrook. Graham Corling was the only one of these bowlers who did not taste defeat. Only Hornibrook and David Brown could be said to have made vital contributions towards winning a game, and the Queenslander's bowling did help Australia to regain the Ashes. On the whole their efforts were largely innocuous.

14

ASSORTED ALL ROUNDERS

A recurring component of Test Match sides has been the 'useful all-rounder.' Batsmen who could bowl a bit, and bowlers who could make a few have often found themselves preferred to more capable specialists. The theory is two players for the price of one place. Occasionally the theory has been practised to excess. A star batsman who can provide useful change bowling is an asset; so is a star bowler who can score a valuable 20 or 30. But sometimes the selectors have chosen useful change bowlers who can make 20 or 30, and this has proved a mistaken policy.

16 cricketers owed their places in these Tests to their all-round potential. Five of them (Freddie Brown, Graham Dilley and Roy Kilner of England; Colin McCool and Roy Minnett of Australia) achieved results with both bat and ball which compared favourably with many of the leading specialists. They will be considered in later chapters. The remaining 11 (4 English, 7 Aussies) fell short in at least one of the requirements of a skilled all-rounder. All four Englishmen were county captains; one of them led his country against Australia. All had reputations for attractive batting; two were leg-break bowlers; one played one of the greatest innings ever seen in a Test; all were excellent fieldsmen. Yet, with all their talent, they could not achieve the consistency required at Test level.

The two leg break bowlers were Percy George Fender and Walter Robins. Fender, captain of Surrey, found short-lived favour in the years following World War I. He went to Australia with Johnny Douglas and played in the last 3 Tests. His batting consisted of a curious mixture of first innings failures and second innings defiances when the cause was lost; 59 at Melbourne, plus a couple of forties at Adelaide and Sydney. Twice he captured 5 victims with his leg-spin (5 for 122 at Melbourne; 5 for 90 at Sydney), and had the distinction of topping the bowling, with an average of 34.16.

Fender got into hot water on this tour by writing some controversial comments on the Tests for an English newspaper. He was — perhaps on account of this — omitted from the early Tests of the 1921 series. England's poor form at this time (8 successive defeats) precipitated regular changes in the side. Fender was recalled for the Old Trafford and Oval matches. He made 44 not out in the first game, but failed at the Oval. His leg breaks claimed 2 wickets for 112 in the two matches. With the not unreasonable batting average of 24.75, Fender might well have kept his place if his bowling had not been so expensive. 14 wickets at 37 apiece were too dear for the selectors.

R.W.V. Robins of Middlesex returned figures very similar to Fender's. Unlike the Surrey skipper, Robins had a split Test career. He started at Trent Bridge in 1930, scoring an unbeaten 50 and taking 7 wickets (4 for 51 plus 3 for 81). He was considerably less successful at Lord's, where Bradman plundered him ruthlessly, but only after Duckworth had missed stumping the Australian champion off Robins. Dick Tyldesley and then Ian Peebles took over the leg-spin duties for the remainder of the series despite Robins' superior batting and fielding. For the next two series Robins was on the sidelines. After Peebles had broken down, Tommy Mitchell of Derbyshire took over the spinner's spot, but without lasting success. When Gubby Allen's side assembled for the 1936-7 tour Robins was back in the ranks. In Australia his only achievement was a bright 61 at Melbourne as England went down by 365 runs, their first reverse of the rubber. Robins, who broke his spinning finger early in the tour, found his leg breaks hopelessly expensive Down Under. In 56 overs he gave away 220 runs, with 4 paltry wickets to compensate him. Robins' final record of 183 runs and 14 costly wickets failed to do justice to his potential. The 1930 selectors should have persevered with him.

The youthful promise of Norman Yardley had its development retarded by World War II. He was 31 years old when he went to Australia as vice-captain to Wally Hammond in 1946. On that ill-fated tour Yardley was one of the few successes. He averaged 31 with the bat and, like Fender after the previous war, headed the bowling averages. A brace of fifties at Melbourne were his best scores; while he three times got rid of Bradman with the ball. Yardley was the natural choice for skipper in 1948. In England Yardley's batting declined, probably because of captaincy worries. He still remained a useful change bowler, though his reluctance to use himself meant that England did not gain full benefit from his skill. Of course, he lost the rubber; Bradman's side was unbeatable. By the time the next series arrived he had retired from Tests. Yardley's Test figures of 402 runs and 19 wickets were a pale reflection of what he might have achieved if his best years had not been wasted by the War.

The remaining Englishman in this group of all rounders is one of the great cricketing names: Gilbert Laird Jessop of Gloucestershire. Because of his awesome reputation one would expect to find Jessop in a chapter on Great Batsmen , but his figures belie his greatness. Jessop, of course, was the complete all-rounder. A fast bowler of merit; a superb cover-point; a rapid scoring batsman, with an impressive range of strokes; Jessop was or should have been very successful. His career against Australia only fleetingly displayed these talents.

'The Croucher' started his Test career at Lord's in 1899. He was then captaining Cambridge University and an illustrious career was predicted for him. In the event luck — never conspicuous on Jessop's behalf — intervened. Jessop began auspiciously, scoring 51 in an hour and helping F.S. Jackson to add 95 for the 7th wicket. It was the best stand of a poor innings by England. Jessop was caught by Trumper at long-on. He then slipped when bowling and strained his back. Despite the injury Jessop bowled 37 overs, taking 3 for 105 and having three catches dropped. Once the game was over his back had to be put in plaster and he missed the rest of the series. When Archie MacLaren embarked his side for the Antipodes in 1901-2, Jessop was on board. He had a poor series, scoring 166 runs in 9 innings, and capturing only 6 wickets. MacLaren's side lost the rubber 4-1 and Jessop returned to England with a question mark against his ability at Test level.

In 1902, Joe Darling's Australians confronted the 'Flower of England's Golden Age'. Jessop, perhaps fortunately, was given a place in the side at Edgbaston. He scored 6 and did not bowl. At Lord's he did not bat in a rain-ruined game. At Sheffied — probably surprised to be still in the team — Jessop, after batting at number 9 in the first knock, was promoted to open the second innings. England, set 339 to win on a wearing wicket, needed a good start; and 'The Croucher' supplied it. He scored 53 in fifty minutes before close of play on the second day and England were 73 for 1 overnight. On the final morning, Jessop was l.b.w. (off his chest!) after adding 2 more runs. The umpire apologised later, but the damage was done. England slid to a substantial defeat before lunch. Having come good, Jessop must have felt that his place was no longer at risk. The selectors promptly dropped him for the Old Trafford Test. (As England lost this game by 3 runs and as Jessop's cover fielding, like Derek Randall's today, regularly saved 20 or 30 runs per innings, this was a crucial mistake.)

With the rubber lost, the Gloucestershire captain was recalled for the Oval game. England's 'best side' (according to Neville Cardus) trailed by 141 on first innings and, though the Australians were tumbled for 121 in their second knock, a third defeat seemed likely. When England's bid for victory on a difficult wicket had reached 48 for 5, it looked all over bar the shouting. Then Jessop arrived. In about half an hour before lunch, he and Jackson put on 39 (29 to Jessop). The wicket eased during break and 'The Croucher' completed his 50 on the resumption in less than quarter of an hour. He lost Jackson at 157; they had put on 109. The next landmark was Jessop's hundred. His second fifty came in 32 minutes, completing one of the best centuries recorded in these games. Jessop scored one more boundary and then was caught behind square leg. He had hit a five and 17 fours in a stupendous display of scientific hitting. The merit of this innings cannot be exaggerated. It is the fastest century in these games; it was scored when England was tumbling to defeat; it wrested the initiative from a strong Australian bowling side (Trumble, Noble, Saunders, Armstrong); and it was launched on an extremely difficult pitch. It must also have had a psychological effect on the English tail. When Jessop departed the score was 187. Lockwood, Lilley and Rhodes clung on in turn while George Hirst collected the bulk of the remaining 86 runs. England's one wicket victory is the most famous triumph in the annals of the Tests.

The remainder of Jessop's career was anti-climax. He never toured again. One Test for a duck's egg in 1905 and two in 1909 were all that remained. In the second of these at Leeds, he strained his back while fielding on the first morning and took no further part in the game. It was his last Test. All told, he batted 18 times against Australia for 433 runs, nearly half of which came from his three best knocks. Those occasions apart, the Australian bowlers obviously had his measure; particularly Hugh Trumble who dismissed him 7 times. Undoubtedly Jessop's impetuosity contributed to his inconsistent returns. His duck in 1905 was a golden one; he tried an uncouth shot to leg and was clean bowled. F.S. Jackson, that series' captain, somewhat unkindly in view of their epic stand three years before, refused to have Jessop in his team for the rest of the games. A little tempering of his flamboyant stroke play might have gone a long way towards keeping Jessop in the Test side. 'The Croucher''s bowling seems to have been over-rated by the selectors. At least twice he was chosen as England's fast bowler rather than for his attacking batting, at a time, too, when there was a wealth of fast bowling round the country. His 10 Test wickets cost 34.6 each and only once (at Sydney in 1902) did he make an appreciable breach in Australia's defences. One talent which Jessop did display consistently was his fielding at cover-point. He was an important restricting force and Archie MacLaren, for once showing sound judgment, always wanted to include him in the side because of 'his ability to run people out'. 'The Croucher' may have been inconsistent, but by thunder he gave full entertainment value!

The Australian all-rounders comprise one who bowled economically and batted just about adequately; two who bowled very poorly, but batted with unexpected success; two who batted well, but disappointed with their bowling; and two who just disappointed.

The economical bowler, though with only limited opportunities, was J.W. Trumble, Hugh's elder brother. Trumble had a short career, his business as a solicitor taking him to the Outback while he was still in his prime. The Victorian was a good defensive player with both bat and ball. He played in successive series in the mid-eighties, scoring 59 in his debut innings at Melbourne. A couple of thirties was all that he achieved in 12 further innings. As a bowler Trumble kept a good length but, to quote George Giffen, he lacked devil. He was used as a change bowler and his best analysis was 3 for 29 at Melbourne in the last Test of 1885. His tour of England in 1886 was disappointing in terms of results and Trumble dropped out of Test cricket on his return to Australia. A batting average of 20.25, plus 10 wickets for 222 runs was his total contribution to the Australian cause.

The two who had poor bowling returns were cricketers of recent vintage: Tom Veivers and Kerry O'Keeffe. Both were chosen for their bowling rather than their batting; both were more successful with the willow. Veivers, an off-spinner from Queensland, visited England in 1964. 11 wickets at 40 each was his haul for the series. With the bat, however, he justified his place, averaging 39.75 and recording two fifties. His 54 at Lord's was the top score in a poor first innings by Australia. At home for the 1965-6 rubber, Veivers had even less success as a bowler. 4 matches provided only as many wickets and he did not even perform the stock bowling function effectively. His batting was still useful; he partnered the young Doug Walters in a stand of 119 for the 6th wicket at Brisbane, finishing with 56 not out. Australia, however, needed an effective slow bowler and Veivers had lost his place by the time the next tour of England was due.

In the seventies Kerry O'Keeffe of New South Wales played in 6 Tests as a leg-break bowler. In 1970-71, he had a bad debut (0 for 116) at Melbourne, but did better (6 for 144) in the final Test at Sydney.

O'Keeffe did not appear against England again until 1977. He was chosen for the Centenary Test at Melbourne. Although his 3 wickets cost him 112 runs, he captured the vital scalps of Derek Randall and Tony Greig in the second innings, at a time when they looked like taking England to victory. On the strength of that performance, O'Keeffe was included in the side to tour England later that year. He played in 3 of the 4 Tests and captured 1 wicket per game. Like Veivers he redeemed himself with some sound batting and, by virtue of 4 not outs, actually topped the Test averages. However batting bowlers are only honoured when they have fulfilled their chief function successfully. O'Keeffe hadn't, so he was dropped after this tour.

The two who batted well but disappointed with the ball were Arthur Richardson and Alan Fairfax. The bespectacled Richardson bowled off-spin and was a good enough bat to open the innings for Australia. He made a belated entry into international cricket at the age of 36. On his debut at Sydney in 1924 the South Australian scored 22 and 98. Ironically he fell to 'Tich' Freeman, caught and bowled off a stroke which should have given him a debut century. Later in that series Richardson scored a solid 69 at Adelaide. His off-spinners yielded only 8 wickets in the 4 Tests which he played in this rubber. In 1926 A.J. toured England with some success. He played in all the Tests of that waterlogged series, scoring exactly 100 − run out − at Leeds. This knock consolidated Australia's position after Charlie Macartney's whirlwind 151. Richardson did little of note in the rest of the matches. His bowling was too defensive. He delivered 150 overs for 273 runs and 4 wickets and seemed over-keen on leg theory. He dropped out of the Australian side after this tour with 403 runs, average 31, but only 12 costly wickets to his name.

In the last game of the succeeding series, Australia introduced Alan Fairfax of New South Wales. He made a fine start with the bat, partnering Bradman in a stand of 183 for the 5th wicket. Fairfax's share was 65 and the partnership kept Australia in the match. His fast-medium bowling made little impact though. Chosen for the 1930 tour, Fairfax was given the chance to establish himself as an opening bowler. He managed 12 wickets in the 4 Tests in which he played, with 4 for 101 at Lord's as his best offering. With the bat Fairfax did better, scoring 53 not out at the Oval, but, with Bradman on the rampage, runs from the lower order were not of vital importance. The New South Welshman moved into Lancashire League Cricket in the early Thirties and played for Australia no more. His batting average was 53.75 and his

14 wickets cost 31 each. Perhaps Australia lost a potential stalwart, but the bowling evidence is rather flimsy.

The two all rounders whose overall record was disappointing enjoyed extensive runs in the Test side. First of these was 'Stork' Hendry of New South Wales. Hendry began as a tail-end batsman and a fast-medium support bowler with Armstrong's 1921 tourists. He played in 4 Tests with negligible results. The same outcome arose from his appearance in the First Test of 1924-5. He was dropped from the rest that series. It was surprising to find him among the 1926 tourists, especially as Charlie Kelleway was omitted. In the event, 'Stork' contracted scarlet fever, played in only 7 games and missed all the Tests. In 1928-29 Hendry found himself back in the Test team – as number 3 batsman! Charlie Macartney had retired; Bradman had not quite arrived; Hendry was the stop-gap. He performed surprisingly well, scoring 227 runs in 8 starts, 112 coming in the second innings at Sydney. This knock was the sole justification for Hendry's prolonged Test career. He assisted Woodfull in a stand of 215 for the second wicket, though as there was a deficit on the first innings of 380 odd, it only had the effect of ameliorating Australia's resounding defeat. Hendry's bowling picked up 8 wickets in this rubber, so that his efforts with bat and ball showed significant improvement over his earlier contributions. However he was now thirty three years old and a member of a fading, well-beaten team, so it was not surprising that his head rolled along with quite a few others at the end of the series.

A modern counterpart of Hendry's was the notorious 'Slasher' Mackay. Mackay, a Queenslander, turned up among Ian Johnson's tourists in 1956. Three Tests on that trip yielded 73 runs, a pair of spectacles and 1 wicket; not an auspicious start. By the time that Peter May's team arrived for the 1958-9 series Mackay was established in Australia's side – as spoiler-in-chief. His defensive play brought only 118 runs and 3 wickets, but he consumed vast quantities of time (Australia's reply to Trevor Bailey – though Mackay was never in Bailey's class as an all rounder). 'Slasher' turned up in England again in 1961. This time he did rather better. 64 at Edgbaston was followed by 54 at Lord's and he also took some wickets. 158 runs and 16 victims represented Mackay's best series return. At the Oval he filled the breach caused by an injury to Alan Davidson. Mackay bowled 107 overs in the match for only 196 runs and 7 wickets.

The 1962-3 series saw 'Slasher''s swansong. At Brisbane, in front of his home crowd, he helped Brian Booth add 103 for the 7th wicket, going on to his highest score against England of 86 not out. If he had only shown a greater sense of urgency — his innings lasted 247 minutes — the 'Slasher' would have recorded a well-earned ton. The writing was on the wall however. Mackay's bowling was beginning to lose its economy and his tortuous batting methods were not popular with the spectators. He survived for only two more Tests and then decided to quit. Mackay's 16 Tests produced 497 runs, average 22, and 24 wickets at 36 each. Probably his main asset to Australia was his economy as a bowler: 2828 balls cost only 875 runs, barely 2 per 8 ball over. The 'Slasher''s record illustrates his character — a determined grafter making as much as possible of a limited technique. Mackay cannot be ranked with the leading all rounders.

Most of these 'Assorted All-Rounders' were not members of highly successful sides. Yardley and Fender were never on a winning team, while O'Keeffe, Trumble and Jessop were frequent losers. Hendry and Robins broke even and Richardson was just on the right side. For the other three success was the story. Fairfax was a winner in 3 of his 5 games; Mackay, after losing Laker's series in 1956, was successful in the next two; while Veivers never lost. Australia only won twice with Veivers in the side, 7 of his 9 Tests ending in draws. Generally speaking, the selection of most of these players was not attended by success for their sides. Perhaps Robins and Fairfax could have achieved consistency if they had continued as regular Test players, but the rest, even Jessop, were tried and found wanting.

Gilbert Jessop (Gloucs.), an all rounder. His innings
of 104 at the Oval in 1902 was one of the greatest
Test innings, but his overall batting (average 24.05)
and bowling (ten wickets at 34.60) were
disappointing. He was a superb cover fielder.

15

SECOND CHOICE STUMPERS

The most specialised position in cricket is that of wicket-keeper. All touring sides arrange to take two stumpers with them in case the first choice breaks down or loses form. Sometimes the best wicket-keeper has not been available to tour so a capable but inferior replacement has been drafted. Consequently a number of stumpers have appeared in Test matches because they were available, not necessarily because they were able. Eight Englishmen and three Australians come within this second choice definition. None of them topped 20 dismissals; only one − Affie Jarvis − played in more than 10 Tests. Most of them made the bulk of their appearances on tour; they lost their places once the better stumpers were available.

The majority of England's group of reserve stumpers played their Tests in the 19th Century (M.C.C. took over the organisation of overseas tours in 1903. Since then the two best current 'keepers have generally been sent abroad). First in chronological order was Dick Pilling of Lancashire who went out with the all pro side of 1881-2. Between then and 1888 Pilling played in 8 Tests dismissing 14 batsmen (about 1 per innings) and conceding 42 byes. Pilling was arguably England's best keeper at this period, but the haphazard organisation of Test matches in England seriously affected his prospects of regular selection. Each authority in charge of a Test venue picked the English side for that game. Consequently Pilling was chosen for the Old Trafford Tests of 1884, 1886 and 1888, but was probably never even considered at Lord's or the Oval. His negligible batting (13 innings brought 91 runs) also told against him.

Contemporary with Pilling was Edmund Fernando Sutton Tylecote, a Kentish amateur who, though perhaps inferior to Pilling as a keeper, was a much superior bat. Tylecote toured with Ivo Bligh in 1882-3 and played a couple of home Tests in 1886. He only dismissed 10 Australians (5 caught, 5 stumped) but he made a major contribution towards winning the match which regained the Ashes in 1883. His first innings 66 against a very much in form Spofforth was an invaluable knock. Coming in at 75 for 5, he went for his shots and partnered Walter Read in a stand of 116 which laid the base for victory. Tylecote, like many of his amateur contemporaries, was never regularly available and he was about twice as costly as Pilling in byes.

A 'tourist only' stumper was Yorkshire's J. Hunter who went out in 1884-5. The five Tests produced 11 victims and 38 byes; better than Tylecote, but not as good as Pilling, Hunter was never more than a competent county keeper and he was not considered for Test teams in England. A first choice keeper who made only a few appearances was Gregor MacGregor, Middlesex's Scotsman. MacGregor played in 8 consecutive games from 1890 to 1893, dismissing 17 batsmen. He was not as adept in keeping down the byes as his county colleague Philipson, but he was certainly more rapacious in claiming victims. It is curious to note that both the Middlesex men toured with W.G.'s team in 1891-2. Philipson, having supported MacGregor on that tour, returned to Australia with Stoddart's team in 1894-5. He played in the last 4 Tests and accounted for 10 Australians. The fact that he was reserve to MacGregor for Middlesex gives a clear indication of his true standing in the line of English stumpers. There were probably half a dozen better men dotted around the counties.

All of these wicket-keepers, apart from Tylecote, were rabbits as batsmen. A man of very different calibre turned up as the wicket-keeper on Stoddart's second tour. This was William Storer, the first man from Derbyshire to be capped. Storer was a versatile cricketer. He made 11 catches, scored 208 runs (and bowled 28 overs!) in the 5 Tests of 1897-8. This was a high scoring series; Stoddart was unavailable for the first two Tests and MacLaren captained in his place; and the weather was excessively hot. Bowlers had a tough time of it, so in 4 of the games Storer discarded his pads for some spells of bowling leg-breaks. He only captured a couple of wickets, but he provided much needed relief for Richardson, Hearne & Co. The Derbyshire man scored a useful 43 at Sydney, followed by 51 at Melbourne and a couple of other good knocks in the last match at Sydney. He later played in the Trent Bridge Test of 1899 but failed to distinguish himself and was replaced by A.A. Lilley.

The next reserve stumper to take over the main role was Warwickshire's 'Tiger' Smith. In 1911-12 Smith went to Australia as deputy to the more experienced Herbert Strudwick. One of England's chief bowlers on this tour was Smith's county captain, Frank Foster. Foster's line of delivery, fast left-arm round the wicket, was considered to present Strudwick with problems, so the reserve was promoted because of his familiarity with Foster's style. Smith retained the place for the Triangular series of 1912. As it turned out, Smith's record was not all that good. In his 7 Tests he dismissed only 13 batsmen, and a mere 4 went off Foster's bowling. One piece of wizardry was the stumping of Clem Hill off Foster at Adelaide; almost the last case of a stumping from a fast delivery in Test matches. Smith was expensive in byes. 126 (about 5%) of Australia's runs came from byes during 'Tiger''s tenure. At this distance in time, it does seem that Strudwick would have been just as, if not more, effective; there was little to choose between them as tail-end rabbits.

The most recent of these wicket-keepers was J.T. Murray of Middlesex. 'John Thomas' was given his chance in a full home rubber in 1961, almost the only one in this group to be so honoured. He responded by dismissing 18 Australians, including 7 of them in one game, the famous Old Trafford Test. Murray was also an economist with the byes. He conceded 36 (about 1.5% of Australia's total) and generally showed himself to be the successor to Godfrey Evans for whom England had been searching. His batting was also useful; he averaged 20 for the series. Then things went wrong. Murray went to Australia in 1962-3, but lost his place for the first two Tests to his deputy, Alan Smith of Warwickshire (Warwickshire stumpers do seem to get favourable consideration on tour). Murray worked his way back into the side for the third match and promptly injured a shoulder in diving to catch Lawry on the leg side. Parfitt had to take over the keeping and Murray's interest in the match had to be confined to stonewalling his way through 100 minutes in England's second innings. He was unable to avert England's defeat. Smith returned for the last two matches and Murray's days against Australia were done. By the time of the 1964 series, Jim Parks had established himself as England's batsman/wicket-keeper.

Australia's trio of stumpers were A.H. Jarvis, Len Maddocks and Barry Jarman. Jarvis, known as 'Affie' (the A.H. stood for Arthur Harwood), was unfortunate in being contemporary with the great Jack Blackham. But for the Victorian's presence, Jarvis would have gained many more caps than the 1·1 he actually received. Jarvis made 4 trips to England. He was merely the deputy stumper on the 1880 tour, when he was a lad of 19, and again in 1893, but he kept in the majority of the Tests in 1886 and 1888. He did not tour in 1882, 1884 or 1890. He was first capped at Melbourne on New Year's Day, 1885. This was the series when Australian domestic relations were in turmoil and Australia used 28 players and changed the captain in each Test. Jarvis played in 3 of the 5 games, dismissing 6 batsmen and scoring 110 runs. 82 of those runs came in his debut innings in a valiant, but futile, attempt to save the follow-on. His performances must have impressed, for he was given the pads and gloves instead of Blackham for the first two Tests of 1886. 3 victims and 36 byes led to Blackham's recall for the final game. In 1888 Jarvis played in two Tests — really to make up the number. Blackham did the keeping, but, with Sammy Jones stricken by smallpox and Boyle a complete back number, the shorthanded Aussies (only 14 players toured) had little alternative. Jarvis scored a paltry 20 runs and was dropped for the final Test. Affie's last appearances came six years later. Blackham, injured in the First Test, was unfit for the remainder of the series. Jarvis captured 8 victims, including 6 stumpings, and scored 110 runs. His final totals, from 9 matches spread over 10 years, were 8 catches, 9 stumpings, 102 byes (about 3% of the opposition's total) and 303 runs (average 16.8). The South Australian spent years in the shadow of Blackham and his record shows it.

An injury to Gil Langley gave Len Maddocks of Victoria the chance to deputise in the last three Tests of 1954-5. With just 7 catches, Maddocks hardly set the world on fire, but he averaged 30 with the bat. His best effort, a robust 69 at Adelaide, was the top Aussie score of that game; but they still lost. In 1956, Maddocks came to England as Langley's deputy. Another injury gave the Victorian the stumper's duties in the Third and Fourth Tests. He picked up 6 victims and scored 6 runs in his 4 innings, which included a pair. Maddocks' one consolation was his parsimony about byes. He was well below Langley's class; the South Australian lifted 28 scalps in these two rubbers as opposed to Maddocks' 13. Each played in 5 of the 10 Tests. Maddocks probably held the edge as a batsman, but his final average of 17.3 was nothing very outstanding.

Barry Jarman bore much the same relationship to Wally Grout as Maddocks had to Langley. An injury to Grout in a state match let Jarman into the team for the first three Tests of 1962-3. 7 dismissals and 23 runs presented no problems to an immediate return for Grout when he had recovered. Jarman played no more Tests until after Grout's retirement. He was chosen as vice-captain to Bill Lawry in 1968 and played in 4 of the 5 Tests. An injury kept him out of the Third game. Jarman's haul was 11 catches and 88 runs; unspectacular figures. Overall he dismissed 18 batsmen (all caught) and allowed 61 byes (nearly 2% of England's total). He was a tail-ender at batting and, like Jarvis and Maddocks, was just a competent deputy for a more brilliant stumper.

Most of these wicket keepers were stop-gap deputies. Hunter, Storer, Philipson, Jarvis, Maddocks and Jarman were all contemporary with superior keepers. Tylecote was probably unduly favoured by the selectors and MacGregor's career was restricted by business commitments. Smith might have had an extended run in England's side but for World War I. The really unlucky stumpers in this group were Pilling and Murray. Selectorial gerrymandering spoiled the Lancastrian's career, while J.T., who has the best record of the 11, suffered through injury and the misguided theory of 'a batsman who keeps wicket being a better choice than a stumper who bats a bit'. If he had not been injured during that 1963 Test, Murray could have joined the ranks of the best.

Teams could be drawn from these bankrupt bats, bountiful bowlers, and assorted all-rounders. England might be represented by: Warner, Spooner, Gooch, Billy Gunn, Mike Smith, Jessop, Yardley, Fender, Emmett, Murray (W.K.) and David Brown. Plum would skipper, because of his record, and there should be some lively — if risky batting. Australia's side could be: Massie, Favell, Arthur Richardson, Bonnor, Len Darling, Fairfax, Jarman (W.K.), Whitty, Bob McLeod, McCormick and Ironmonger. Hugh Massie would lead, as he never lost a Test, and the bowling would be interesting to say the least. If all the hitters on both sides came off at the same time the match could well resemble something out of Barnum and Bailey.

A.H. ('Affie') Jarvis (South Australia) played in nine
Tests between 1885 and 1894, taking 8 catches and
making 9 stumpings. His career was overshadowed by
that of Jack Blackham.

16

SOLID WORKMEN

To earn his keep at Test level a batsman should average more than 25 runs per innings. A bowler should take his wickets at a cost of less than 30 runs each. A batsman with a touch of quality above and beyond the dependable will probably average 35 plus; a bowler with similar attributes will probably capture his victims for less than 25 apiece. Among our Lesser Lights (less than 500 runs; less than 25 wickets) there remain 44 players to fit into the above categories. With 38 it is easy: 21 are dependables ; 17 showed that touch of quality. The remaining 6 are a problem: they certainly weren't dependable; neither did they show genius. This chapter will deal with the 21 Solid Workman , the following chapter with the mercurial 6. The 21 included 10 Englishmen, 10 Australians and that Anglo-Australian, Billy Midwinter. To dispose of Mr. Midwinter once and for all (his career has already been outlined and analysed in the discussion of the Australian Pioneers), he was the first of the Solid Workmen.

In the English ranks we find 5 batsmen, 4 bowlers and an all rounder. Two of the batsmen played in one overseas series each. Norman Druce toured with Stoddart's 1897-8 team. He reached double figures in all of his 9 innings; but his top score was 64 at Sydney in the last Test. Druce was a young Surrey amateur of whom, as of J.R. Mason of Kent, great things were expected. He batted a good deal better than Mason did, but not brilliantly enough to command a place at home. Ten years later Joseph Hardstaff senior, a Nottinghamshire professional, went to Australia with his county skipper, Arthur Jones. He played in all 5 Tests as a middle order batsman and scored 311 valuable runs. Three fifties were included in his efforts and he finished third in the averages behind George Gunn and Jack Hobbs. Hardstaff's peak performance was in the Third Test (at Adelaide) when he scored 61 and 72. With Len Braund he made a stand of 113 for the 4th wicket in the second innings; but was unable to stave off defeat. Hardstaff should probably have been given a chance against the 1909 Australians; an examination of the English batting averages in that rubber would indicate that better results may have been obtained with him and George Gunn in the side. Like many solid pros of that era, he had to make way for questionably 'gifted' amateurs. Joe senior deserved more of his country.

Both Druce and Hardstaff were members of teams which lost by the wide margin of 4 Tests to 1. Another batsman on the losing end was Lancashire's Geoffrey Pullar. Pullar, known as 'Noddy' because of a phlegmatic capacity to doze off, opened England's innings for the best part of two rubbers in the early sixties. Without making any excessively large scores, Pullar provided consistent, solid batting through most of his 9 Tests. A stylish left-hander, Pullar was chosen in 1961 to partner Raman Subba Row in coping with the problems posed by Alan Davidson. They only succeeded in passing 50 for the first wicket on two occasions, and six times it was Pullar who departed first. Nevertheless the Lancastrian notched 287 runs in the series, averaging 31, and scoring 53 at Leeds and 63 at Manchester. In 1962-3, Pullar was not quite so successful. This time he had the Reverend David Sheppard for his opening partner. At first they prospered with stands of 62 and 114 at Brisbane, where Pullar scored 56 in the second innings; after that they fell apart. Pullar's only other innings of note was a 53 at Sydney in the Third Test. He failed in the Second and Fourth and a knee injury kept him out of the last game. By the time that the party returned home it was a foregone conclusion that Pullar's Test days were numbered. He dropped out of the side with 457 runs under his belt and an average of 26.88.

A contemporary batsman with a similar record to Pullar's is Chris Tavaré of Kent. Called to the colours in 1981, Tavaré commenced with 68 and 78 in the Fifth Test at Old Trafford. These two workmanlike efforts occupied 710 minutes; shades of Scotton and Alec Bannerman. At the Oval Tavaré took another 171 minutes to score 32. These stone-walling qualities ensured Tavaré a place among the 1982-3 tourists. In Australia however he was less impressive, his 10 innings realising only 218 runs. Another 1100 minutes went by while the Kent batsman crawled to that total. Twice his tally reached 89, but it seemed as if 5 days would never be long enough to enable him to reach the magic ton. Tavaré's 397 for an average of 28.36 at a rate of 1 run every 5 minutes places him squarely in the Solid Workman class.

Another contemporary Test player is Mike Gatting, the Middlesex batsman. He made his debut at Lord's in the 1980 Centenary Test, scoring 12 and 51 not out; the latter a dour knock which helped Geoffrey Boycott to ensure a draw for England, but which did little to please the spectators. In the 1981 series Gatting was ever present. He batted consistently in the middle order, averaging 30.83 from 370 runs, with a top score of only 59. His brilliant fielding was also a potent asset to England and it seemed that Gatting's solid workmanship would be a feature of England teams for some years to come. Nevertheless his impressive batting average of 33.31 — almost identical with David Gower's and considerably superior to Graham Gooch's — did not induce the selectors to include him in the 1982-3 side.

The four bowlers consist of two ancients and two moderns. The ancients both hailed from Nottinghamshire and the first of them, Alfred Shaw, has already been considered in the account of the Lillywhite Boys. The other Notts. man, Wilfrid Flowers, has some claims to consideration as an all-rounder. He was the first professional to do the Double in an English season (W.G. Grace, of course, had already beaten him to it), but his batting in Tests was not really up to the mark. Flowers toured with the all-pro side in 1884-5 with barely average success. His length bowling brought only 11 wickets in the five games and he finished at the foot of the averages. His best effort with the bat and ball, almost his only one, was in the Sydney Test of 1885. He scored 24 and 56, the top score in each innings of a keenly contested game. Combined with his 5 for 46 in Australia's first innings these added up to a first class all-round performance. Sadly his other efforts failed to reach the same standard. Flowers toured again in 1886-7, bowling in only one of the two Tests. It was fairly clear, at this this stage, that his presence in the side was due to his availability to tour; he had never been considered for an English side at home. He faded from the scene after this tour.

Then out of the blue Flowers was drafted into the side for the Lord's Test of 1893. In an attack headed by Peel, Lockwood and Mold he bowled 11 overs for 21 runs and a tail-end wicket. He was unwell for the next game and was never chosen again. Flowers' 14 Test wickets cost him 21 runs each. His main asset was economy; he bowled 858 balls in giving away only 296 runs, about 2 per over. He was one of the earliest stock bowlers.

The two modern bowlers are still playing first class cricket. It is possible that both John Lever of Essex and Graham Dilley of Kent will cross swords with the Australians again. So far their efforts have been sound and steady. Lever, left arm fast-medium, made his debut in the Melbourne Centenary Test. He bagged a couple of wickets in each innings, setting the pattern for the rest of his Test career to date. Three Tests in the home series of 1977, plus one appearance in each of the following trips to Australia brought him a further 14 victims. He seemed to be more effective Down Under, for he captured 5 for 48 in the Perth match in 1978-9 and 4 for 129 at Melbourne a year later. However as the selectors have treated him as an expendable bowler for home rubbers, it is not surprising that 13 of his 18 scalps were taken in Australia. Lever's economy, only 500 runs from 1300 deliveries, shows his value as a stock bowler.

Graham Dilley, a fast bowler, was a surprise choice for Brearley's 1979-80 tourists. In Australia he played in 2 of the 3 Tests but claimed only 3 wickets for 143 runs. The 3 victims were bagged at Perth on his debut, but he was only given 17 overs at Sydney and lost his place for the last game at Melbourne. He gained greater distinction by averaging 40.00 with the bat in his two games. In 1981 Dilley was recalled for the first three Tests. He performed creditably, capturing 14 wickets at less than 20 runs each. He also batted well, hitting a belligerent and invaluable 56 in the second innings at Headingley. His stand of 117 with Ian Botham carried England from apparently certain defeat to a position from which they gained a famous victory. Just as it seemed that Dilley had assured himself of a permanent place in the side, injury laid him low. He missed the last three Tests, so his bowling record remains at 17 wickets at 24.59 runs each; impressive, but not fully proven until he produces the goods in Australia. Nevertheless with a batting average of 38.33 for 230 runs, Dilley has a sound claim to be accorded all-rounder status and the selectors would be well-advised to keep him on their short list.

In 1924-5 Roy Kilner, a Yorkshire all-rounder, went with Arthur Gilligan's side to recover the Ashes. He was originally regarded as a supporting player, but poor performances by the leg-spinners, Freeman and Dick Tyldesley, in the first two matches resulted in his selection for the Third Test. Kilner kept his place for the rest of the rubber and for most of the 1926 one as well. An experienced cricketer, 34 years old, he bowled left-hand spinners and batted solidly in the lower order. Injuries to others plunged him into a marathon bowling stint on his debut and he emerged with 8 wickets for 178 runs from 78 overs, a highly creditable performance. Five victims at Melbourne and 4 at Sydney placed him second to the redoubtable Maurice Tate with an average of 23.47. In that high scoring series this represented fine bowling. With the bat Kilner made a substantial contribution to England's only win of the series. He went to the wicket with England's first innings showing 394 for 6, and promptly helped 'Dodge' Whysall to add another 133. Kilner's 74 was a purposeful, attacking knock — just the right approach for squeezing the maximum advantage from tired bowlers.

In 1926 Kilner played in the first four Tests. The dreadful weather restricted his opportunities, though he did take 4 for 70 at Lord's. When the side was chosen for the final, deciding match, Kilner's record showed 45 runs (he only batted twice) and 7 wickets and he was at the bottom of the bowling averages. It was this fact that probably decided the selectors to gamble with the veteran Wilfrid Rhodes, Kilner's county colleague and predecessor in the Test team. Kilner's full figures against Australia are: 174 runs, average 29.00; 24 wickets, average 28.12. He was knocking on a bit when he came into the side and illness tragically led to his death before the 1928-9 series could begin. Possibly England should have tried him in 1920; he would surely have done better than E.R. Wilson and Bill Hitch.

Eight of the ten Australians were batsmen. Furthest back in time was Dr. Henry Scott of Victoria, who played in 8 Tests between 1884 and 1886. Scott, not a stylish bat, had a confident defence and could hit hard when occasion required. He toured England in 1884 and scored 220 in 3 completed innings, top scoring with 75 at Lord's and making 102 of Australia's mammoth 551 at the Oval. He partnered his captain, Billy Murdoch, in a stand of 207 for the 3rd wicket. Back in the Antipodes Scott played in only one game of the 1884-5 rubber, without success. Then he was given the captaincy for the 1886 tour of England. His side was reasonably strong on paper, but contained too many players who were either untried or over the hill. Australia was whitewashed. Scott's own Test performances bore little resemblance to his earlier tour's. 47 at Old Trafford was his best effort in 6 knocks. He retired to his country medical practice with a batting average of 27.61.

At about the time Scott was at his peak, Jack Worrall, also of Victoria, appeared. Worrall, a short, thickset hard-hitting batsman, had an uneven Test career. During the decade 1885-95 he made 6 Test appearances in 4 different series, generally batting so low in the order that it was impossible for him to make any sort of mark. He toured England in 1888, making 14 runs in the three Tests, and played at home in 1885, 1888 and 1895, one Test each time. By the end of the 1894-5 series, his tally was 72 in 10 completed innings, a complete and utter flop. Worrall's redeeming asset was his brilliant fielding at mid-off. It seems that his early appearances were made on the basis that he was bound to save runs galore and he *might* come off with the bat. By one of those curious quirks of fate, Worrall was recalled for the last Test of the 1897-8 rubber. 34 years old, Worrall found himself batting at number 4 in place of the out of form Frank Iredale. He seized his chance, scoring 26 and 62. In the second innings he assisted Joe Darling in a match-winning partnership of 193 for the 3rd wicket. That knock booked Worrall's passage for the 1899 tour. In England again, 11 years after his previous visit — when he had averaged 11.00 for the whole tour — Worrall missed the First Test. Iredale, who had opened the innings, failed again, and Worrall replaced him at Lord's. The rest of the series was a triumph for the Victorian. He did just enough at Lord's to keep the opener's place and in his remaining 6 innings he hit 289 runs, including 4 fifties. His finest effort came at the Oval where he scored 55 and 75 helping to save the game and prevent England from squaring the rubber. Worrall and Charlie McLeod put on 116 for the first wicket in the second innings. The Victorian, with 45.42, was third to Clem Hill and Monty Noble in the series averages. His success in these last half a dozen matches redeemed his previous woeful record and Worrall retired from Tests with an average of 25.15 for his 478 runs. He also made 13 catches, a contribution in keeping with his pre-eminence as a fielder.

Between Worrall's two tours of England, Harry Graham, known as the 'Little Dasher', started and finished his Test career. Graham, from Victoria, was 22 years old when he toured England in 1893. He began in a blaze of glory by scoring 107 at Lord's on his Test debut. With Sid Gregory, Graham added 142 for the 6th wicket and steered Australia past the follow-on. The game was drawn. Graham also hit 42 at the Oval and finished the tour at the head of the averages. However, his form seems to have fallen away after the side's return to Australia and he was omitted from the first three Tests against Stoddart's '94 side. With the Aussies 2-1 down, he was recalled for the Fourth Test which proved to be a sensational match. Bad weather had spoiled the wicket and Stoddart put Australia in. They lost 4 wickets for 26, then Graham, who had arrived at the fall of the 3rd wicket, began to hit. He went down the pitch to Richardson, twice hitting the fast bowler high to the long field. Two more wickets fell, but at 51 for 6 Darling supported Graham in a stand of 68. Then Albert Trott, in his second Test, came in. Graham and Trott laid about them so well that 112 were added for the 8th wicket. The 'Little Dasher''s brilliantly audacious knock ended after 135 minutes when he was stumped by Philipson off Johnny Briggs for 105. Australia totalled 284 and, after further rain, tumbled England out twice for a paltry 137 to square the rubber. That superb innings gave Graham the unique distinction of compiling a ton in his debut Test innings at home and abroad. Yet his Test career was virtually over. He failed in the final Test, went to England with the 1896 side, scored only half as many runs as he amassed in 1893, failed in the First Test there, was dropped from the side, and disappeared from Test cricket at the age of 25. The reasons for his rejection are difficult to ascertain. His Test average of 30 was superior to several contemporaries who played on in the side for some seasons. Graham was not the most certain of catchers in the outfield, so perhaps the Australian insistence on top-class fielding weighed against him. It does seem though that he was prematurely discarded with a lot of fine batting still in him.

In 1911-12 Roy Minnett, a New South Wales batsman with pretensions to being an all-rounder, was capped in all 5 games against Johnny Douglas' side. He began in great style with 90 on his Sydney home ground. This match provided Australia's sole win of the series and Minnett helped Victor Trumper to add 109 for the 6th wicket; a stand which consolidated the base for victory. Minnett continued his good work with fifties in the Fourth and Fifth Tests. He averaged 30.50 for the series and also picked up a few wickets with his change bowling. This good form, plus the vacancies caused by the 'Big Six' in their squabble with the Board of Control, guaranteed Minnett's place in the Triangular Tests team. He had a disappointing tour. The dismal weather reduced his effectiveness with bat and ball and his only contribution to the Tests was 4 for 34 in England's first innings at the Oval. When World War I broke out Minnett was only 26, so it is surprising that he failed to reappear in 1920. Like many cricketers in both wars he seemed to have lost that vital spark during the non-cricketing years.

In the mid nineteen thirties Alan Chipperfield of New South Wales played in 9 Tests. Chipperfield, an all rounder for his state, confined his Test contributions to batting. At Trent Bridge in 1934 Chipperfield, prematurely balding, made one of the most unusual debuts of any Test cricketer. He was 99 not out at lunch time on the second day. Chipperfield fretted his way through the break, worrying about that single run, with the inevitable result. He touched the first ball after lunch, from Ken Farnes to Leslie Ames behind the wicket. All Chipperfield's remaining innings were anti-climax. The rest of his scores in 1934 were negligible with one exception. At Lord's, on a wicket worsened by heavy rain, Chipperfield made 37 not out against a Hedley

Verity on the kill. He ran out of partners 7 short of saving the follow-on. Australia collapsed to an innings defeat. The 1936-7 rubber found Chipperfield in difficulties. Two Tests yielded 67 runs. He was dropped for the Third Test. His replacement, Len Darling, also failed, so 'Chipper' was recalled for the Adelaide match.

Australia were struggling at 206 for 5 with all of their big guns gone. Chipperfield came in to score 57 of the 82 runs added for the last 5 wickets. He was undefeated at the end, and had just about kept the Aussies in the game. 31 in the second innings clinched his place in the team again. Before the last Test Chipperfield was injured and had to withdraw. He was chosen for the 1938 tour but played in only one Test. This was due to firstly a finger injury and then to appendicitis. The New South Welshman failed at Lord's and missed the last 3 Tests. At least he avoided the Oval debacle. Chipperfield's 356 runs for an average of just under 30 were not his only contribution to Australia's cause. Thirteen slip catches in as many innings are a clear testimony of his value in the field. He deserved better luck in 1938.

In the post-war years Graeme Hole of South Australia looked a good prospect. He played 9 Tests between 1951 and 1955, but never succeeded in claiming a permanent place in Australia's team. The Australians blooded Hole in the last game versus Freddie Brown's side (as they were 4-0 ahead, some gambles were justified). Hole batted elegantly in the second innings, top-scoring with 63, but Australia lost. In 1953 Hole was ever-present, contributing 273 runs, including fifties at Old Trafford and Leeds. He helped Neil Harvey add 173 in the former match, but was very much the junior partner. At home for the 1954-5 series, Hole kept his place for 3 more games. 57 at Brisbane in another stand with Harvey (131 this time) helped Australia to a total of 601 and victory by an innings. Then Tyson and Statham got at him and his next four innings totalled 28. He was dropped and never recalled. As Hole was only 24, the selectors' treatment seems prematurely final. The South Australian's final tally was 439 runs averaging 25.82, while his competent slip fielding yielded 10 catches; unspectacular but useful.

One of the greater disappointments in recent years was the comparative failure of schoolteacher Paul Sheahan in Tests against England. Sheahan, a spectacular right hand batsman from Victoria, came to England in 1968 with a glowing reputation. Great things were expected from a bat who possessed 'the greatest driving technique seen for years.' Perhaps the Antipodean euphoria was too much for Sheahan. Certainly, on the evidence of his figures, it was premature. Playing in all the Tests, Sheahan collected only 213 runs. Indeed on the tour as a whole he didn't even top 1,000. Yet he began in ominous form. At Old Trafford, coming in at 173 for 3, Sheahan lost Walters almost immediately and then embarked on a partnership of 152 with Ian Chappell. He looked set for a century when John Snow dismissed him early in the second day. Like Minnett and Chipperfield before him, Sheahan never did as well again. This 88 was the only time he scored more than 50 in the 9 Tests he played against England. In Australia, Sheahan batted poorly against Illingworth's team. He was dropped after Two Tests had produced only 38. Consequently it was a surprise when he turned up in England in 1972. This time his tour average was a more impressive 41, but he did not regain his Test place until the last two matches. Then he scored a not out forty in each game, steering Australia to the Oval victory which squared the series. Teaching commitments forced Sheahan to make himself unavailable for future tours. In view of his run of-the-mill achievements, 341 runs at 26.23, it is unlikely that Australia was greatly weakened by his loss.

John Dyson of New South Wales is the final batsman in this group. He played in the first five Tests of the 1981 series and at Headingley be batted throughout the first day for 102 runs, nearly half of his total output for the rubber. His unimpressive average (20.60) surprisingly did not deter the Australian selectors from picking him for all 5 games in 1982-3. This time he did rather better with 283 runs at an average of 35. Overall Dyson's 10 Tests have produced 489 runs, average 27.17, unspectacular but solid. Australia has tried many worse batsmen in their problem opening position in recent years.

The two Australian bowlers in this group operated before World War I. Thomas McKibbin made 5 appearances in the nineties under circumstances of some controversy. He was adept at making the ball break, sometimes quite prodigiously, from the off at a lively pace. Australian public opinion was not impressed when this New South Wales country boy ousted the famous Charlie Turner from the last Test of 1894-95. As McKibbin only took a couple of expensive wickets, public opinion seemed vindicated. McKibbin made the boat for the 1896 tour however. He was given little cricket in the first half of the tour, (perhaps Harry Trott was mourning the absence of brother Albert, who probably lost out to McKibbin) and he missed the First Test. From the end of June McKibbin had so much work that he took 100 wickets and headed the bowling averages. In two Tests he captured 11 victims for 162; not spectacular, but very economical wicket-taking. There was concern under the surface, about his bowling action though. He was considered by many, and *Wisden* of 1897 said so in print, to throw his off-break. No doubt he began to receive conflicting advice which, as always in such cases, reduced his effectiveness when he tried to put it into practice. Two unsuccessful Tests in 1897-8 gave the relieved selectors a chance to drop him and a chucking storm was probably averted. McKibbin's 17 wickets eventually cost nearly 30 runs each, so his omission was fully justified, despite that fine tour of England.

Shortly after McKibbin's departure, New South Wales supplied Arthur Hopkins to Test cricket. Hopkins, a good all rounder at state and county level, visited England three times (1902, 1905 and 1909) and got through a lot of work with both bat and ball. He first appeared in Test matches in 1901-2, playing in the last 2 games and making a modest start with 43 in his first knock at Sydney. For the next two rubbers Hopkins was ever-present. It is difficult to understand why. By the time he reached the end of the 1903-4 matches, Hopkins had scored 321 runs in 20 innings and taken 13 wickets. This meagre return did not deter the selectors from taking him to England again in 1905. Only 3 Test appearances fell to his lot in that rubber, and he maintained his reputation for mediocrity.

Hopkins missed the whole of the 1907-8 series, but turned up in England with the 1909 side. A couple of Tests in that rubber brought one of the strangest of Australian careers to a close. The Australians are generally ruthless in dropping players who fail to produce results, yet Hopkins was allowed to amble through 17 Tests for 434 runs and 21 wickets, about 25 runs and 1 wicket per game. He topped 40 only 3 times, never reaching 50, and his only real bowling contribution was 7 wickets for 149 in the match at Adelaide in 1904, which Australia won. There are no indications that Hopkins was especially economical as a bowler, but he played a supporting role in a number of valuable batting partnerships. Like most Australians, he was a sound fieldsman, though his haul of 10 catches is nothing out of the ordinary for a man who played so often. Hopkins enjoyed the friendship of Monty Noble and Frank Laver, the 'strong men' of Australian cricket in his day, which may explain his long tenure in the Test side.

Alfred Shaw (Notts.), co-organiser of the Lillywhite Boys' tour
to Australia in 1876-7. He took 8 wickets in the First Test.

Warwick Armstrong's Australians: (Back row) W. Bardsley, J.S. Ryder, H.L. Hendry, J.M. Gregory, E.R. Mayne, T.J.E. Andrews, Sydney Smith (manager). (Middle row) A.A. Mailey, E.A. McDonald, H.L. Collins, W.W. Armstrong (capt.), C.G. Macartney, H. Carter, J.M. Taylor. (Front row) C.E. Pellew, W.A. Oldfield.

17

A MERCURIAL SIX

Half a dozen cricketers completed their Test careers with totals and averages which place them squarely in the Solid Workmen class. An examination of those totals, however, show that each is based on a purple patch, when those cricketers transcended their normal play. If these cricketers had been able to produce their purple patches regularly, they would have left the ranks of the Lesser Lights and become stars. If they had never experienced a purple patch at all, they would have remained with the small fry (Three Time Losers, Nearly Men, and so on). Because they fell between the two extremes they are dealt with here — an appendage to the more reliable Solid Workmen. There are four Englishmen and two Australians among the six. Four were batsmen, two bowlers. One captained England. One was among the half dozen best fieldsmen these games have seen. All of them made one superb contribution to Anglo-Australian Tests.

Two of these players started their Test careers in the same series, one on each side. Gerry Hazlitt of Australia did not shine; his great day was ahead. Kenneth Hutchings of England was the man of the moment. 1907-8 was a bad series for England. Beaten 4-1, beset by illness and injury, weakly led, ill-served behind the stumps, there was not a lot to be proud about. Yet this series introduced Hobbs and George Gunn to Test matches, had Barnes and Fielder providing high quality opening bowling, and also provided opportunities for two gifted amateurs to display their talents. One of these was Jack Crawford, the other was Ken Hutchings. Hutchings of Kent reached his twenty fifth birthday early in the tour. A right hand bat, possessed of a good back-foot defence, he was highly regarded in England for the power of his straight and on-driving. He got the power from his exceedingly strong wrists and forearms, a power which also made him a superb thrower from the out-field. England had great expectations of Hutchings, and to an extent he realised them. At Sydney he began with 42, helping George Gunn to retrieve a bad start. Then came the Melbourne Test — and Hutchings' purple patch. This match saw Jack Hobbs' debut. Australia started with 266; when Hutchings joined Hobbs, England had lost 2 wickets for 61. They made steady progress, adding 99 before Hobbs fell. Hutchings, who had been driving powerfully, now accelerated. With Len Braund as partner, he reached his century in 125 minutes; his second 50 virtually coming in even time. On the third day he went on to 126 before Cotter bowled him. 90 of his runs came from boundaries; one of the great Test innings. His efforts steered England to a substantial first innings lead. In the end England nearly frittered it away. Australia fought back and Barnes and Fielder had to squeeze 39 runs out of England's last wicket to win the match. Hutchings' second knock brought him 39. His form declined during the rest of the series. Six more innings brought only 49 runs. He finished fourth in England's averages behind the professional trio of Gunn, Hobbs and the solid Hardstaff.

In 1909 Hutchings was ignored for the first three Tests. His county form had started to decline, and anyway, MacLaren was skipper so he probably didn't have much use for members of a defeated touring side. (George Gunn and Hardstaff were overlooked as well.) By the time of the Fourth Test. MacLaren had managed to go one down in the rubber. Injuries forced changes on England and Hutchings was summoned to Old Trafford. He made 9 and England drew. At the Oval Hutchings was relegated to number 8, behind the untried Frank Woolley and Ernie Hayes. Australia made 325. England were 206 for 6 when Hutchings joined Lancashire's Jack Sharp. They added 142 in 105 minutes, took England into the lead and then fell at the same total. Hutchings' share was 59, an innings which emphasised his potential quality. He never played for England again. The Kent amateur's 341 against Australia were gathered at the rate of 28.41 per innings, figures within touching distance of greatness, but lacking the necessary consistency. If he had played throughout 1909 the story might have been different.

In that same 1907-8 series, Gervys 'Gerry' Hazlitt a nineteen year old, fast medium bowler from Victoria played in the first two Tests. Hazlitt possessed a jerky action which enabled him to wobble the ball in the air. In the Sydney Test he was only given 13 overs without success, but he batted usefully, being twice not out for 18 and 34. His partnership with Cotter in the second innings realised 56 runs and took Australia to a two-wicket win. At Melbourne Hazlitt again failed to get a wicket. His most significant contribution was an ill-judged shy at the stumps at the end of the second English innings, when Barnes and Fielder were going for the winning run. Hazlitt missed and Australia lost. He played no more Tests until 1911-12. In that series he played in the last match at Sydney, taking 4 fairly expensive wickets.

Nevertheless, like Jimmy Matthews and Bill Whitty, Hazlitt was given a place on the 1912 tour; there wasn't anyone else. Hazlitt had a good tour, taking 98 wickets. From the Tests he emerged with 12 victims, the same number as Whitty, at the relatively cheap cost of 18.16. His best effort was reserved for England's last innings of the rubber. At Kennington Oval Hazlitt bowled 21.4 overs, 8 maidens and took 7 for 25; one of the most impressive analyses in Test history. Hazlitt actually demolished the last 5 wickets for 1 run as the pitch began to dry after heavy overnight rain. Australia, batting last, had the worst of the wicket and lost heavily. World War I effectively finished Hazlitt as a Test cricketer. His final bag of 16 wickets at 27.68 would have looked far less workmanlike if he had not enjoyed his purple patch at the Oval.

The great Australian side of 1948 contained a number of cricketers who, in other times, would have had no difficulty in establishing themselves as permanent Test players. In Bradman's side they were of reserve standard. One such was Sam Loxton of Victoria. Loxton, a hard-hitting bat and a lively pace bowler, was a superb all-round fieldsman, particularly brilliant close to the wicket. It took him nearly half the tour to battle his way to a Test place. Loxton made his debut at Old Trafford, where he scored 36 in his only innings. He was retained in the team for the Fourth Test at Headingley. In that match Loxton bowled 26 overs in England's first innings, rolling up the tail-enders with 3 for 55. England totalled 496 and quickly had Australia in trouble at 68 for 3. Keith Miller and Neil Harvey, in his first Test innings, added 121 in 90 minutes and, when Miller departed, Loxton arrived at number 6. The next two and a quarter hours were absolute mayhem. Loxton and Harvey added another 105 in 95 minutes, with Harvey batting beautifully and Loxton indulging in a sustained bout of colossal hitting. Loxton hit 5 sixes as well as 9 fours, the highest number of six-hits in these matches. He was bowled by Norman Yardley with his score at 93, just missing a much deserved century. At this stage of his career, Loxton was a glutton for work, always full of enthusiam; a truly fighting cricketer who fully merited his place in that great Australian side. The rest of Loxton's efforts against England were small beer compared with the champagne of that 93. One more innings in 1948 was followed by 5 knocks in the first three games of 1950-51. He scored just 90 more runs, 3 less than in his finest innings. Loxton's only achievement of note in this latter series was to grab 5 catches in the Brisbane Test — 4 in the second innings. His decline in form included his bowling and he was dropped in favour of the young Jim Burke at

Adelaide. His final batting average of 27.37 was disappointing after that breakneck beginning.

In the series that saw Loxton drop out, Reg Simpson of Nottinghamshire had his finest hour for England. The English batting in that rubber apart from Len Hutton was almost non-existent. Simpson played in all the Tests achieving nothing in the first two, and scoring a useful 49 in the Third. He did better with 29 and 61 in the Fourth, and England lost all four games. At Melbourne for the last Test, Australia began with a weakly compiled 217. This was England's opportunity. They had lost Cyril Washbrook at 40 when Simpson joined Hutton. Together they carried the score to 171 by confident batting, with Simpson matching Hutton run for run. Then England collapsed; seven wickets fell to Miller and Lindwall for the addition of 75 runs. Simpson was 92 not out when last man Tattersall joined him, with England's lead a meagre 29. The last wicket stand was epic. Tattersall defended stoutly and made 10 while the Nottinghamshire man scored another 64. When Miller knocked over Tattersall's wicket, Simpson's individual total was 156 and England's lead had increased to 103. The rest is history. England disposed of the Aussies for 197 and lost only 2 wickets, Simpson's being one of them, in recording her first post-war victory. For Simpson there were no more great moments. He played three Tests in 1953 and one in 1954-5 for a total of 85 runs. His average, if his 156 not out is excluded, is the mediocre one of 18.53. When his purple patch is added, it jumps to 28.93. Reg Simpson had only one *tour de force* against Australia — but what a performance!

A man who could have joined the ranks of the great Anglo-Australians, but who promised more than he achieved, was Johnny Wardle, Yorkshire's left-hand spin bowler of the 1950s. Wardle had an in and out Test career because of the competition from Surrey's Tony Lock. The Yorkshire man's failure to bowl consistently well against the Australians must have been due, partly at least, to lack of certainty about his Test place. In 1953 Wardle was selected ahead of Lock for the first three Tests. He had little chance to shine at Trent Bridge, (Alec Bedser had a monopoly of the wickets there), but his 4 for 77 at Lord's tore the middle out of Australia's first innings. The Third Test at Old Trafford was rain plagued. Wardle's 3 for 70 in the first innings was in the nature of a tail-end mop up. England took a long time due to rain interruption in saving the follow on, and there was little time left when Australia began their second knock. The finish was almost sensational. In 5 overs Wardle captured 4 for 7 and, with Bedser and Laker taking two Australian wickets each, the visitors had fallen to 35 for 8 when time expired. Lock replaced Wardle for the remainder of the series! It was touch and go as to who would be preferred for the 1954-5 tour of Australia; Wardle was in fact the one favoured.

He was omitted from the Brisbane Test. At Sydney, Melbourne and Adelaide he did little more than make up the number. 34 overs in the three games yielded 2 expensive wickets; Tyson and Statham, with support from Trevor Bailey and Bob Appleyard, were not leaving sufficient pickings for a third-change spinner to achieve much. The final Test at Sydney gave Wardle his opportunity. With the rubber already won, Len Hutton was more inclined to use a varied attack. The first three days were lost to rain and after England had declared at 371 for 7, Australia were confronted by a new style Wardle. The Yorkshire man changed from the orthodox left hand spin, which he had employed defensively in the previous Tests, to over-the-wrist Chinamen. In 24.4 overs he removed 5 Australians for 79 and forced them to follow on. He then went on to capture 3 of the 5 second innings wickets which fell before the match petered out in a draw. His full match haul was 8 for 130; the Australians' vulnerability to spin had been fully, if belatedly, exposed. That was the virtual end of Wardle's tussles with Australia. By 1956 Tony Lock had again come into favour and it was surprising to find Wardle getting preference over him for the Lord's Test. The Yorkshire man did not shine in that game, collecting a pair and taking one expensive wicket. Lock was recalled for the rest of the series.

In view of Wardle's tardy success in 1954-5 he was invited to tour in 1958-9. Unfortunately he had become embroiled in controversy within the Yorkshire club and the county dispensed with his services. He immediately aired his grievances in vigorous terms in the Press. The M.C.C. then withdrew the invitation and Wardle played for England no more. Wardle's 8 Tests against Australia brought him 24 wickets at 26.33 each. He enjoyed 1½ purple patches: that fine display at Sydney, plus his Old Trafford performance in 1953, which, though impressive in figures, was helped by some careless Australian batting. He also provided some useful tail-end batting, averaging 18 from 12 innings. If he had avoided controversy, Wardle might well have engineered bowling feats to match his illustrious Yorkshire predecessors Verity, Rhodes and Peel. As events turned out his record is fairly unimpressive except for that Sydney Test.

Last on the list of these one night standers comes Mike Denness of Kent, captain of England in 1974-5. Denness had a bad time as skipper, losing the rubber 4-1. For most of the series he didn't have too good a time with the bat either. The first 3 Tests found him sadly out of form. Lillee and Thomson didn't help of course. After 6 innings the Scot had scored a princely 65 runs. Under pressure from all sides. Denness dropped himself from the fourth game; an almost unprecedented occurrence. After recovering some form in state and country matches, Denness returned to the colours at Adelaide. Batting number 4, he top scored with 51 out of 172, but England lost again.

The Englishmen arrived at Melbourne seeking to salvage something from the wreckage of the series. Circumstances now were in their favour. Jeff Thomson was absent from the Australian team with a shoulder injury, and Lillee broke down after bowling 6 overs. England had made their best start of the rubber by dismissing Australia for 152, due chiefly to Peter Lever, and they proceeded to make the most of their opportunity. Denness led the way, going to the wicket at a score of 18 for 2 and partnering John Edrich in a stand of 149. When Edrich went for 70 the skipper carried on, adding another 192 with Keith Fletcher. When Denness gave a return catch to Max Walker, he had batted 8½ hours, made the highest score by an England captain in Australia (188), and been missed three times (at 36, 98 and 121). Denness' timing of his off-side strokes was impeccable and he must have gained a good deal of personal satisfaction from the innings, after his experiences earlier in the tour. England won by an innings.

The Kent man led England just once more at Edgbaston in 1975. He gambled on putting Australia in, but got caught on a wet wicket when England batted, followed on 258 behind and lost by an innings. With personal contributions of 3 and 8, it was inevitable that Denness should lose both the captaincy and his place in the side. Denness had a batting average against Australia of 29.9. If his 188 is excluded, that average from 10 innings drops to 14.1. But for his purple patch Denness would have been classified with failures like J.R. Mason and Arthur Jones.

16 of these 25 players were very much on the losing end of the Tests in which they played. Chipperfield, Sheahan, Worrall, Lever and Tavare broke even in terms of wins and losses. Gatting, Hopkins, Flowers and Wardle played for the more successful sides, though they were all in losing teams at least once. Sammy Loxton, with 5 wins and 1 draw in his six Tests, was the player of the group on whom fortune smiled most. A couple of reasonably good sides could be assembled from these Solid Workmen. There is not much pace bowling amongst

them and a brace of stumpers would be needed. In batting order the teams might be: *England*: Denness, Tavaré, Simpson, Hutchings, Gatting, Hardstaff, Kilner, Murray (wicket-keeper), Dilley, Shaw and John Lever. *Australia*: Worrall, Dyson, Scott, Graham, Chipperfield, Loxton, Midwinter, Hopkins, Jarvis (wicket-keeper), Hazlitt and McKibbin. For England, Kilner's batting gives him the edge on Wardle; and Hutching's flair makes him a better prospect than Druce. On the Australian side, Hole and Sheahan lose out because of their slightly inferior batting averages, though perhaps Roy Minnett should replace Midwinter or Hopkins. The Australian bowling looks thinner than England's and the batting seems to have less quality too. Denness and Scott could lead, but I fear that a war of attrition might ensue.

R.E. Foster (Worcs.) made the most brilliant debut of any Test cricketer, scoring 287 at Sydney in December 1903. His 5 Tests brought 486 runs at an average of 60.75. Private commitments and ill health curtailed his playing career.

18

SHOOTING STARS

Seventeen lesser lights remain. Each of them performed so well in their limited number of appearances that the brevity of their careers seems, in most cases, an aberration. Thirteen were English, only four Australian, a clear indictment of the inconstancy of English selectors. Eleven of the seventeen were batsmen, four were bowlers, the remaining two all-rounders. The batsmen scored 5,329 runs between them at an average of 43, the bowlers captured 110 wickets at 23 each; figures a good deal more impressive than most long-serving Test players outside the super-star class. Certainly their fount of talent was largely wasted by the impermanence of their Test careers.

Of the English batsmen, three were amateurs whose private circumstances dictated that their cricketing days should be fleeting. Each of them was present throughout one series, making their mark by scoring over 400 runs in their five games. First in point of time was the Corinthian, Reginald Erskine Foster. Third of the famous Foster brothers of Malvern College and Worcestershire, R.E. was a brilliant all-round sportsman. He gained Blues for association football as well as cricket and he went on to represent England at both sports. His soccer caps were gained before his Tests, Foster representing England 6 times between 1900 and 1902. On at least one occasion he gained preference at inside forward over the legendary Steve Bloomer, and he captained England against Wales in 1902, the rest of the side being made up of professionals. 'Tip' Foster's cricketing skills had been developed at Malvern College. His style mixed magnificent off-driving with superb late-cutting, and he was an automatic choice for the Oxford sides of 1897-1900. Foster captained Oxford in his last year and scored a brilliant 171 in the Varsity match. It was inevitable that the Malvernian should gain a Test place sooner or later. Foster's opportunity arrived in 1903-4 when he visited Australia with Plum Warner's side. He was destined to make his name in cricket history.

At Sydney in December 1903 Foster played the greatest debut innings in the history of the Tests. Australia won the toss and started with the useful total of 285. Foster marked his first day of Test cricket by diving for a left-handed slip catch to get rid of Victor Trumper for 1.

He later grabbed another, also from the bowling of his county colleague, Ted Arnold, to dismiss the Aussie skipper Monty Noble. Before he had even raised his bat, 'Tip' proved his value. On the second day, England was off to a bad start. Warner went for a duck , Hayward followed for 15, and Arnold., batting surprisingly high in this list, succumbed for 27. Foster joined Johnny Tyldesley at 73 for 3 and supported the Lancastrian while the total went past 100. At 117 Noble bowled Tyldesley for 53 and England's prospects seemed less than rosy. At this juncture Len Braund arrived. Foster had been very uncertain at first, but he had derived encouragement from Tyldesley's positive batting and Braund's confident approach helped him to conquer his nerves. The pair matched each other, run for run, and by close of play England had reached the safe position of 243 for 4: Foster 73, Braund 67.

On the third morning, Foster found the wicket playing faster and this suited his free-stroking style. He reached his century one over ahead of Braund, who was bowled almost immediately by Howell for 102. Their stand was worth 192 and had seen England into the lead. Three more wickets fell quickly, so that England, with 8 men gone were a mere 47 ahead. Albert Relf joined Foster, who started the third phase of his innings. He scored nearly 3 runs to Relf's 1, off-driving and cutting with lavish freedom. They added 115 priceless runs, and, when Relf was out just before tea, Foster had completed his double century. But he was not finished yet. With the competent Wilfred Rhodes as partner, Foster embarked on a last wicket stand which realised another 130 runs in only 66 minutes. Rhodes' share was 40, but the Worcestershire crack added another 84 to his tea-time tally. He looked set for the first treble century in Test matches, when Noble held on to a catch at mid-off when Foster drove Saunders. Foster's innings lasted seven hours and he included 37 boundary hits in his 287. Thanks to this wonderful debut knock, which is still the highest individual score by an English batsman in a Test in Australia, England led by 292. Australia fought back, but the visitors ran out comfortable winners. Foster, the prime architect of this victory, looked set for a long occupation of the star batsman's role in the England team.

The rest of his performances in this rubber were almost inevitably less impressive. Foster was a diabetic and he was afflicted by a bout of illness during the Second Test at Melbourne. In the first innings he scored 49 out of a 99 stand with J.T. Tyldesley, then had to retire. He took no further part in that match. Foster's remaining six innings of the series yielded only 131 runs. Nevertheless, he headed the English list with 486 runs at 60.75 per innings, one of the highest averages in the history of these games. 'Tip' returned to England to enjoy a triumph, tempered with concern over his ill-health. Back at home his business commitments as a stock-broker combined with his diabetes to restrict his appearances in the first class game. Though he continued to show his best form for some years at county level and against the South Africans, Foster never again played against the Australians. He died in 1914 of diabetes at the sadly early age of 36. If circumstances had been different, Reginald Erskine Foster would indubitably have taken his place alongside Hobbs and Hammond among the great names of cricket.

Another Worcestershire amateur joined the English ranks in 1934. Cyril Walters, a stylish opening batsman, had made his initial impact on first class cricket with the new county Glamorgan in the nineteen twenties. He became the Worcestershire secretary and qualified to play for them in 1930. By 1933 he had graduated to the county captaincy and Test cricket. When Woodfull's second tourists arrived in the aftermath of Bodyline, Walters had established himself as Sutcliffe's best opening partner since Jack Hobbs' retirement. The Worcestershire bat made an unique debut at Trent Bridge. R.E.S. Wyatt, the chosen captain, broke his thumb just before the match, and Walters, by virtue of his captaincy of Worcestershire, took over the leadership. He lost the toss and England fielded to an Aussie total of 374. When England batted Walters lasted an hour as Sutcliffe's junior partner. Then he fell leg before to Grimmett's straight one for 17. England trailed by over 100, Australia piled on a further 273, and England was faced with 4¾ hours on a wearing pitch to save the game. This time Sutcliffe went first, and Walters set his side a fine example by batting steadily for 2¼ hours. Then O'Reilly bowled him. England collapsed and Australia won with twenty minutes to spare. Walters' 46 was the top score of the innings.

Freed of captaincy worries for the rest of the rubber, Walters set about proving his worth. At Lord's he played a pedigree innings on the first day. His strokes were rapid and wristy; he conjured 82 out of England's 130 for 4 and looked set for a century when he hit precipitately at O'Reilly's slower ball. England, thanks to Ames and Leyland, went on to 440; then Hedley Verity's bowling squared the rubber. At Old Trafford Walters launched a brilliant onslaught on Grimmett and O'Reilly. He reached 52 out of 68 in an hour, with 8 boundaries. A break for drinks was his undoing. The first delivery on the resumption, O'Reilly's slow ball again, deceived him and a vintage innings was nipped in the bud. This was a high-scoring match which petered out in a draw. England, with a lead of 136 and only a few hours left, batted unhurriedly in their second innings. Walters and Sutcliffe put on 123 undefeated in 145 minutes before Wyatt made a token declaration. The Worcestershire bat scored his second fifty of the match. At Headingley Walters scored a couple of forties. He followed this with 64 at the Oval, another century stand with Sutcliffe. Then with England facing a colossal deficit of 707, he fell to the innocuous McCabe for 1, his only real failure of the series. Walters' 401 runs, which included 4 fifties, averaged 50 for the series. He looked a fixture in the side for years to come, but before the next series fell due he had retired prematurely from the first-class game. On his 1934 form he could have held his place at least until the Second World War.

The last of this trio of amateurs was Raman Subba Row of Cambridge University, Surrey and Northants. Subba Row, born in Croydon, was nearly thirty years old when he first faced Australia in 1961. A very useful all-rounder, he had been forced to migrate to Northants. because of the difficulty of clinching a permanent place in the strong Surrey side of the middle fifties. His sound play got him a place with Peter May's 1958-9 tourists, but a broken finger put him out of action for a long spell and he failed to make the Test team. England's batting troubles on that tour led to a deal of experimenting with the opening positions in the interim before the arrival of Richie Benaud's men in 1961. The Australians found a left-handed duo, Subba Row and 'Noddy' Pullar awaiting them. By this ploy England hoped to counter the difficulties posed by Alan Davidson's line of attack.

Subba Row started in fine style with 59 and 112 at Edgbaston. The 59 was the top score in a rain interrupted first day. England were all out for 195 early on the second morning. Australia replied with 516 for 9, but time was fairly short as England struggled to avoid an innings defeat. Subba Row's 112, another debut century, was solidly stroked from stands of 93 with Pullar and 109 with Dexter. England saved the match and a lot of the credit was due to the Northants. left-hander.

The next 3 Tests found Subba Row continuing to make useful scores. His 48 at Lord's was England's top first innings score; at Old Trafford his second innings 49 helped Dexter to set England on the road to victory. Unfortunately sloppy batting against Benaud by the middle order and tail frittered away that opportunity. England lost both games and went to the Oval 1 down. There, Subba Row scored 12 in England's first knock of 256, but Australia led by 238. Once again he was required to fight a rearguard action. His first four partners were all back in the pavilion before the total reached 100, but the Northants. man then received solid support from Ken Barrington. They added 172 for the fifth wicket, despite Subba Row's pulled muscle which necessitated the employment of a runner. All told, the left-hander batted for seven hours forty minutes before he gave a return catch to Richie Benaud. His 137 had virtually saved England's bacon, though Murray and Allen had to bat out the last two hours to make sure.

Subba Row announced his retirement from first-class cricket after this Test; another unpaid cricketer with his way to make in the world. He thus achieved the distinction (shared with Maurice Leyland, another great left-hander) of scoring centuries in both his first and last Tests against Australia. Subba Row's 46.80 average from his 10 Test innings compares very favourably with most of England's post-war openers. His early retirement was just as great a loss as Cyril Walters', for, though he lacked the Worcestershire man's flashing stroke play, his phlegmatic grafting and consistent scoring were much needed by the brittle English teams of his period.

A number of pointers indicate that most of the remaining English batsmen in this group were denied their just deserts by fickle selectors. Albert Ward and J.T. Brown in the nineties, Phillip Mead, Jack Russell and Ernest Tyldesley in the twenties, and Bob Barber of more recent vintage all made their mark on the Ashes matches. Every man-jack of them had a better batting average against the Aussies than, for example, Colin Cowdrey, Archie MacLaren, Frank Wooley and W.G. Grace. Indeed Mead and Russell were only surpassed by Hobbs, Sutcliffe, Hutton, Barrington, R.E. Foster, Maurice Leyland and Eddie Paynter. Yet none of the six was able to retain his Test place for longer than the space of half-a-dozen games.

With Brown and Ward the reason is fairly easy to deduce. They were very competent professional batsmen who had to face fierce competition from the 'gifted' amateurs of the 'Golden Age'. In England that competition restricted their opportunities; overseas their abundant talent had freer range. Albert Ward of Lancashire took over from Dick Barlow as the county's sheet-anchor batsman. A tall right-hander with a long reach, he adopted sound defence as the basis of his play. Nevertheless, he drove well once he was set and his style had a purity which prevented him from being dull to watch. Ward was also a fine fieldsman in the deep, with one of the safest pair of hands in the game. It was common practice for the next man in to pick up his bat whenever a skier went in Ward's direction. He always took such catches level with his eyes, as if he were plucking the ball from the sky. The Lancastrian made his debut in the Second Test of 1893. He had been selected for the first match at Lord's but his county begged him off. His debut commenced with England in the comfortable position of 200 for 3 and Ward contributed a sound 55 to a stand of 103 for the 4th wicket with Arthur Shrewsbury. England went on to their then record home score of 483. Australia collapsed in their first knock and eventually succumbed by an innings, so Ward went from the Oval to Old Trafford well satisfied with his efforts. In front of his own supporters, he scored 13 and 0. This could well have brought his Test career to a premature end, but he continued his good county form in 1894 and was invited by Andrew Stoddart to tour Australia that winter.

On that tour Ward was joined by J.T. Brown of Yorkshire. Brown only made the trip because Bobby Abel had declined the invitation. The two pros averaged over 40 in the Tests, heading the list in front of Stoddart and MacLaren, and making the major batting contributions towards winning the rubber. In the First Test at Sydney Ward achieved the distinction of top-scoring in each innings. Australia led off with 586 and, though Ward's 75 steered England to a reply of 325, they forced the follow-on. The Lancastrian did even better in the second knock, scoring 117. He and Brown added 102 for the 3rd wicket, the Yorkshireman passing his fifty, and they took England well along the road towards making the Aussies bat again. Rain in the early hours of the last day gave England a chance to snatch victory from the jaws of defeat; and they managed it by 10 runs. Without Ward's double effort, they wouldn't have had a hope. The next Test, also won by England, saw a couple of workmanlike knocks by Ward of 30 and 41. He failed in the third and fourth games, Australia taking both to square the rubber and set up a grandstand finish at Melbourne.

Meanwhile Jack Brown was not doing as well as his Roses rival. After four Tests his total was only 173 from 8 innings, whereas Ward had 294 under his belt. In the decider neither got beyond the thirties in their first innings, and the amateurs MacLaren and Stoddart had to lead the fight back against Australia's 414. Eventually England were set 297 to win. The visitors lost 2 wickets for 28, then Brown, with rain threatening, joined Ward. Lancashire defended while Yorkshire attacked. Brown square-drove his first ball and hooked his second for a boundary apiece. He hammered 51 in 28 minutes, still the fastest half ton in these Tests, and went on to score 140 superlative runs in 2 hours 25 minutes. When the Yorkshireman was caught at slip, he had made

Raman Subba Row (Northants.) played 5 Tests in 1961, averaging 46.80 from 10 innings. *(Northamptonshire Cricket Club)*

J.T. Brown (Yorks.) *(above)* and Albert Ward (Lancs.) *(right).*
Brown played 8 Tests in 1894-6, scoring 470 runs at an average of
36.15. Ward played 7 Tests in the same period, scoring 487 runs at
an average of 37.46. They shared a partnership of 210 at
Melbourne in 1895. Both were professionals discarded to make
way for 'gifted' amateurs.

F.R. Brown (Northants.) captained England in 1950-1 in Australia. His batting (260 runs at an average of 26.00) and bowling (26 wickets at 23.81) were achieved after the age of forty.

his runs out of 210 added for the 3rd wicket, two thirds of the total. Ward, whose stout defence had proved the perfect foil to Brown's onslaught battled on towards his own century. With MacLaren stroking the ball well it became problematic whether Albert would reach his personal target before England won the game. In the event he was bowled by Harry Trott for 93, 19 runs short of victory. England won comfortably, but it would not have been possible without the pros' great stand; at that time the highest Test partnership and England's first to exceed 200.

Ward and Brown probably anticipated lengthy Test careers after this triumph, but the selectors thought otherwise. Brown played twice in 1896, scoring 86 in 4 innings and losing his place to the overrated Captain Wynyard at the Oval. He made one further appearance at Leeds in 1899, scoring 27 and 14 not out in a drawn match. Five years later he was dead. If Jack Brown's treatment by the selectors subsequent to 1894-5 was somewhat grudging, Albert Ward's was downright scandalous. The Lancastrian was never chosen again after his return from Australia. Those selectors who preferred Billy Gunn to Ward for the First Test of 1896 were guilty of ingratitude to a deserving player. Ward's 487 runs were gathered in 7 Tests at an average of 37.46. Jack Brown's figures were slightly inferior, 470 from 8 Tests at 36.15. Stoddart could have done with both of them for his second tour in 1897-8. He could have left J.R. Mason and Ted Wainwright at home then and avoided the 4-1 drubbing that accrued. Still the two professionals always had that triumphant partnership at Melbourne to relish.

One of the most underrated bats in Test history was Charles Philip Mead of Hampshire. Mead laboured under several handicaps. His unattractive left-hand batting, though based on a very sound defensive technique, compared unfavourably with the flowing stroke-play of his great contemporary Frank Woolley. The heavily-built Mead was not a particularly active fielder, neither did he bowl regularly. Woolley was a first-class man at both. In addition Hampshire was not a fashionable county and had little influence on selection committees. Consequently Mead played in only 7 Tests against the Aussies, spread over 17 years. His first opportunity came in 1911-12. Mead, two months older than Woolley, lined up with his rival for the first 4 Tests. The Hampshire man was given the traditional left-hander's spot of number 5, while Woolley, regarded as an all-rounder, occupied number 8. Mead failed to seize his chance. Three matches produced only 84 runs and he was dropped to number 8 for the fourth game. He scored 21 and promptly lost his place for the last Test. On the return to England, Mead was — quite rightly on his form — omitted from the Triangular series of 1912. World War I broke out two years later.

When cricket re-started after the Great War Mead was 32. Nevertheless his form was good, as demonstrated by three useful innings against the Australian Imperial Forces team in 1919. Yet Makepeace, Hendren and Russell were preferred for the 1920-21 trip to the Antipodes. Hendren and Russell were only marginally younger than the Hampshire crack, while Makepeace was 6 years older, a real veteran. Mead had good reason to feel aggrieved by his omission. The 1920-21 side took a 5-0 drubbing. The following season in England, Mead was at last recalled to the colours. No doubt through the influence of his county skipper, Lionel Tennyson, now leading England, the left-hander played at Old Trafford and the Oval. Both matches were rain-affected and resulted in draws. Mead's contributions were a painfully slow 47 at Manchester and a much livelier 182 not out at the Oval. In this latter innings Mead actually scored 109 before lunch on the last day, but the session lasted 2½ hours rather than the normal 2. He looked set for a double century, but Tennyson declared when England passed 400 with 8 wickets down. As it was, Mead's 182 was the highest individual score for England in England up to that time, a record that lasted until Eddie Paynter beat it in 1938.

After this fine innings Mead could have been excused for taking his place on the 1924-5 trip for granted. If he did, his awakening was rude in the extreme. His dependability was discarded in favour of the more flamboyant left-hand style of the young Percy Chapman. Perhaps that was forgiveable, for Mead was 13 years older than the Kentish amateur. What was less forgivable was the inclusion of 'Dodge' Whysall the Notts. batsman in the team, for Mead's record was far superior. Whysall's potential as reserve stumper must have clouded the selectors' thinking. In 1926 Mead, then nearly forty, was hardly considered. He missed that series too, and then must have been astounded to be invited to tour with Chapman's team in 1928. That great side was so strong in batting that the Hampshire man was only used in the First Test. He scored 8 of England's first innings 521, and then helped himself to an easy 73 against a depleted Australian attack when England batted again nearly 400 in front. It was his Test match swansong. Thus Philip Mead batted 10 times against Australia over a period of 17 years. He scored 415 runs, averaging 51.87, a very imposing record. The selectors should have sent him Down Under in 1920 and, probably, 1924, and he should have played throughout the 1921 rubber at home. A prolific left-hander, Phil Mead was a batsman whose talents were set at discount by short-sighted selectors.

A.C. 'Jack' Russell played some fine cricket for Essex during the twenties. Born in 1887, he was one of many cricketers who lost some prime years to the Great War. He was 33 when he went to Australia with Johnny Douglas' side. He owed his selection, at least partly, to the fact that his county skipper was leading England. An opening batsman, Russell partnered Jack Hobbs in the First Test at Sydney. He made 0, bowled by Charlie Kelleway first ball, and 5. In the Second Test he was relegated to number five and made the same scores. It was touch and go whether Russell would retain his place; he did so as number six and at Adelaide came good. England, two down in the series were 161 for 4 in reply to Australia's 354, when Russell joined Woolley. They added 89 for the 5th wicket. With Woolley out, Russell started another long partnership with his captain, Douglas. While J.W.H.T. grafted, Russell went on to an almost faultless hundred. They added 124 (Douglas 60) and Russell's only blemish was an escape from a stumping when his tally was 52. With his captain gone and England in the lead Russell steered the tail into squeezing a further 73 runs from the Australian bowling. His century took only 3 hours and he was undefeated with 135 at the end of the innings. England, 93 ahead, failed to contain the Aussies' second innings. Set 494 to win they managed 370, with Russell contributing 59 after Hobbs had set them going with a hundred before lunch on the last day. Russell and Patsy Hendren made a brave stand, but Mailey bowled both of them and then wrapped up the tail. England, now 3 down, kissed the rubber goodbye. Jack missed the next Test with an injured thumb. He returned at Sydney, where he made 19 and 35. Third in the Test averages behind Hobbs and Douglas, Russell must have expected to keep his Test place for the return series in England.

1921 was, as we have seen, a boom year for Test hopefuls. Russell was left on the sidelines while it seemed every possible alternative batsman was selected in turn to play. By the time the Fourth Test arrived England had tried almost every permutation and had lost the rubber. Russell was recalled at Old Trafford to take the place of a Hobbs stricken by appendicitis. The first day was lost to rain. England won the toss and batted, making 362 for 4. The Essex man's contribution was 101, 81 of which accrued by indulging his penchant for leg-side strokes. He was missed twice (at 6 and 86) but became the first Englishman to make a ton in that sorry series. It took him four hours to compile. Retained at the Oval, Russell repeated his feat. After making 13 in the first innings, when there was some doubt about the catch which Oldfield made to dismiss him, Russell got his revenge by plundering the Australians' occasional bowlers. The match petered out in a draw, but Russell managed to complete his century (102 not out) just before the close of play. That game was Russell's last fling. His 6 Tests had produced 474 runs, with 3 centuries, and an average of 52.66. By the time of the next tour Russell, like Mead, was 37, but his county form was still good and he would surely have been as good a bet as Whysall or J.L. Bryan of Kent who both made the trip. Veteran professional batsmen, particularly if their fielding is no more than adequate, are always at risk when young tyros are available.

A contemporary of Mead and Russell was Ernest Tyldesley, the Lancashire batsman. 16 years younger than his famous brother, J.T., Ernest was considered by some good judges to have been the better bat. Against Australia however Tyldesley was never given sufficient opportunities to prove his case. Like so many others Tyldesley played his first game for England against Warwick Armstrong's Australians. At Trent Bridge Jack Gregory dismissed Donald Knight in the fifth over of the match. Tyldesley came in to face his first ball in Test cricket, was beaten by the pace and played on as it broke back viciously. This was a chastening start to his Test career, but bad comes before and worse remains behind. The worse arrived in the second innings when a bouncer hit the Lancastrian on the jaw as he tried to hook and felled him. Before this calamity Tyldesley had defended staunchly for over half an hour, scoring a mere 7 runs, but showing signs of coping successfully with the extreme pace of Gregory and McDonald. Poor Tyldesley was knocked cold by the blow; it took some time to bring him round. He was helped to the pavilion by the sympathetic Australians, only then to discover that he was out: the ball had dropped from his jaw on to his wicket. Tyldesley was one of the first victims of the 1921 selectors' panic policy. He was omitted at Lord's and Headingley, but with the series already lost got his second chance at his Old Trafford home ground. England had the better of this rain ruined game, and Tyldesley seized his opportunity. Batting at number five, he appeared when England was 217 for 3 wickets; he was still there with 78 fine runs to his credit when Tennyson declared. Tyldesley and Percy Fender added an unbeaten 102 in their 5th wicket stand. Retained at the Oval, Tyldesley scored 39 in his only innings, so that he emerged from the rubber with an average of 41 for his 4 knocks. He looked a safe bet for the number 3 position for some years to come.

Like Mead's and Russell's, his hopes were dashed. When Gilligan's men set out for Australia in 1924-5, the only Tyldesley in the party was the rotund Richard. Probably Ernest's age was a deciding factor. He was then 35, and the selectors plumped for new blood. Consequently Tyldesley had to wait until 1926 before he had another chance to meet the Aussies. Even then he had to wait through three drawn games before he was chosen for the Old Trafford match. After some uncertain moments against Mailey, Tyldesley settled down to a top-scoring 81 in England's unfinished reply to Australia's 335. Rain spoiled this game too, and the teams went to the Oval for the Ashes decider. They went without Tyldesley. Once again the selectors rejected him after he had played an innings of some worth. England, seeking the Ashes, decided that an extra bowler, Geary, would be needed and Tyldesley was the unlucky batsman who had to make way. The Ashes were won, but the Lancastrian had every right to feel aggrieved.

By no stretch of the imagination could Tyldesley have expected to be a serious contender for a place in the 1928-9 side. He was 39, rising 40, when Chapman's side was chosen and a number of young batsmen (Hammond, Jardine, Leyland etc.) had come to the fore in the meantime. To everyone's surprise, including, probably, his own Tyldesley was selected for his only trip to Australia. The selectors had at long last decided to dispense with Hearne and Woolley as front line batsmen. Their replacements however were the almost equally ancient Mead and Tyldesley. The two veterans found themselves in competition with Maurice Leyland for the last batting place in the Test side. In the event each of them played in one Test on the tour. Tyldesley's appearance was delayed until the final Test at Melbourne. With Sutcliffe and Chapman under the weather, the Lancastrian played in England's only defeat of the series, scoring 31 and 21. It was the last of his 5 appearances against Australia and he left the Test scene with the very respectable average of 42.83 for his 257 runs. The chief stumbling block to Tyldesley in his quest for a regular place must have been Patsy Hendren. The Middlesex man was almost ever-present throughout the Twenties and it was probably his sharper fielding which clinched the issue between them. Tyldesley, Mead and Russell were three fine batsmen whose potential was never fully developed by England.

A modern batsman, whose talents were largely wasted by mistaken selectorial policies, was Bob Barber of Warwickshire. Barber, a left-handed opening bat, had had a somewhat mixed career prior to his debut at the Oval in 1964. Captain of Lancashire in 1960 and 1961, Barber had left that county after an uneasy period during which the county committee had demoted him in favour of the virtually untried J.R. Blackledge. He joined Warwickshire in 1963, and comparatively late in the 1964 season Barber hit the headlines by hammering a hundred before lunch for his new county against Bobby Simpson's tourists. At the Oval Barber scored a couple of twenties. In the following season his energetic method of opening the innings complemented the much more stolid style of Geoffrey Boycott. They both travelled to Australia as members of Mike Smith's 1965-6 team.

Barber began that tour moderately at Brisbane and Melbourne with 87 runs in 3 innings, and he finished even less spectacularly with 56 in 4 innings at Adelaide and Melbourne. But in between, at Sydney, he played one of the greatest individual innings in the history of these contests. England won the toss and batted. With Boycott playing the support role, Barber set about the Australian attack in unequivocal fashion. 93 for 0 at lunch-time, they stretched their stand to 234 in four hours before Boycott gave a return catch to leg-spinner Philpott. Boycott's share was 84, by which time Barber had completed a scintillating century and was well on the way towards 150. The Warwickshire man's ton occupied only 190 minutes and he went on to 185 in 5 hours. When he became the second English wicket to fall the score had reached 303 and Barber had played the most dominating innings by an English batsman in post-war Ashes games. He batted without giving a chance, showing exceptional strength in his driving and making room to indulge some wristy cutting. Australia wilted under Barber's onslaught and when he was finally bowled by Neil Hawke, England was firmly established on the way to victory. The Australians went down by an innings and the man chiefly responsible was Bob Barber.

Sadly Barber played only once more against Australia. By the first match of 1968 he had been dropped down the batting order to number 6. At Old Trafford he scored 20 and 46 in a match where England batted badly and lost by a hefty margin. Barber was one of five players axed for the Lord's game and he was never recalled. The left-hander's 7 matches against Australia produced 447 runs at an average of 37.25. But for that brilliant 185, these figures would look a good deal less impressive, so perhaps the experts who considered him too impetuous and erratic were right. Nevertheless Barber, like Gilbert Jessop, had established his place in cricketing history.

Alan Lamb, Northamptonshire's South African born batsman, made his debut for England in the 1982-3 series. He started well at Perth with 46 and 56, followed with 72 and 12 at Brisbane, 82 and 8 at Adelaide, 83 and 26 at Melbourne, and failed at Sydney. 414 runs in 10 innings constituted an impressive beginning and this fine cricketer will probably graduate to the ranks of the star batsmen in the fairly near future.

In the years after the Great War several fine cricketers figured in prominent supporting roles in Warwick Armstrong's all-conquering sides. One such was Clarence 'Nip' Pellew of South Australia. Pellew, 27 years old when he made his debut at Sydney in 1920, had already lost some of his best years to the War. Blessed with a big match temperament, he promptly set about making up for lost time. In the Australian side of 1920 that wasn't easy for an unproven young batsman. Pellew found himself at number 8 in the list with every prospect of not being needed to display his wares very often. He started modestly with 36 and 16. The second match at Melbourne saw him move one place up the order. When he went to the wicket, Australia's tally was a moderate 220 for 5. By the end of that first day the score had advanced to 282 for 6, Pellew not out 33. On the second morning, the Australians lost Ryder immediately, only for Pellew to be joined by the belligerent Jack Gregory. In just over two hours they added 173 sparkling runs, causing the English attack to wilt in the extreme heat. 'Nip''s century arrived in exactly three hours, a superb maiden effort. Gregory too completed his ton and Australia went on to win by an innings. The next Test, on Pellew's home ground, found the South Australian continuing his fine form. He was run out in the first innings for 35 of Australia's reasonable total of 354. England, for the only time in the series, led on first innings, but the Aussies set that right with a massive 582 in their second knock. Pellew plundered tired bowling towards the end of the fourth day, and on the fifth became the third century maker of the innings. When he departed with 104 to his credit, the Australian total had advanced to 477. 149 runs accrued while Pellew was at the wicket. For much of the time he was partnering the monumentally patient Charlie Kelleway, so it was no great surprise to find Pellew collecting 84 of their stand of 126 for the 6th wicket. 'Nip' raced to his ton by taking 16 off an over by Harry Howell. At this stage of his career Pellew seemed set to become a permanent batting star in

Australia's firmament.

Sadly his career had already reached its zenith. He made only 12 at Melbourne, and then had the mortifying experience of being dropped to make room for Charlie Macartney who had missed the three previous Tests through illness. Why Pellew should have been discarded instead of either Johnny Taylor or Jack Ryder, both of whom had far inferior batting records, is very hard to fathom. Possibly the selectors shunned the difficulties of omitting Taylor from a Test on his home ground of Sydney, and of confronting Warwick Armstrong with the news that his Victorian colleague, Ryder, should be dropped. The South Australian was probably more easily expended. Nevertheless Pellew was in the ranks when Armstrong's team sailed for England. There his batting disappointed. He played in all 5 Tests, making 43 at Lord's and 52 at Leeds, and finishing well down the averages. He played for Australia only once more, against South Africa on the voyage home. Despite his disappointing tour, Pellew's haul against England was 478 runs from 9 Tests, averaging just under 40. Allied to these sound batting credentials was his deserved reputation as an outfielder. A dashing, happy man, his chasing, gathering and returning of the ball was fast, clean and accurate. Sixty years later he is still recalled as one of Australia's two or three greatest men in the deep. When this run-saving ability is added to his run-making, it is extremely hard to understand why his Test career was so short.

The bowlers who enjoyed uninterrupted, but short-lived, success in these games are only four in number. Two Englishmen, John Gunn and Bob Appleyard, and two Australians, Jack Iverson and Jim Higgs, achieved respectable averages. Indeed in Iverson's case the figures were extremely impressive.

First in chronological order came John Gunn. Gunn, a member of the famous Nottinghamshire family, toured Australia with Archie MacLaren's side in 1901-2. He occupied a minor place in the great Archie's strategy during the first two Tests, but the break-down of Sydney Barnes enforced a change of tactics for the rest of the rubber. In the Adelaide Test Gunn bowled 64 overs of his left-hand medium-pace stuff, more than any other Englishman, and captured 8 wickets. His 5 for 76 in the first innings was a tail-wrapping operation, but he collected 3 good wickets in the second before Australia's victory was complete. Gunn continued the good work with 3 more victims at Sydney, and 6 in the final Test at Melbourne. England lost both games, but Gunn had the pleasure of coming second in the bowling averages to the great Barnes. His 17 wickets cost only 360 runs, a much better return than Colin Blythe, the principal left-hand bowler among the tourists, achieved. Gunn also claimed a wicket every 51 deliveries whereas Blythe required 58 for his. Unfortunately for the Nottinghamshire man, he not only had Blythe to contend with back in England, but also Yorkshire's Hirst and Rhodes. Consequently, he played no Tests in 1902. Omitted from Warner's 1903-4 side, Gunn had probably ceased to dream of Test matches, when, in 1905, he was chosen for the Trent Bridge game. He bowled only 6 overs in a match which was won by Bosanquet's googlies. The selectors promptly discarded Gunn, for good this time. John Gunn's 18 Test wickets averaged 21.50. If the competition from Rhodes & Co. had not been so fierce he could well have extended his Test career and become a permanent member of the English attack. He certainly bowled very tightly in an outclassed side on the 1901-2 tour.

Another bowler who might have been great was Bob Appleyard of Yorkshire. Appleyard, a purveyor of seamers and off breaks at a lively pace, had captured 200 wickets in 1951, his first full campaign in first class cricket. Unhappily his health was not good and his county appearances in 1952 and 1953 were minimal. He reappeared in 1954, again topping the Yorkshire averages and he was selected for Hutton's tour that winter, gaining precedence over Jim Laker. Down Under Appleyard performed well enough to justify his selection. His 4 Tests brought him 11 wickets, 3 in each innings at Adelaide being his best effort. Significantly his average was marginally better than Frank Tyson's, though he only bowled half the overs that Tyson did. All his victims came from the top half of Australia's batting order, eloquent testimony to the quality of his economical bowling. On his return to England Appleyard ran into more spells of illness and injury. He played just once more against the Aussies, at Trent Bridge in 1956, when he captured 2 more wickets to bring his record versus Australia to 13 scalps at 21 apiece. By 1959 Appleyard's cricket career was over. He had achieved the almost unique distinction of never being on a losing side against Australia and he had shown that, with better health, he had the talent to take his place among England's greatest bowlers.

Jimmy Higgs, Australia's most recent leg-spin and googly merchant, captured 19 English wickets in his 6 Tests. The whole 19 were taken during the 1978-79 series, when Higgs provided unexpectedly strong support to the pace duo of Hogg and Hurst. In that rubber the

Australian 'Reserves' were outclassed with the bat and in the field by Brearley's competent team, but their three main bowlers lost little in comparison with the English. Higgs, who was probably fortunate to be picked in the light of the current negative thinking about the expensiveness of leg-spinners, took his wickets at a cost of 24.63 each; quite an economical rate. His first Test, at Brisbane, yielded no wickets in 18 overs, so he was left out of the side at Perth, where conditions were expected to favour the quicker bowlers. Recalled at Melbourne, his home ground, Higgs picked up 3 for 61 in 35 overs in the match, good figures for a stock bowler, let alone a leg-spinner. His economy was an appreciable factor in Australia's only win in the rubber. At Sydney the Victorian made his mark much more emphatically. 3 for 42 in the first innings was augmented by a marathon bowl (59 overs and 6 balls) in the second. Higgs captured 5 for 148, mopping up England's tail in the process. 3 for 84 at Adelaide and 5 for 81 at Sydney completed Higgs' haul for the rubber. He looked well-established in the side, despite the prospective competition from the Packerites on their return to the fold. Higgs did play in the Sydney Test of 1979-80. Unimaginative captaincy by the seam-obsessed Greg Chappell restricted the Victorian to one over in the whole match. He was promptly dropped from the Melbourne game and he also missed out on selection for 1980 and 1981 visits to England and the 1982-3 home rubber. Whether he will have a chance to improve his record against England is debatable, but Jim Higgs has already done sufficient to prove himself Australia's best leg-break bowler since Richie Benaud.

Last, but best, of this small group of bowlers comes Jack Iverson of Victoria. Iverson, the mystery bowler of the nineteen fifties, played in only one series against England. He was 35 years old when he appeared in the ranks against Freddie Brown's side. Iverson a tall, burly, ungainly man had developed an unusual bowling grip while experimenting with ping-pong balls during the years of World War II. His technique involved doubling the middle finger of his right hand underneath the ball and then propelling the ball from his hand by flicking that finger forward. In developing this talent, Iverson learned to make the ball break either way — a daunting prospect for batsmen who were generally unable to read his hand. Additionally Iverson had excellent control of length and direction, so, all in all, he was a formidable proposition. Iverson's role in 1950-51 was to provide relief to and contrast from the Aussies' main attack, the pace of Lindwall, Miller and Bill Johnston. This he achieved admirably. At Brisbane he was not required in the first innings. In the second he accounted for 4 wickets at a cost of only 43 and was the prime element in England's defeat. In the next game, at Melbourne, he helped himself to 6 for 73 in the match and bowled 38 overs in doing it. England went down again, Iverson sharing the bowling honours with 'Big Bill' Johnston. Then came the Sydney match which decided the series. England started with 290 (Iverson 0 for 25) and Australia replied with 426 against an English attack depleted by injuries. By the fourth day the wicket was wearing and Iverson ripped the heart from England's second knock. He disposed of Hutton, Simpson and Washbrook for 43 between them, and, after a brief rest, he came back to finish the match by clean bowling Brown, Bedser and Warr. His 6 scalps cost a mere 27 runs in 19.4 overs of excellent, mainly off-spin, bowling. The last two Tests provided the Victorian with 5 more victims. Iverson completed his only rubber with 21 wickets at the amazingly low cost of 15.23 apiece. He had added a further dimension to an already powerful Australian attack. Iverson was a Nine Day Wonder. As Australian cricketers go, he was already ancient in years. Since he was also a poor field and a negligible bat, his Test place depended on his bowling skill alone. Before the next tour of England fell due the Victorian had become dissatisfied with his form and retired from top-class cricket. All the indications were that, at his best, he would have reaped a harvest on English pitches. Jack Iverson, with an earlier start to his career, could well have challenged the records of the best.

Two all-rounders remain. Both were fine cricketers who attained a high standard of success in the limited Test match careers allowed to them by importunate selectors. The first of them to appear in Ashes games was the Queenslander, Colin McCool. McCool's debut at Brisbane in 1946 was not quite perfect. He went to the wicket with Australia's score in this first post-war Test at 428 for 4. McCool plundered a demoralised attack for 95 scintillating runs before he put his leg in front of a Doug Wright delivery. Like Arthur Chipperfield in 1934, McCool got within a whisker of putting his name in the record books at the first time of asking. McCool's first opportunity for purveying his leg-spin bowling came in the Second Test at Sydney. His first Test were the illustrious ones of Denis Compton and Wally Hammond. That put England in the parlous position of 99 for 4 and later McCool bagged Edrich. England, out for 255, then fielded while Australia ran together a little matter of 659. In England's first innings McCool, despite his illustrious victims, had been outshone by off-spinner Ian Johnson. The tourists' second knock was the Queenslander's all the way. He bowled 32.4 overs to take 5 for 109 and win the match by an innings. Having established his credentials with ball as well as bat, McCool added further to his stature at Melbourne. For the first time in the rubber Australia was in comparative difficulty at 188 for 5. At that juncture McCool went to the wicket and, though another batsman quickly fell, he took complete charge and steered Australia to 255 for 6 by close of play. Two wickets fell quickly the following day, but McCool, striking cleanly off the back foot, scored 64 of a 9th wicket stand of 83 with Bruce Dooland. The Queenslander completed his century in the process and was undefeated with 104 when the innings ended. McCool continued the good work with 43 in his second knock and he also picked up 3 more wickets, though England scrambled a draw.

At this stage of his short career, McCool was one of the brightest of Australia's new stars. He failed at Adelaide; but in the final Test at Sydney it was again his googly bowling which destroyed England's second innings and set up an Australian victory. McCool's 5 for 44 in 22 overs set the seal on one of the most successful all-round sequences in Test history. His final returns were 272 runs at 54.40 per innings and 18 wickets at a cost of 27.27, outstanding figures in one of Australia's outstanding teams. McCool was an automatic choice for the 1948 trip to England. Sadly he was far from fit and this affected his batting. Then an injury to his spinning finger prevented him from compensating with his bowling. By the time he had regained his form, the Test side had been settled and McCool was unable to command a place again. He gradually faded from the first-class game after this tour, only to re-appear some seasons later when he joined Somerset. McCool, at his best, merited a place in Bradman's Test side and his disappearance in 1948 brought a promising career to a sad end.

Our final Shooting Star is Freddie Brown of Cambridge University, Surrey and Northants. Brown led a sub-standard team in 1950-51 and inspired it by personal example. His excellent all-round figures in that series clearly demonstrated that, even at 40 years old, the skipper was of real Test class. Why F.R. was excluded from pre-war sides against the Aussies is a mystery. As a youngster of 22 Brown toured with Jardine's team, but Tommy Mitchell of Derbyshire was preferred for the Tests. Brown's strengths were an aggressive, hard-hitting approach to batting, and an ability to bowl either steady medium-paced swingers or slower, flighted leg-breaks and googlies. But above all he was a fighting captain. Though his side lost the rubber 4-1, they could, with a better rub of the green, have won it 3-2.

Brown, as a player, took some time to find his feet. The First Test involved a couple of freak declarations which set up a thrilling finish but gave Brown little personal satisfaction. As he had been neither first, nor second choice for the tourists' leader, it soon became a pressing matter for him to establish his playing credentials. Brown's chance came at Melbourne. Australia had been dismissed for a mediocre 194. England then collapsed to 54 for 5. If ever a captain's innings was needed, this was the occasion; Brown duly obliged. While Trevor Bailey defended, the burly skipper played a rousing innings of 62 in two hours, featuring some full-blooded, straight driving. After Bailey was out he received more support from Godfrey Evans, and England gained a slender lead. In Australia's second innings Brown the bowler took over. After the front-line bowlers had held Australia to 126 for 4, Brown brought his medium-paced seamers into play. In a thirty minute spell either side of the tea interval he accounted for Hassett, Loxton, Lindwall and Tallon. The Aussies were reduced to 156 for 8. Brown's wickets cost him 26 runs only in a very tight 12 over spell. Despite requiring only 179 to win, the English batsmen made a mess of it and lost a match which their skipper's bowling had placed within their grasp.

Brown, an apostle of the John Wayne principle, 'Hell! *That* was yesterday! What're we going to do to-day?', set about winning the Third Test. He lost that one too, but not before he had contributed another aggressive innings as well as a marathon bowling feat. In two and a half hours Brown hammered 79 runs (9 boundaries), the top score in England's 290. Unfortunately two of England's bowlers, Bailey and Wright, were injured in the latter stages of that innings. This threw a hefty burden on the rest of the attack and Brown toiled through 44 overs while Australia ran up 426. The captain's 4 wickets for 153 were the result of determination, persistence and perspiration. As a batsman Brown had now shot his bolt. No more exhilarating barrages ensued, but he still had some bowling to do. At Adelaide he did little of note while England went four down, but he found some hidden reserves for the final Test. Australia won the toss and had 100 on the board with only one wicket down. Then Brown, though handicapped by a shoulder injured in a motor accident, broke the back of the innings. His medium-pacers dismissed Morris, Harvey and Miller and he later got rid of Hassett and Iverson. Australia totalled 217, Brown 5 for 49 in 18 overs; fine bowling. England this time made no mistake and gained her first post-war victory over the Aussies.

Freddie's Test career was not quite over. In 1953, he was called up for the Lord's Test under Len Hutton's captaincy. A couple of twenties, plus 4 for 82 with his leg breaks in Australia's second knock were useful contributions to saving a game which was frequently tilted in the Australians' favour. Then, at the age of 43, Brown retired from Test cricket.

260 runs, average 26.00, plus 22 wickets at 23.81 represented Brown's final record against Australia. When it is remembered that the whole of that tally was compiled after Freddy had passed the age of 40, this short career must rank as one of the minor *tours de force* in the history of the Ashes.

Four hundred and ten 'Sundry Extras' have now been appraised. Most of them were extremely lucky to be selected; a few, less than 10%, were unlucky not to become regular members of the sides. Certainly Test honours have been profusely scattered by the selection panels over the years. Nevertheless two quite redoubtable sides could be selected from these four hundred and ten lesser lights. A Test Match in Elysium between these two teams (in batting order) would be well worth watching:

England: C.F. Walters, A.C. Russell, R.E. Foster, K.S. Duleepsinjhi, D. Steele,. G. Brown (Wicket-keeper), F.R. Brown (Captain), H. ('Sailor') Young, W. Brearley, F. Martin, F. Morley.
Australia: C. Bannerman, A. Jackson, R. Gregory, C. McCool, B. Shepherd, C. Pellew (Captain), A. Trott, B. Barnett (Wicket-keeper), R. Massie, T. Kendall, J. Iverson.

Steele just gets the verdict over Phil Mead because of his better fielding; while 'Nip' Pellew, who captained South Australia in his time, seems the likeliest skipper for Australia.

England's first six and Australia's first four all have batting averages of 50 plus in these games, while Shepherd and Pellew averaged more than forty and Albert Trott tops the lot with 102.50. In bowling, Young, Martin, Morley, Massie, Kendall and Iverson took their wickets at a cost of less than 20 runs each. Brearley, Trott and F.R. Brown captured theirs at just above the 20 mark. England's fielding looks weaker, but their attack is more varied: fast right (Brearley), fast left (Morley), medium pace (Young), slow left hand (Martin), and leg-spin (F.R. Brown). The Aussies with Kendall (fast left), Massie (medium pace swervers), Trott (off-breaks) and Iverson (off-breaks plus 'funny ones') would have to work harder for their wickets, though Colin McCool's leg-breaks and googlies (1947 vintage) could tip the scale in their favour.

Many selectors, beset by the difficulties of choosing balanced sides for their various eras, would probably be only too pleased to nominate the above teams to battle for the Ashes. Yet 13 of these players were rejected after their initial selection — some of them in cavalier, not to unkind, fashion. Foster, Duleep, Morley, Bannerman and Jackson were laid low by illness, while F.R. Brown, Iverson, Gregory and Barnett had their careers truncated by World War II. If they could all come together at their various peaks what a battle royal would ensue!

STATISTICAL APPENDIX

SUMMARY OF THE PLAYERS

ENGLAND				Glamorgan		3
				Leicestershire		2
Middlesex		31		Ireland		1
Lancashire		28				
Yorkshire		28		Total		233
Surrey		21				
Kent		19				
Nottinghamshire		15		*AUSTRALIA*		
Gloucestershire		14				
Sussex		13		Victoria		74
Essex		12		New South Wales		50
Northamptonshire		12		South Australia		24
Warwickshire		12		Queensland		17
Worcestershire		8		Western Australia		10
Derbyshire		6		Tasmania		2
Hampshire		4				
Somerset		4		Total		177

One Test	71	53		Assorted All Rounders	4	7
Two Tests	45	33		Second Choice Stumpers	8	3
Three Tests	29	31		Solid Workmen	14	13
Four Tests	23	12		Shooting Stars	13	4
Bankrupt Batsmen	20	12				
Bountiful Bowlers	6	9		Total	233	177

I. One Test Appearance: English Batting

Batsmen	County	Debut	Age	Inns.	N.O.	Runs	H.S.	Av.	Ct.	St.
Macaulay, G G.	Yorks.	1926	28	1	0	76	76	76.00	-	-
Allott,P.	Lancs.	1981	24	2	1	66	52	66.00	-	-
Wood,A	Yorks.	1938	39	1	0	53	53	53.00	3	-
Penn, F.	Kent	1880	29	2	1	50	27*	50.00	-	-
Prideaux, R.M.	Northants.	1968	28	2	0	66	64	33.00	-	-
King, J.H.	Leics.	1909	38	2	0	64	60	32.00	-	-
Absolom, C.A.	Kent	1879	32	2	0	58	52	29.00	-	-
Shuter, J.	Surrey	1888	33	1	0	28	28	28.00	-	-
Kinneir, S.P.	Warwicks.	1911	40	2	0	52	30	26.00	-	-
Dipper, A.E.	Gloucs.	1921	35	2	0	51	40	25.50	-	-
Wellard, A.W.	Somerset	1938	36	2	0	42	38	21.00	-	-
Schultz, S.S.	Lancs.	1879	21	2	1	20	20	20.00	-	-
Holmes, P.	Yorks.	1921	34	2	0	38	30	19.00	-	-
Gay, L.H.	Somerset	1894	23	2	0	37	33	18.50	3	1
Keeton, W.W.	Notts.	1934	29	2	0	37	25	18.50	-	-
Grace, E.M	Gloucs.	1880	38	2	0	36	36	18.00	1	-
Christopherson, S.	Kent	1884	22	1	0	17	17	17.00	-	-
Cranston, J.	Gloucs.	1890	31	2	0	31	16	15.50	1	-
Hardinge, H.T.W.	Kent	1921	35	2	0	30	25	15.00	-	-
Vernon, G.F.	Middlesex	1882	26	2	1	14	11*	14.00	-	-
Newham, W.	Sussex	1887	26	2	0	26	17	13.00	-	-

continued

Batsmen	County	Debut	Age	Inns.	N.O.	Runs	H.S.	Av.	Ct.	St.
Gibb, P.A.	Yorks.	1946	33	2	0	24	13	12.00	1	-
Taylor, K.	Yorks.	1964	28	2	0	24	15	12.00	-	-
Royle, V.P.	Lancs.	1879	24	2	0	21	18	10.50	2	-
Coxon, A.	Yorks.	1948	32	2	0	19	19	9.50	-	-
Tate, F.W.	Sussex	1902	35	2	1	9	5*	9.00	2	-
Evans, A.J.	Kent	1921	32	2	0	18	14	9.00	-	-
Wood, H.	Surrey	1888	33	1	0	8	8	8.00	1	1
Durston, F.J.	Middlesex	1921	27	2	1	8	6*	8.00	-	-
Jackson, L.	Derbys.	1961	40	1	0	8	8	8.00	1	-
Pocock, P.	Surrey	1968	21	2	0	16	10	8.00	2	-
Warren, A.R.	Derbys.	1905	30	1	0	7	7	7.00	1	-
Fishlock, L.B.	Surrey	1947	40	2	0	14	14	7.00	1	-
Hone, L.	Ireland	1879	25	2	0	13	7	6.50	2	-
Wynyard, E.G.	Hants.	1896	35	2	0	13	10	6.50	-	-
Hayes, E.	Surrey	1909	32	2	0	13	9	6.50	-	-
Parker, P.	Sussex	1981	25	2	0	13	13	6.50	-	-
Denton, D.	Yorks.	1905	31	2	0	12	12	6.00	-	-
Thompson, G.	Northants.	1909	31	1	0	6	6	6.00	2	-
Sinfield, R.	Gloucs.	1938	37	1	0	6	6	6.00	-	-
Bairstow, D.	Yorks.	1980	28	1	0	6	6	6.00	2	1
Andrew, K.	Northants.	1954	24	2	0	11	6	5.50	-	-
Downton, P.	Middlesex	1981	24	2	0	11	8	5.50	2	-
Wilson, E.R.	Yorks.	1921	41	2	0	10	5	5.00	-	-
Cranston, K.	Lancs.	1948	30	2	0	10	10	5.00	-	-
Emmett, G.M.	Gloucs.	1948	35	2	0	10	10	5.00	-	-
Insole, D.J.	Essex	1956	30	1	0	5	5	5.00	-	-
Athey, W.	Yorks.	1980	22	2	0	10	9	5.00	1	-
McIntyre, A.J.	Surrey	1950	32	2	0	8	7	4.00	1	-
Mead, W.	Essex	1899	31	2	0	7	7	3.50	1	-
Wood, R.	Lancs.	1886	25	2	0	6	6	3.00	-	-
Richmond, T.L.	Notts.	1921	30	2	0	6	4	3.00	-	-
Price, W.F.	Middlesex	1938	36	2	0	6	6	3.00	2	-
Barlow, G.	Middlesex	1977	27	2	0	6	5	3.00	-	-
MacKinnon, F.A.	Kent	1879	30	2	0	5	5	2.50	-	-
Ducat, A.N.	Surrey	1921	35	2	0	5	3	2.50	1	-
Webbe, A.J.	Middlesex	1879	23	2	0	4	4	2.00	-	-
Haig, N.E.	Middlesex	1921	33	2	0	3	3	1.50	-	-
Martin, F.	Kent	1890	28	1	0	1	1	1.00	-	-
Watkins, A.J.	Glamorgan	1948	26	2	0	2	2	1.00	-	-
Dolphin, A.	Yorks.	1920	35	2	0	1	1	0.50	1	-
Grace, G.F.	Gloucs.	1880	29	2	0	0	0	0.00	2	-
Carr, D.W.	Kent	1909	37	1	0	0	0	0.00	-	-
Goddard, T.W.	Gloucs.	1930	29	1	0	0	0	0.00	-	-
Hollies, W.E.	Warwicks.	1948	36	2	1	0	0*	0.00	-	-
Parker, C.W.L.	Gloucs.	1921	38	1	1	3	3*	-	-	-
Hallows, C.	Lancs.	1921	26	1	1	16	16*	-	-	-
Nichols, M.S.	Essex	1930	29	1	1	7	7*	-	-	-
Moss, A.E.	Middlesex	1956	25	-	-	-	-	-	-	-
Rumsey, F.E.	Somerset	1964	28	1	1	3	3*	-	-	-
Russell, W.E.	Middlesex	1965	29	1	1	0	0*	-	-	-

II. One Test Appearance: English Bowling

Bowlers	County	Balls	Maidens	Runs	Wickets	Average
Martin, F.	Kent	287	21	102	12	8.50
Wilson, E.R.	Yorks.	126	5	36	3	12.00
Parker, C.W.L.	Gloucs.	168	16	32	2	16.00
Nichols, M.S.	Essex	126	5	33	2	16.50
Warren, A.R.	Derbys.	236	9	113	6	18.83
Jackson, H.L.	Derbys.	264	16	83	4	20.75
Allott, P.	Lancs.	138	4	88	4	22.00
Goddard, T.W.	Gloucs.	193	14	49	2	24.50
Tate, F.W.	Sussex	96	4	51	2	25.50
Schultz, S.S.	Lancs.	34	3	26	1	26.00
Pocock, P.J.	Surrey	348	15	156	6	26.00
Hollies, W.E.	Warwicks.	336	14	131	5	26.20
Durston, E.J.	Middlesex	202	2	136	5	27.20
Carr, D W	Kent	414	3	282	7	40.28
Wellard, A.W.	Somerset	192	3	126	3	42.00
Richmond, T.L.	Notts.	114	3	86	2	43.00
Haig, N.E.	Middlesex	138	4	88	2	44.00
Rumsey, F.E.	Somerset	215	4	99	2	49.50
Coxon, A.	Yorks.	378	13	172	3	57.33
Sinfield, R.	Gloucs.	378	16	123	2	61.50
Christopherson, S.	Kent	136	13	69	1	69.00
Cranston, K	Lancs.	127	1	79	1	79.00
Mead, W.	Essex	265	24	91	1	91.00
King, J.H.	Leics.	162	5	99	1	99.00
Macaulay, G.G.	Yorks.	192	8	123	1	123.00
Royle, V.P.	Lancs.	16	1	6	0	–
Penn, F.	Kent	12	1	2	0	–
Thompson, G	Northants.	24	0	19	0	–
Hayes, E.	Surrey	36	0	24	0	–
Watkins, A.J.	Glamorgan	24	1	19	0	–
Moss, A.E.	Middlesex	24	3	1	0	–
Taylor, K.	Yorks.	12	0	6	0	–

III. One Test Appearance: Australian Batting

Batsmen	State	Debut	Age	Inns.	N.O.	Runs	H.S.	Av.	Ct.	St.
Welham, D.	N.S.W.	1981	22	2	0	127	103	63.50	-	-
Malone, M.	W. Australia	1977	26	1	0	46	46	46.00	-	-
Hartkopf, A.E.V.	Victoria	1924	35	2	0	80	80	40.00	-	-
Hamence, R.A.	S. Australia	1947	31	2	1	31	30	31.00	-	-
Lee, P.K.	S. Australia	1933	28	2	0	57	42	28.50	-	-
Sincock, D.J.	S. Australia	1966	23	2	0	56	29	28.00	-	-
Nothling, O.E.	Queensland	1928	28	2	0	52	44	26.00	-	-
Allen, R.C.	N.S.W.	1887	28	2	0	44	30	22.00	2	-
Ebeling, H.I	Victoria	1934	29	2	0	43	41	21.50	-	-
Harvey, M.	Victoria	1947	28	2	0	43	31	21.50	-	-
Nagel, L.	Victoria	1933	27	2	1	21	21*	21.00	-	-

continued

Batsmen	State	Debut	Age	Inns.	N.O.	Runs	H.S.	Av.	Ct.	St.
Moule, W.H.	Victoria	1880	22	2	0	40	34	20.00	1	-
Alexander, H.H.	Victoria	1933	27	2	1	17	17*	17.00	-	-
Nash, L.J.	Victoria	1937	26	1	0	17	17	17.00	2	-
Taber, H.B.	N.S.W.	1968	28	1	0	16	16	16.00	2	-
Morris, S.	Victoria	1885	29	2	1	14	10*	14.00	-	-
Guest, C.	Victoria	1963	25	1	0	11	11	11.00	-	-
Reedman, J.C.	S. Australia	1894	29	2	0	21	17	10.50	1	-
Watson, W.	N.S.W.	1955	24	2	0	21	18	10.50	-	-
Cooper, B.B.	Victoria	1877	32	2	0	18	15	9.00	2	-
Musgrove, H.	Victoria	1885	24	2	0	13	9	6.50	-	-
Coningham, A.C.	Queensland	1894	31	2	0	13	10	6.50	-	-
Walters, F.H.	Victoria	1885	25	2	0	12	7	6.00	2	-
Gregory, E.J.	N.S.W.	1877	37	2	0	11	11	5.50	1	-
Groube, T.U.	Victoria	1880	23	2	0	11	11	5.50	-	-
Slight, J.	Victoria	1880	24	2	0	11	11	5.50	-	-
Allan, F.E.	Victoria	1879	29	1	0	5	5	5.00	-	-
Travers, J.F.	S. Australia	1901	31	2	0	10	9	5.00	1	-
Saggers, R.A.	N.S.W.	1948	31	1	0	5	5	5.00	3	-
McIlwraith, J.	Victoria	1886	28	2	0	9	7	4.50	1	-
Harry, J.	Victoria	1894	37	2	0	8	6	4.00	1	-
Love, H.S.	N.S.W.	1933	37	2	0	8	5	4.00	3	-
Rackemann, C.	Queensland	1982	24	1	0	4	4	4.00	1	-
Laughlin, T.	Victoria	1978	27	2	0	7	5	3.50	2	-
Gaunt, R.A.	Victoria	1961	27	1	0	3	3	3.00	1	-
Duncan, J.	Victoria	1971	26	1	0	3	3	3.00	-	-
Marr, A.P.	N.S.W.	1885	22	2	0	5	5	2.50	-	-
Robinson, R.H.	N.S.W.	1936	22	2	0	5	3	2.50	1	-
Eastwood, K.	Victoria	1971	35	2	0	5	5	2.50	-	-
Cottam, J.T.	N.S.W.	1887	19	2	0	4	3	2.00	1	-
Hilditch, A.	N.S.W.	1979	22	2	0	4	3	2.00	2	-
Pope, R.J.	N.S.W.	1885	20	2	0	3	3	1.50	-	-
Robertson, W.R.	Victoria	1885	23	2	0	2	2	1.00	-	-
Park, R.L.	Victoria	1920	28	1	0	0	0	0.00	-	-
Moroney, J.A.	N.S.W.	1950	31	2	0	0	0	0.00	-	-
Crawford, P.	N.S.W.	1956	22	2	1	0	0*	0.00	-	-
Coulthard, G.	Victoria	1882	25	1	1	6	6*	-	-	-
McLaren, J.W.	Queensland	1912	24	2	2	0	0*	-	-	-
Mayne, E.R.	Victoria	1912	28	-	-	-	-	-	-	-
Freer, F.W.	Victoria	1947	31	1	1	28	28*	-	-	-
Slater, K.N.	W. Australia	1958	23	1	1	1	1*	-	-	-
Allan, P.J.	Queensland	1966	29	-	-	-	-	-	-	-
Dell, A.	Queensland	1971	23	2	2	6	3*	-	-	-

IV. One Test Appearance: Australian Bowling

Bowlers	State	Balls	Maidens	Runs	Wickets	Average
Moule, W.H.	Victoria	51	4	23	3	7.66
Malone, M.	W. Australia	342	24	77	6	12.83
Travers, J.F.	S. Australia	48	2	14	1	14.00
Dell, A.	Queensland	343	11	97	5	19.40
Allan, F.E.	Victoria	180	15	80	4	20.00
Nash, L.J.	Victoria	197	2	104	5	20.80
Eastwood, K.	Victoria	40	0	21	1	21.00
Reedman, J.C.	S. Australia	57	2	24	1	24.00
Freer, F.W.	Victoria	160	3	74	3	24.66
Gaunt, R.A.	Victoria	276	10	86	3	28.66
Ebeling, H.I.	Victoria	186	9	89	3	29.66
Morris, S.	Victoria	136	14	73	2	36.50
Coningham, A.C.	Queensland	186	9	76	2	38.00
Lee, P.K	S. Australia	316	14	163	4	40.75
Allan, P.J.	Queensland	192	6	83	2	41.50
Rackemann, C.	Queensland	200	11	96	2	48.00
Slater, K N	W Australia	256	9	101	2	50.50
Nagel, L.	Victoria	262	9	110	2	55.00
McLaren, J W	Queensland	144	3	70	1	70.00
Hartkopf, A.E.	Victoria	240	2	134	1	134.00
Alexander, H.H.	Victoria	276	3	154	1	154.00
Robertson, W.R	Victoria	44	3	24	0	–
Marr, A.P.	N.S.W.	48	6	14	0	–
Park, R.L.	Victoria	6	0	9	0	–
Nothling, O.E.	Queensland	276	15	72	0	–
Crawford, P.	N.S.W.	29	2	4	0	–
Guest, C.	Victoria	144	0	59	0	–
Sincock, D.J.	S. Australia	160	1	98	0	–
Duncan, J	Victoria	112	4	30	0	–
Laughlin, T.	Victoria	200	6	60	0	–

V. Two Test Appearances: English Batting

Batsmen	County	Debut	Age	Inns.	N.O.	Runs	H.S.	Av.	Ct.	St.
Hill, A.	Yorks.	1877	33	4	2	101	49	50.50	1	-
Vine, J.	Sussex	1912	36	3	2	46	36	46.00	-	-
Freeman, A.P.	Kent	1924	36	4	2	80	50*	40.00	1	-
Milburn, C.	Northants.	1968	26	3	0	109	83	36.33	2	-
Sharpe, P.J.	Yorks.	1964	27	3	1	71	35*	35.50	-	-
Mortimore, J.B.	Gloucs.	1959	25	3	1	67	44*	33.50	-	-
Sugg, F.H.	Lancs.	1888	26	2	0	55	31	27.50	-	-
Bradley, W M.	Kent	1899	24	2	1	23	23*	23.00	-	-
Young, H.	Essex	1899	23	2	0	43	43	21.50	1	-
Larkins, W.	Northants.	1980	26	4	0	86	34	21.50	1	-
Stevens, G.T.S.	Middlesex	1926	25	3	0	63	24	21.00	3	-
Greenwood, A.	Yorks.	1877	29	4	0	77	49	19.25	2	-
Parkhouse, W.G.A.	Glamorgan	1950	25	4	0	77	28	19.25	1	-
Jupp, H.	Surrey	1877	35	4	0	68	63	17.00	2	-
Townsend, C.L.	Gloucs.	1899	22	3	0	51	38	17.00	-	-
Jupp, V.W.C.	Sussex	1921	30	4	0	65	28	16.25	-	-
Charlwood, H.R.J.	Sussex	1877	30	4	0	63	36	15.75	-	-
Fagg, A.E.	Kent	1936	21	3	0	42	27	14.00	2	-
Swetman, R.	Surrey	1959	25	4	0	56	41	14.00	3	-
Knight, D.J.	Surrey	1921	27	4	0	54	38	13.50	1	-

continued

Batsmen	County	Debut	Age	Inns.	N.O.	Runs	H.S.	Av.	Ct.	St.
Dollery, H.E.	Warwicks.	1948	33	3	0	38	37	12.67	-	-
Palairet, L.C.H.	Somerset	1902	32	4	0	49	20	12.25	2	-
Armitage, T.	Yorks.	1877	29	3	0	33	21	11.00	-	-
Close, D.B.	Yorks.	1950	19	4	0	42	33	10.50	3	-
McGahey, C.P.	Essex	1901	30	4	0	38	18	9.50	1	-
Milton, C.A.	Gloucs.	1958	30	4	0	38	17	9.50	1	-
Peebles, I.A.R.	Middlesex	1930	22	3	2	9	6	9.00	-	-
Lillywhite, J.	Sussex	1877	35	3	1	16	10	8.00	1	-
Smith, T.P.｀ʌ`	Essex	1946	38	4	0	32	24	8.00	1	-
Kenyon, D.	Worcs.	1953	29	4	0	29	16	7.25	1	-
Oakman, A.S.M.	Sussex	1956	26	2	0	14	10	7.00	7	-
Young, R.A.	Sussex	1907	22	4	0	27	13	6.75	6	-
O'Brien, T.C.	Middlesex	1884	22	4	0	24	20	6.00	1	-
Hopwood, J.L.	Lancs.	1934	30	3	1	12	8	6.00	-	-
Shuttleworth, K.	Lancs.	1970	26	2	0	9	7	4.50	1	-
Waddington, A.	Yorks.	1920	27	4	0	16	7	4.00	1	-
Southerton, J.	Surrey	1877	49	3	1	7	6	3.50	2	-
Loader, P.J.	Surrey	1958	29	4	2	7	6*	3 50	-	-
Pollard, R.	Lancs.	1948	36	2	1	3	3	3.00	1	-
Cartwright, T.W.	Warwicks.	1964	29	2	0	4	4	2.00	-	-
Higgs, K.	Lancs.	1965	28	3	0	6	4	2.00	1	-
Sims, J.M.	Middlesex	1936	33	2	0	3	3	1.50	5	-
Warr, J J.	Middlesex	1950	23	4	0	4	4	1.00	-	-
Dean, H.	Lancs.	1912	27	2	1	0	0*	0.00	1	-
Clark, E.W.	Northants.	1934	31	3	3	6	2*	-	-	-

VI. Two Test Appearances: English Bowling

Bowlers	County	Balls	Maidens	Runs	Wickets	Average
Southerton, J.	Surrey	263	24	107	7	15.28
Lillywhite, J.	Sussex	340	37	126	8	15.75
Dean, H.	Lancs.	324	19	97	6	16.16
Hill, A.	Yorks.	340	37	130	6	21.66
Young, H.	Essex	556	38	262	12	21.83
Townsend, C.L.	Gloucs.	140	5	75	3	25.00
Loader, P.J.	Surrey	482	10	193	7	27.57
Jupp, V.W.C.	Sussex	235	4	142	5	28.40
Shuttleworth, K.	Lancs.	605	13	242	7	34.51
Stevens, G.T.S.	Middlesex	384	7	184	5	36.80
Bradley, W.M.	Kent	625	49	233	6	38.83
Peebles, I.A.R.	Middlesex	756	17	354	9	39.33
Clark, E.W.	Northants.	608	15	324	8	40.50
Pollard, R.	Lancs.	612	29	218	5	43.60
Cartwright, T.W.	Warwicks.	834	55	228	5	45.60
Higgs, K.	Lancs.	591	25	223	4	55.75
Freeman, A.P.	Kent	968	16	459	8	57.37
Close, D.B.	Yorks.	104	2	61	1	61.00
Sims, J.M.	Middlesex	408	2	244	3	81.33
Smith, T.P.B.	Essex	376	1	218	2	109.00
Waddington, A.	Yorks.	276	7	119	1	119.00
Mortimore, J.B.	Gloucs.	382	14	163	1	163.00
Warr, J.J.	Middlesex	584	6	281	1	281.00
Armitage, T.	Yorks.	12	0	15	0	—
Hopwood, J.	Lancs.	462	32	155	0	—
Oakman, A S.M.	Sussex	48	3	21	0	—

VII. Two Test Appearances: Australian Batting

Batsmen	State	Debut	Age	Inns.	N.O.	Runs	H.S.	Av.	Ct.	St.
Gregory, R.	Victoria	1937	20	3	0	153	80	51.00	1	-
Shepherd, B.	W. Australia	1963	24	3	1	94	71*	47.00	1	-
Hartigan, R.	Queensland	1908	28	4	0	170	116	42.50	1	-
Barrett, J.E.	Victoria	1890	23	4	1	80	67*	26.66	1	-
Wiener, J	Victoria	1979	24	4	0	104	58	26.00	2	-
Kelly, T.	Victoria	1877	32	3	0	64	35	21.33	1	-
Thompson, N.	N.S.W.	1877	38	4	0	67	41	16.75	3	-
Dooland, B.	S. Australia	1947	23	3	0	49	29	16.33	2	-
Smith, D.	Victoria	1912	27	3	1	30	24*	15.00	-	-
Craig, I	N.S.W.	1956	21	4	0	55	38	13.75	-	-
Kendall, T.	Victoria	1877	25	4	1	39	17*	13.00	2	-
Alexander, G.	Victoria	1880	29	4	0	52	33	13.00	2	-
Freeman, E.	S. Australia	1968	23	3	0	37	21	12.33	1	-
Ring, D.	Victoria	1948	29	3	0	34	18	11.33	-	-
Burn, K.	Tasmania	1890	26	4	0	41	19	10.25	-	-
Bromley, E.	Victoria	1933	20	4	0	38	26	9.50	2	-
Wright, K.	W. Australia	1979	25	4	0	37	29	9.25	7	1
Gilmour, G.	N.S.W.	1975	24	3	0	26	16	8.67	-	-
Charlton, P.	N.S.W.	1890	23	4	0	29	11	7.25	-	-
Eady, C.	Tasmania	1896	25	4	1	20	10*	6.67	2	-
Cooper, W.	Victoria	1881	32	3	1	13	7	6.50	1	-
Hill, J.	Victoria	1953	29	4	2	12	8*	6.00	1	-
Carlson, P.	Queensland	1979	28	4	0	23	21	5.75	2	-
Watson, G.D.	W. Australia	1972	27	4	0	21	13	5.25	1	-
Gehrs, D.	S. Australia	1904	23	4	0	19	11	4.75	4	-
Waite, M.	S. Australia	1938	27	3	0	11	8	3.67	1	-
Hodges, J	Victoria	1877	20	4	1	10	8	3.33	-	-
Burton, F.	N.S.W.	1887	21	4	2	4	2*	2.00	1	1
Whitney, M.	N.S.W.	1981	22	4	0	4	4	1.00	-	-
Kline, L.	Victoria	1958	24	2	2	5	4*	-	2	-
Rorke, G.	N.S.W.	1959	20	2	2	2	2*	-	-	-
Misson, F.	N.S.W.	1961	22	1	1	25	25*	-	1	-
Emery, S.	N.S.W.	1912	25	-	-	-	-	-	-	-

VIII. Two Test Appearances: Australian Bowling

Bowlers	State	Balls	Maidens	Runs	Wickets	Average
Charlton, P.C.	N.S.W.	45	1	24	3	8.00
Hodges, J.	Victoria	136	9	84	6	14.00
Kendall, T.	Victoria	563	56	215	14	15.35
Eady, C.	Tasmania	223	14	112	7	16.00
Rorke, G.	N.S.W.	565	17	165	8	20.62
Gilmour, G.	N.S.W.	380	18	190	9	21.11
Hill, J.	Victoria	396	18	158	7	22.57
Cooper, W.H.	Victoria	466	31	226	9	25.11
Watson, G.D.	W. Australia	240	14	92	3	30.67
Thompson, N.	N.S.W.	112	16	31	1	31.00
Freeman, E	S. Australia	407	17	186	6	31.00
Emery, S.	N.S.W	114	2	68	2	34.00
Misson, F.	N.S.W.	456	18	243	7	34.71
Dooland, B.	S. Australia	784	9	351	8	43.87
Alexander, G.	Victoria	168	13	93	2	46.50

continued

Bowlers	State	Balls	Maidens	Runs	Wickets	Average
Whitney, M.	N.S.W.	468	16	246	5	49.20
Carlson, P.	Queensland	368	10	99	2	49.50
Ring, D.	Victoria	426	20	171	3	57.00
Waite, M.	S. Australia	552	23	190	1	190.00
Hartigan, R.	Queensland	12	0	7	0	–
Bromley, E.	Victoria	60	4	19	0	–
Gregory, R.	Victoria	24	0	14	0	–
Kline, L	Victoria	200	6	77	0	–
Wiener, J.	Victoria	64	3	22	0	–

IX. Three Test Appearances: English Batting

Batsmen	County	Debut	Age	Inns.	N.O.	Runs	H.S.	Av.	Ct.	St.
Steele, D.S.	Northants.	1975	33	6	0	365	92	60.83	4	-
Brown, G.	Hants.	1921	33	5	0	250	84	50.00	2	2
Sharp, J.	Lancs.	1909	31	6	2	188	105	47.00	1	-
Roope, G.	Surrey	1975	29	4	0	149	77	37.25	1	-
Fowler, G.	Lancs.	1982	25	6	0	207	83	34.50	1	-
Hemmings, E.	Notts.	1983	33	6	1	157	95	31.40	2	-
Pataudi (Snr.)	Worcs.	1932	22	5	0	144	102	28.80	-	-
Pringle, D.	Essex	1982	24	6	2	108	47*	27.00	-	-
Sharpe, J.W.	Surrey	1890	23	6	4	44	26	22.00	2	-
Relf, A.E.	Sussex	1903	29	5	2	64	31	21.33	4	-
Bean, G.	Sussex	1891	27	5	0	92	50	18.40	4	-
Crapp, J.F.	Gloucs.	1948	35	6	1	88	37	17.60	6	-
Knight, A.E.	Leics.	1903	31	6	1	81	70*	16.20	1	-
Sherwin, M.	Notts.	1886	35	6	4	30	21*	15.00	5	2
Worthington, S.	Derbyshire	1936	31	6	0	74	44	12.33	3	-
Price, J.E.	Middlesex	1964	27	4	2	24	19*	12.00	2	-
Brearley, W.	Lancs.	1905	29	4	2	21	11*	10.50	-	-
Sandham, A.	Surrey	1921	31	5	0	49	21	9.80	-	-
Cook, G.	Northants.	1982	31	6	0	54	26	9.00	1	-
Humphries, J	Derbys.	1907	31	6	1	44	16	8.80	7	-
Edmonds, P.	Middlesex	1975	24	5	1	33	13*	8.25	2	-
Dewes, J.G.	Middlesex	1948	21	6	0	34	10	5.67	-	-
Young, J.A.	Middlesex	1948	35	5	2	17	9	5.67	2	-
Mitchell, T.B.	Derbys.	1933	30	4	1	14	9	4.67	1	-
Tattersall, R.	Lancs.	1951	28	4	0	18	10	4.50	3	-
Hornby, A.N.	Lancs.	1878	31	6	0	21	9	3.50	4	-
Tyldesley, R.	Lancs.	1924	27	5	0	17	6	3.40	-	-
Mold, A.	Lancs.	1893	30	3	1	0	0*	0.00	1	-
Root, F.	Worcs.	1926	36	-	-	-	-	-	1	-

X. Three Test Appearances: English Bowling

Bowlers	County	Balls	Maidens	Runs	Wickets	Average
Hornby, A.N.	Lancs.	28	7	0	1	0.00
Steele, D.	Northants.	70	5	21	2	10.50
Brearley, W.	Lancs.	669	23	355	17	20.88
Root, F.	Worcs.	642	47	194	8	24.25
Relf, A.E.	Sussex	448	24	173	7	24.71
Sharpe, J.W.	Surrey	975	61	305	11	27.72
Mold, A.	Lancs.	491	32	234	7	33.42
Sharp, J.	Lancs.	183	3	111	3	37.00
Edmonds, P.	Middlesex	591	22	251	6	41.83
Hemmings, E.	Notts.	1131	59	409	9	45.44
Tattersall, R.	Lancs.	717	17	338	7	48.28
Price, J.E.	Middlesex	595	11	365	7	52.14
Tyldesley, R.	Lancs.	830	26	370	7	52.85
Pringle, D.	Essex	443	12	214	4	53.50
Young, J.A.	Middlesex	936	64	292	5	58.40
Mitchell, T.B.	Derbyshire	468	12	285	4	71.25
Worthington, S.	Derbyshire	80	0	78	0	–
Cook, G.	Northants.	36	3	23	0	–

XI. Three Test Appearances: Australian Batting

Batsmen	State	Debut	Age	Inns.	N.O.	Runs	H.S.	Av.	Ct.	St.
Trott, A.E.	Victoria	1895	20	5	3	205	85*	102.50	4	-
Bannerman, C.	N.S.W.	1877	25	6	2	239	165*	59.75	-	-
Thomas, G.	N.S.W.	1965	27	4	0	147	52	36.75	1	-
Archer, K.	Queensland	1950	21	5	0	152	48	30.40	-	-
Kent, M.	Queensland	1981	27	6	0	171	54	28.50	6	-
Laird, B	W. Australia	1979	28	6	0	162	74	27.00	1	-
A'Beckett, E.L.	Victoria	1928	21	5	0	133	41	26.60	4	-
Rigg, K.E.	Victoria	1936	30	5	0	118	47	23.60	2	-
Serjeant, C.	W. Australia	1977	25	5	0	106	81	21.20	1	-
Colley, D.	N.S.W.	1972	25	4	0	84	54	21.00	-	-
Gregory, D.W.	N.S.W.	1877	31	5	2	60	43	20.00	-	-
Oxenham, R.	Queensland	1928	37	5	0	88	39	17.60	-	-
Tribe, G.	Victoria	1946	26	3	1	35	25*	17.50	-	-
Callaway, S.T.	N.S.W	1891	22	6	1	87	41	17.40	-	-
O'Brien, L.	Victoria	1932	25	6	0	104	61	17.33	2	-
Robinson, R.	Victoria	1977	31	6	0	100	34	16.67	4	-
De Courcy, J	N.S.W.	1953	26	6	1	81	41	16.20	3	-
Chappell, T	N.S.W.	1981	28	6	1	79	27	15.80	2	-
Turner, A.	N.S W.	1975	24	5	0	77	37	15.40	2	-
Jennings, C B.	S. Australia	1912	28	4	1	44	21	14.66	4	-
Sievers, M.	Victoria	1936	24	6	1	67	25*	13.40	4	-
Edwards, W.	W. Australia	1974	24	6	0	68	30	11.33	-	-
Cosier, G	S. Australia	1977	23	6	0	66	47	11.00	4	-
Francis, B.	N.S.W.	1972	24	5	0	52	27	10.40	1	-
Edwards, J.D.	Victoria	1888	26	6	1	48	26	9.60	1	-
Blackie, D.	Victoria	1928	46	6	3	24	11*	8.00	2	-
Philpott, P.I.	N.S.W	1965	31	4	1	22	10	7.33	2	-
Woods, S.M.J.	N.S.W.	1888	21	6	0	32	18	5.33	1	-
McShane, P.	Victoria	1885	28	6	1	26	12*	5.20	2	-
Carkeek, W	Victoria	1912	33	2	1	5	5	5.00	2	-
Giffen, W.F.	S. Australia	1887	23	6	0	11	3	1.83	1	-

XII. Three Test Appearances: Australian Bowling

Bowlers	State	Balls	Maidens	Runs	Wickets	Average
Sievers, M.	Victoria	602	25	161	9	17.88
Trott, A.E.	Victoria	474	17	192	9	21.33
Callaway, S T.	N.S.W.	471	33	142	6	23.66
Woods, S.M.J.	N.S.W.	217	18	121	5	24.20
Blackie, D.	Victoria	1260	51	444	14	31.71
Philpott, P.I.	N.S.W.	801	9	371	8	46.37
McShane, P.	Victoria	108	9	48	1	48.00
Oxenham, R.	Queensland	1202	72	349	7	49.85
Colley, D.	N.S.W.	729	20	312	6	52.00
A'Beckett, E.L.	Victoria	936	41	282	3	94.00
Tribe, G.	Victoria	760	9	330	2	165.00
Gregory, D.W.	N.S.W.	20	1	9	0	–
Cosier, G	S. Australia	96	3	35	0	–

XIII. Four Test Appearances: English Batting

Batsmen	County	Debut	Age	Inns.	N.O.	Runs	H.S.	Av.	Ct.	St.
Duleepsinhji, K.S.	Sussex	1930	25	7	0	416	173	59.42	2	-
Tennyson, L.H.	Hants.	1921	31	5	1	229	74*	57.25	2	-
Makepeace, H.	Lancs.	1920	39	8	0	279	117	34.87	-	-
Wood, B.	Lancs.	1972	29	8	0	262	90	32.75	-	-
Whysall, W.W.	Notts.	1925	37	7	0	209	76	29.85	7	-
Harris, Lord	Kent	1879	27	6	1	145	52	29.00	2	-
Lloyd, D.	Lancs.	1974	27	8	0	196	49	24.50	6	-
Fane, F.	Essex	1907	32	8	0	192	50	24.00	1	-
Hampshire, J.	Yorks.	1971	29	8	0	168	55	21.00	4	-
Lyttleton, A.	Middlesex	1880	23	7	1	94	31	15.66	2	-
Leslie, C.F.	Middlesex	1882	21	7	0	106	54	15.14	1	-
Midwinter, W.	Gloucs.	1881	30	7	0	95	36	13.57	5	-
Carr, A.W.	Notts.	1926	33	1	0	13	13	13.00	1	-
Smith, A.C.	Warwicks.	1962	26	5	1	47	21	11.75	13	-
Cowans, N.	Middlesex	1982	21	7	1	68	36	11.33	3	-
Bligh, I.	Kent	1882	23	7	1	62	19	10.33	7	-
Haigh, S.	Yorks.	1905	34	5	1	40	14	10.00	1	-
Jones, I.J.	Glamorgan	1965	24	5	2	29	16	9.66	-	-
Flavell, J.	Worcs.	1961	32	6	2	31	14	7.75	-	-
Howell, H.	Warwick.	1920	30	8	6	15	5	7.50	-	-
Coldwell, L.	Worcs.	1962	29	6	4	9	6*	4.50	-	-
Studd, G.B.	Middlesex	1882	23	7	0	31	9	4.42	8	-
Morley, F.	Notts.	1880	29	6	2	6	2*	1.50	4	-

XIV. Four Test Appearances: English Bowling

Bowlers	County	Balls	Maidens	Runs	Wickets	Average
Lyttleton, A.	Middlesex	48	5	19	4	4.75
Leslie, C.F.	Middlesex	96	10	44	4	11.00
Morley, F.	Notts.	972	124	296	16	18.50
Midwinter, W.	Gloucs.	776	79	272	10	27.20
Haigh, S.	Yorks.	372	21	139	4	34.75
Jones, I.J.	Glamorgan	1032	15	533	15	35.53
Cowans, N.	Middlesex	642	14	396	11	36.00
Coldwell, L.	Worcs.	840	19	317	7	45.28
Flavell, J.	Worcs.	792	25	367	7	52.42
Howell, H.	Warwicks.	798	18	490	7	70.00
Harris, Lord	Kent	32	1	29	0	–
Whysall, W.W.	Notts.	16	0	9	0	–
Wood, B.	Lancs.	36	2	16	0	–

XV. Four Test Appearances: Australian Batting

Batsmen	State	Debut	Age	Inns.	N.O.	Runs	H.S.	Av.	Ct.	St.
Jackson, A.	N.S.W.	1929	19	6	0	350	164	58.33	1	-
Wessels, K.	Queensland	1982	25	8	0	386	162	48.25	8	-
Barnett, B.A.	Victoria	1938	30	8	1	195	57	27.85	3	2
Darling, W M.	S. Australia	1978	21	8	0	221	91	27.63	4	-
Jenner, T.	S. Australia	1970	26	7	1	136	74	22.67	5	-
Davis, I.	N.S W.	1977	23	8	0	180	68	22.50	2	-
Thomson, A.	Victoria	1970	24	5	4	22	12*	22.00	-	-
O'Connor, J.	S. Australia	1907	32	8	1	86	20	12.28	3	-
MacLean, J.	Queensland	1978	32	8	1	79	33*	11.29	18	-
Ward, F	S Australia	1936	27	8	2	36	18	6.00	1	-
Massie, R.A.	W Australia	1972	25	5	0	22	18	4.40	-	-
Meckiff, I.	Victoria	1958	23	4	0	9	5	2.25	1	-

XVI. Four Test Appearances: Australian Bowling

Bowlers	State	Balls	Maidens	Runs	Wickets	Average
Meckiff, I	Victoria	898	24	292	17	17.17
Massie, R.A.	W. Australia	1195	58	409	23	17.78
O'Connor, J.	S. Australia	692	24	340	13	26.15
Jenner, T.	S. Australia	862	25	312	9	34.67
Ward, F.	S. Australia	1268	30	574	11	52.18
Thomson, A.	Victoria	1519	33	654	12	54.50

XVII Bankrupt Batsmen

England	County	Debut	Age	Mat.	Inns.	N.O.	Runs	H.S.	Av.	Ct.
Mason, J.R.	Kent	1897	23	5	10	0	129	32	12.90	3
Jones, A O.	Notts.	1899	26	12	21	0	291	34	13.85	15
Willey, P.	Northants.	1979	30	8	15	0	219	82	14.60	2
Wainwright, E.	Yorks.	1893	28	5	9	0	132	49	14.66	2
Amiss, D L.	Warwicks.	1968	25	11	21	1	305	90	15.25	7
Brockwell, W.	Surrey	1893	28	7	12	0	202	49	16.83	6
Ikin, J.T.	Lancs.	1946	28	5	10	0	184	60	18.40	4
Read, J.M.	Surrey	1882	23	15	26	2	447	5	18.62	8
Ford, F.G.J.	Middlesex	1894	28	5	9	0	168	48	18.66	5
Quaife, W.G.	Warwicks.	1899	27	7	13	1	228	68	19.00	4
Smith, M.J.K.	Warwicks.	1961	27	9	15	2	248	41	19.08	8
Lucas, A.P.	Surrey	1879	21	5	9	1	157	55	19.62	1
Gooch, G.	Essex	1975	21	16	31	0	618	99	19.93	12
Studd, C.T.	Middlesex	1882	21	5	9	1	160	48	20.00	5
Watson, W.	Yorks.	1953	33	7	13	0	272	109	20.92	1
Spooner, R.H.	Lancs.	1905	24	7	11	0	233	79	21.18	2
Parfitt, P.H.	Middlesex	1962	25	9	15	1	302	80	21.57	12
Gunn, W.	Notts.	1887	28	11	20	2	392	102*	21.77	5
Selby, J.	Notts.	1877	27	6	12	1	256	70	23.27	1
Warner, P.F.	Middlesex	1903	30	7	13	1	287	79	23.91	2

Australia	State	Debut	Age	Mat.	Inns.	N.O.	Runs	H.S.	Av.	Ct.
Donnan, H.	N.S.W.	1892	27	5	10	1	75	15	8.33	1
Badcock, C.L.	S. Australia	1936	22	7	12	1	160	118	14.54	3
Toohey, P.	N.S.W.	1978	24	6	12	1	171	81*	15.54	6
Massie, H.H.	N.S.W.	1881	27	9	16	0	249	55	15.56	5
McAlister, P.	Victoria	1904	34	8	16	1	252	41	16.80	10
Bonnor, G.J.	Victoria	1880	25	17	30	0	512	128	17.06	16
Horan, T P.	Victoria	1877	23	15	27	2	471	124	18.84	6
Moses, H	N.S.W.	1887	28	6	10	0	198	33	19.80	1
Inverarity, J.	W. Australia	1968	24	5	9	1	160	56	20.00	2
Darling, L.S.	Victoria	1933	23	7	12	0	245	85	20.41	6
Jones, S.P.	N.S.W.	1882	21	12	24	4	432	87	21.60	12
Favell, L.E.	S. Australia	1954	25	6	10	1	203	54	22.55	3

XVIIa Bankrupt Batsmen *(Bowling Figures)*

England	County	Balls	Maidens	Runs	Wickets	Average
Studd, C.T.	Middlesex	384	60	98	3	32.67
Jones, A.O.	Notts.	228	14	133	3	44.33
Gooch, G.	Essex	308	14	95	2	47.50
Brockwell, W.	Surrey	582	31	309	5	61.80
Mason, J.R.	Kent	324	13	149	2	74.50
Willey, P.	Northants.	254	5	98	1	98.00
Ford, F.G.J.	Middlesex	210	6	129	1	129.00
Wainwright, E.	Yorks.	127	6	73	0	–
Ikin, J.T.	Lancs.	56	0	48	0	–
Quaife, W.G.	Warwicks.	15	1	6	0	–
Smith, M.J.K.	Warwicks.	16	0	8	0	–
Lucas, A.P.	Surrey	120	13	54	0	–
Parfitt, P.	Middlesex	12	0	10	0	–

Australia	State	Balls	Maidens	Runs	Wickets	Average
Horan, T.	Victoria	373	45	143	11	13.00
Jones, S.P.	N.S.W.	262	26	112	6	18.67
Inverarity, J.	W. Australia	372	26	93	4	23.25
Bonnor, G.J.	Victoria	164	16	84	2	42.00
Donnan, H.	N.S.W.	54	2	22	0	–
Darling, L.S.	Victoria	162	7	65	0	–

XVIII Bountiful Bowlers

England	County	Mat.	Debut	Age	Balls	M.	Runs	W	Average
Gilligan, A.E.R.	Sussex	5	1924	29	1087	14	519	10	51.90
Hitch, W.	Surrey	6	1911	25	462	5	325	7	46.42
Gifford, N.	Worcs.	5	1964	24	702	41	256	6	42.66
Brown, D.J.	Warwicks.	8	1965	23	1728	48	810	23	35.21
Emmett, T.	Yorks.	7	1877	35	728	92	284	9	31.55
Knight, B.	Essex	5	1962	24	1168	29	463	15	30.86

Australia	State	Mat.	Debut	Age	Balls	M.	Runs	W.	Average
Matthews, T.J.	Victoria	5	1912	27	680	28	277	3	92.33
Evans, E.	N.S.W.	6	1881	32	1247	166	332	7	47.42
Hornibrook, P.	Queensland	6	1929	29	1579	63	664	17	39.06
Corling, G.	N.S.W.	5	1964	22	1159	50	447	12	37.25
Bright, R.J.	Victoria	10	1977	22	2051	135	667	18	37.06
Ironmonger, H.	Victoria	6	1928	46	2446	155	711	21	33.85
Whitty, W.	S. Australia	6	1909	22	1302	71	498	15	33.20
McLeod, R.W.	Victoria	6	1892	23	1089	67	384	12	32.00
McCormick, E.L.	Victoria	7	1936	30	1356	26	661	21	31.47

XVIIIa Bountiful Bowlers *(Batting Figures)*

England	County	Debut	Age	Inns.	N.O.	Runs	H.S.	Av.	Ct.
Hitch, J.W.	Surrey	1911	25	9	2	103	51*	14.71	3
Emmett, T.	Yorks.	1877	35	13	1	160	48	13.33	9
Knight, B.	Essex	1962	24	7	2	52	27*	10.40	2
Gifford, N.	Worcs.	1964	24	8	2	57	16*	9.50	3
Gilligan, A.E.R.	Sussex	1924	29	9	2	64	31	9.14	1
Brown, D.J.	Warwicks.	1965	23	9	0	34	14	3.77	3

Australia	State	Debut	Age	Inns.	N.O.	Runs	H.S.	Av.	Ct.
McLeod, R.W.	Victoria	1892	23	11	0	146	31	13.27	3
Bright, R.	Victoria	1977	22	16	1	198	33	13.20	7
Matthews, T.J.	Victoria	1912	27	7	0	74	53	10.57	4
Evans, E.	N.S.W.	1881	32	10	2	82	33	10.25	5
Hornibrook, P.M.	Queensland	1929	29	7	1	60	26	10.00	7
Whitty, W.	S. Australia	1909	22	8	4	35	14	8.75	2
McCormick, E.L.	Victoria	1936	30	9	2	35	17*	5.00	7
Ironmonger, H.	Victoria	1928	46	12	3	18	8	2.00	2
Corling, G.	N.S.W.	1964	22	4	1	5	3	1.66	-

England	County	Debut	Age	Mat	Inns	NO	Runs	HS	Aver	Ct	Balls	M	Runs	Wkts	Aver	Diff
Yardley, N.W.D.	Yorkshire	1946	31	10	19	2	402	61	23.64	4	1416	37	576	19	30.31	− 6.67
Jessop, G.L.	Gloucs.	1899	25	13	18	0	433	104	24.05	7	660	28	346	10	34.60	−10.55
Fender, P.G.H.	Surrey	1921	28	5	9	1	198	59	24.75	3	806	16	522	14	37.28	−12.53
Robins, R.W.V.	Middlesex	1930	24	6	10	2	183	61	22.87	2	960	10	558	14	39.85	−16.98

Australia	State	Debut	Age	Mat	Inns	NO	Runs	HS	Aver	Ct	Balls	M	Runs	Wkts	Aver	Diff
Fairfax, A.G.	N.S.W.	1929	22	5	6	2	215	65	53.75	10	1010	38	439	14	31.35	+22.40
Trumble, J.W.	Victoria	1885	21	7	13	1	243	59	20.25	3	600	59	222	10	22.20	− 1.95
Richardson, A.J.	S. Australia	1924	36	9	13	0	403	100	31.00	7	1812	91	521	12	43.41	−12.41
Mackay, K.D.	Queensland	1956	30	16	23	1	497	86*	22.59	7	2828	126	875	24	36.45	−13.86
Hendry, H.S.	Victoria	1921	26	9	15	2	284	112	21.84	6	1430	65	504	14	36.00	−14.16
Veivers, T R	Queensland	1964	27	9	10	2	242	67*	30.25	5	1904	84	694	15	46.26	−16.01
O'Keeffe, K.J	N.S.W.	1971	21	6	11	4	181	48*	25.86	4	1437	67	677	12	56.42	−30.56

XX Second Choice Stumpers

England	County	Debut	Age	Mat.	Ct.	St.	Total	M.A.	Byes	Inns.	N.O.	Runs	H.S.	Average
Murray, J.T.	Middlesex	1961	26	6	18	1	19	3.17	51	10	1	163	40	18.11
MacGregor, G.	Middlesex	1890	20	7	14	3	17	2.43	71	11	3	96	31	12.00
Philipson, H.	Middlesex	1891	25	5	8	3	11	2.20	33	8	1	63	30	9.00
Hunter, J.	Yorks.	1884	29	5	8	3	11	2.20	38	7	2	93	39*	18.60
Smith, E.J.	Warwicks.	1911	25	7	12	1	13	1.86	126	9	1	69	22	8.62
Storer, W.	Derbys.	1897	30	6	11	0	11	1.83	65	11	0	215	51	19.54
Pilling, R.	Lancs.	1881	26	8	10	4	14	1.75	42	13	1	91	23	7.58
Tylecote, E.F.S.	Kent	1882	33	6	5	5	10	1.67	71	9	1	152	66	19.00

Australia	State	Debut	Age	Mat.	Ct.	St.	Total	M.A.	Byes	Inns.	N.O.	Runs	H.S.	Average
Maddocks, L.V.	Victoria	1954	28	5	12	1	13	2.60	22	9	0	156	69	17.33
Jarman, B.N	S. Australia	1962	26	7	18	0	18	2.57	61	11	3	111	41	13.87
Jarvis, A.H.	S. Australia	1885	24	9	8	9	17	1.89	102	17	3	283	82	20.21

XXI   Solid Workmen *(Batting Figures)*

England	County	Debut	Age	Mat.	Inns.	N.O.	Runs	H.S.	Av.	Ct.
Dilley, G.	Kent	1979	20	5	10	4	230	56	38.33	2
Gatting, M.W.	Middlesex	1980	23	7	14	1	433	59	33.31	9
Hardstaff, J., snr.	Notts.	1907	25	5	10	0	311	72	31.10	1
Denness, M.	Kent	1974	33	6	11	0	329	188	29.91	7
Kilner, R.	Yorks.	1924	34	7	7	1	174	74	29.00	5
Simpson, R.T.	Notts.	1950	30	9	17	2	434	156*	28.93	5
Hutchings, K.L.	Kent	1907	25	7	12	0	341	126	28.41	9
Tavaré, C.J.	Kent	1981	26	7	14	0	397	89	28.36	3
Druce, N.F.	Surrey	1897	22	5	9	0	252	64	28.00	5
Pullar, G.	Lancs.	1961	25	9	18	1	457	63	26.88	-
Wardle, J.H.	Yorks.	1953	30	8	12	3	166	38	18.44	1
Flowers, W.	Notts.	1884	28	8	14	0	254	56	18.14	3
Shaw, A.	Notts.	1877	34	7	12	1	111	40	10.09	4
Lever, J.K.	Essex	1977	28	6	10	0	97	22	9.70	3

Australia	State	Debut	Age	Mat.	Inns.	N.O.	Runs	H.S.	Av.	Ct.
Graham, H	Victoria	1893	22	6	10	0	301	107	30.10	3
Chipperfield, A.	N S.W.	1934	28	9	15	3	356	99	29.66	13
Scott, H.J.H.	Victoria	1884	25	8	14	1	359	102	27.61	8
Loxton, S.J.	Victoria	1948	27	6	8	0	219	93	27.37	7
Dyson, J.	N.S.W.	1981	27	10	20	2	489	102	27.17	6
Sheahan, A.P.	Victoria	1968	21	9	16	3	341	88	26.23	5
Minnett, R.B.	N.S.W.	1911	23	6	12	0	309	90	25.75	-
Hole, G.B.	S. Australia	1951	20	9	17	0	439	66	25.82	10
Worrall, J.	Victoria	1885	21	11	22	3	478	76	25.15	13
Hopkins, A.J.	N.S.W.	1902	28	17	28	2	434	43	16.69	10
McKibbin, T.	N.S.W.	1895	24	5	8	2	88	28*	14.66	4
Hazlitt, G.R.	Victoria	1907	19	6	9	3	87	34*	14.50	4
Midwinter, W.	Victoria	1877	25	8	14	1	174	37	13.38	5

XXIa   Solid Workmen *(Bowling Figures)*

England	County	Balls	Maidens	Runs	Wickets	Average
Flowers, W.	Notts.	858	92	296	14	21.14
Shaw, A.	Notts.	1099	155	285	12	23.75
Dilley, G.	Kent	1012	29	418	17	24.59
Wardle, J.H.	Yorks.	1661	82	632	24	26.33
Lever, J.K.	Essex	1319	44	505	18	28.06
Kilner, R.	Yorks.	2164	63	675	24	28.12
Hutchings, K.L.	Kent	90	1	81	1	81.00
Gatting, M.W.	Middlesex	18	1	13	0	—

Australia	State	Balls	Maidens	Runs	Wickets	Average
Minnett, R.B.	N.S.W.	415	15	213	9	23.66
Midwinter, W.	Victoria	949	102	333	14	23.78
Hopkins, A.J.	N S.W.	1183	47	581	21	27.66
Hazlitt, G	Victoria	1107	50	443	16	27.68
McKibbin, T.	N.S.W.	1032	41	496	17	29.17
Hole, G.B.	S. Australia	150	8	46	1	46.00
Loxton, S.J.	Victoria	450	11	174	3	58.00
Chipperfield, A.	N S.W.	870	27	409	5	81.80
Worrall, J.	Victoria	255	29	127	1	127.00
Scott, H J.H.	Victoria	28	1	26	0	–

XXII Shooting Stars *(Batting Figures)*

England	County	Debut	Age	Inns.	N.O.	Runs	H.S.	Av.	Ct.	St.
Foster, R.E.	Worcs.	1903	25	9	1	486	287	60.75	8	-
Russell, A.C.	Essex	1920	33	11	2	474	135*	52.66	3	-
Mead, C.P.	Hants.	1911	24	10	2	415	182*	51.87	3	-
Walters, C.F.	Worcs.	1934	28	9	1	401	82	50.12	5	-
Subba Row, R.	Northants.	1961	29	10	0	468	137	46.80	2	-
Tyldesley, E.	Lancs.	1921	32	7	1	257	81	42.83	2	-
Lamb, A J.	Northants.	1982	28	10	0	414	83	41.40	5	-
Ward, A.	Lancs.	1893	27	13	0	487	117	37.46	1	-
Barber, R.W.	Warwicks.	1964	28	13	1	447	185	37.25	4	-
Brown, J.T.	Yorks.	1894	25	16	3	470	140	36.15	7	-
Brown, F.R.	Northants.	1950	39	10	0	260	79	26.00	5	-
Appleyard, R.	Yorks.	1954	30	6	3	45	19*	15.00	4	-
Gunn, J.R.	Notts.	1901	25	8	1	70	42	10.00	6	

Australia	State	Debut	Age	Inns.	N.O.	Runs	H.S.	Av.	Ct.	St.
McCool, C.L.	Queensland	1946	30	7	2	272	104*	54.40	3	-
Pellew, C.E.	S. Australia	1920	27	13	1	478	116	39.83	4	-
Higgs, J.D.	Victoria	1978	28	11	4	48	16	6.86	-	-
Iverson, J B.	Victoria	1950	35	7	3	3	1*	0.75	2	-

XXIIa Shooting Stars *(Bowling Figures)*

England	County	Balls	Maidens	Runs	Wickets	Average
Appleyard, R.	Yorks.	812	32	273	13	21.00
Brown, F.R.	Northants.	1184	23	524	22	23.81
Gunn, J.R.	Notts.	1438	60	445	17	26.18
Barber, R.W.	Warwicks.	573	4	371	6	61.83
Brown, J.T.	Yorks.	35	0	22	0	–

Australia	State	Balls	Maidens	Runs	Wickets	Average
Iverson, J.B.	Victoria	1108	29	320	21	15.23
Higgs, J D	Victoria	1582	47	471	19	24.79
McCool, C.L.	Queensland	1456	27	491	18	27.27
Pellew, C.E.	S. Australia	78	3	34	0	–

INDEX

Index